DATE DUE

AUG 2 3 1997	
SEP 2 5 2020	

BRODART, CO.   Cat. No. 23-221-003

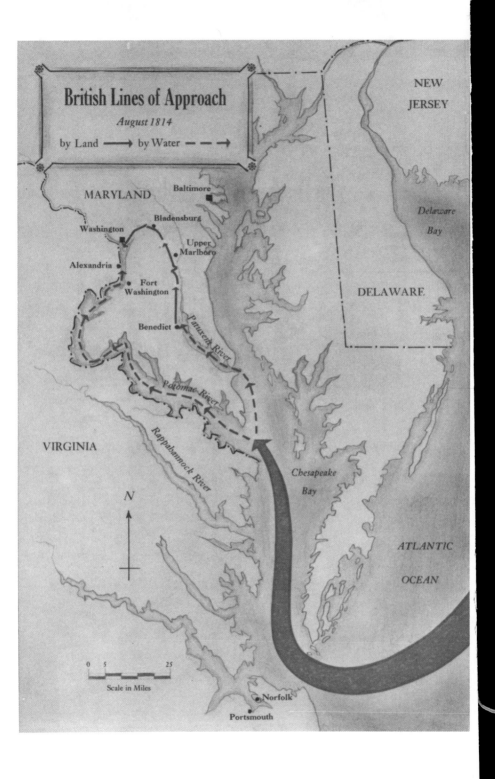

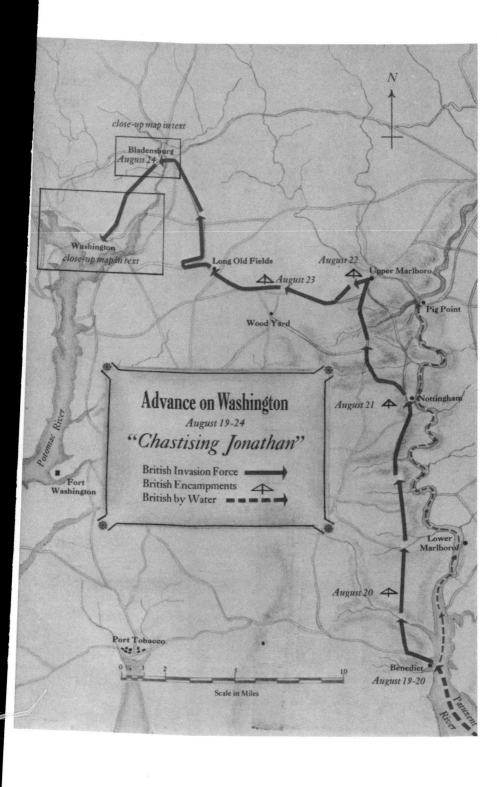

N

close-up map in text

Bladensburg
August 24

Washington
close-up map in text

Long Old Fields

August 22 Upper Marlboro

Pig Point

△ *August 23*

Wood Yard

Potomac River

Advance on Washington
August 19-24
"Chastising Jonathan"

British Invasion Force →
British Encampments △
British by Water ┄┄→

August 21 △ Nottingham

Fort
Washington

Lower
Marlboro

August 20 △

Port Tobacco

0 ¼ 1 2 5 10
Scale in Miles

Benedict
August 19-20

Patuxent River

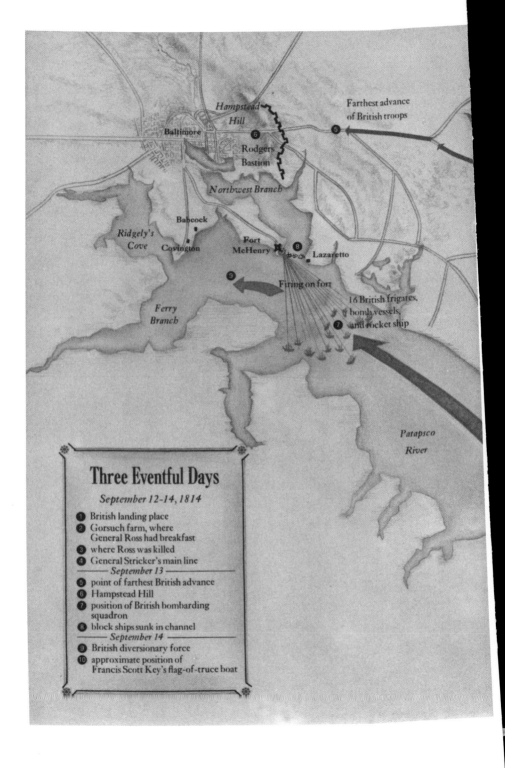

Farthest advance of British troops

Hampstead Hill

Baltimore

⑥ Rodgers Bastion

⑤

Northwest Branch

Babcock

Ridgely's Cove   Covington

Fort McHenry   ⑧   Lazaretto

⑨   Firing on fort

Ferry Branch

16 British frigates, bomb vessels, and rocket ship

⑦

Patapsco River

Three Eventful Days

September 12-14, 1814

① British landing place
② Gorsuch farm, where General Ross had breakfast
③ where Ross was killed
④ General Stricker's main line
—— September 13 ——
⑤ point of farthest British advance
⑥ Hampstead Hill
⑦ position of British bombarding squadron
⑧ block ships sunk in channel
—— September 14 ——
⑨ British diversionary force
⑩ approximate position of Francis Scott Key's flag-of-truce boat

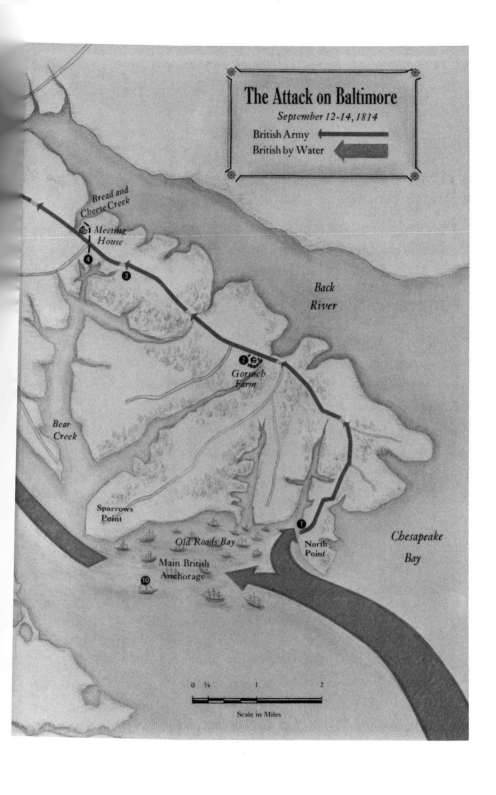

Publisher's Note

Works published as part of the Maryland Paperback Bookshelf are, we like to think, books that have stood the test of time. They are classics of a kind, so we reprint them today as they appeared when first published. While some social attitudes have changed and knowledge of our surroundings has increased, we believe that the value of these books as literature, as history, and as timeless perspectives on our region remains undiminished.

Also Available in the Series:

The Amiable Baltimoreans, by Francis F. Beirne
Mencken, by Carl Bode
Run to the Lee, by Kenneth F. Brooks, Jr.
The Lord's Oysters, by Gilbert Byron
*The Mistress of Riversdale: the Plantation Letters of Rosalie Stier
    Calvert, 1795-1821,* edited by Margaret Law Callcott
The Potomac, by Frederick Gutheim
Spring in Washington, by Louis J. Halle
Bay Country, by Tom Horton
The Bay, by Gilbert C. Klingel
*Tobacco Coast: A Maritime History of Chesapeake Bay in the Colonial
    Era, by* Arthur Pierce Middleton
Watermen, by Randall S. Peffer
Young Frederick Douglass: The Maryland Years, by Dickson J.
    Preston
Miss Susie Slagle's, by Augusta Tucker

WALTER LORD

The Dawn's Early Light

THE JOHNS HOPKINS UNIVERSITY PRESS
BALTIMORE AND LONDON

To Marielle Mactier Hoffman

Originally published by W. W. Norton & Company, 1972
Johns Hopkins Paperbacks edition, 1994

The Johns Hopkins University Press
2715 North Charles Street
Baltimore, Maryland 21218-4319
The Johns Hopkins Press Ltd., London

Library of Congress Cataloging-in-Publication Data

Lord, Walter, 1917–
The dawn's early light / by Walter Lord.
p.   cm. — (Maryland paperback bookshelf)
Includes bibliographical references and index.
ISBN 0-8018-4864-4 (pbk. : acid-free paper)
1. Maryland—History—War of 1812—Campaigns. 2. United States—
History—War of 1812—Campaigns. I. Title. II. Series.
E355.L67   1994
973.5´23—dc20   93-43700

A catalog record for this book is available from the British Library.

Contents

	List of Illustrations	11
	Foreword	13
ONE	Sails on the Chesapeake	19
TWO	"Chastise the Savages"	33
THREE	Face to Face	59
FOUR	Sleepless Hours	91
FIVE	Time Runs Out	101
SIX	Bladensburg	123
SEVEN	Ordeal by Fire	145
EIGHT	Shock Waves	189
NINE	Focus on Baltimore	227
TEN	North Point	259
ELEVEN	Fort McHenry	277
TWELVE	Britain Struggles with Herself	301
THIRTEEN	"The Dawn's Early Light"	323
	Acknowledgments	345
	Chapter Notes	351
	Index	371

List of Illustrations

A 16-page section follows page 192:

    President James Madison

    Dolley Madison

    Vice Admiral Sir Alexander Cochrane

    Rear Admiral George Cockburn

    Brigadier General William H. Winder

    Commodore Joshua Barney

    Secretary of State James Monroe

    Three views of Washington burning

    The President's House before the fire

    The President's House after the fire

    "The fall of Washington or Maddy in full flight"

    The Capitol after the fire

    Benjamin H. Latrobe's drawing of fire damage
        to the Capitol

    Major General Samuel Smith

    Major George Armistead

    Francis Scott Key

    The death of General Ross

    The Battle of North Point

    Bombardment of Fort McHenry

11

The Star-Spangled Banner, the flag itself
Receipted bill for the flag
Andrew Jackson's victory at New Orleans

The following maps appear as indicated:

British Lines Of Approach   2
Advance on Washington   3
Three Eventful Days   4
Bladensburg   109
Washington D.C.   159
North Point   265
The Approach to the Mississippi   327
Final Repulse of the British at New Orleans   333

Foreword

Today, it is called the War of 1812. Then, it was often called the Second War of Independence, and a glimpse of America during those trying times suggests the reasons why.

Caught in the cross-fire of the Napoleonic Wars, the young republic was scorned as a real nation by the European powers. Both the French and the English ignored America's "neutral rights," but Britain's immense sea power made her the chief offender. For years she had impressed American sailors on the high seas; had issued a series of Orders in Council forbidding trade with Continental Europe; had not only blockaded the French coast but seized American vessels suspected of trading with the enemy, wherever found on the oceans.

For years America had proclaimed her rights in vain. Threats, lures, embargo, a Non-Intercourse Act—all were tried in turn, and nothing worked. Meanwhile other sores were festering too. The agricultural south saw its crop prices drop in the wake of British trade restrictions. Western settlers feared British intrigue among the Indians. Land-hungry "war hawks" openly longed for Canada.

Finally President James Madison came to the end of the road. Perhaps it would have been different if he had known

that London had for domestic reasons already decided to re-
peal the hated Orders in Council. But the step was taken and
the news arrived too late. On June 18, 1812, the United
States formally declared war on Great Britain.

Yet the very vote for war showed how nearly right Europe was in refusing to take the new country seriously. The
results showed anything but a strong, united people. All the
Federalists in Congress voted against the declaration. In the
Senate the margin was only 19 to 13, with New England almost solidly opposed. To the banking and shipping circles of
the east, the loss of an occasional ship or sailor was a small
price to pay for the profits to be made.

Nor did the war itself weld the nation together. "Let the
southern *Heroes* fight their own battles," advised the Reverend
Elijah Parish of Massachusetts. In New York and New England a lively smuggling trade developed, supplying the British
armies in Canada. To stop this traffic, Madison tried an embargo on all shipping. It was soon abandoned; it only increased the dissent that tore at the country.

Economically, America seemed almost hopelessly weak.
Committed to low taxes, the administration tried to finance
the war by borrowing, but money proved hard to get. Foreign banks were leary; while New England, the wealthiest
section of the country, declined to cooperate. Soon Washington was practically broke—Congress felt it couldn't even
afford $6,000 to pay the salaries of two Assistant Secretaries
of War.

Militarily too the picture was bleak. The *Constitution* beat
the *Guerrière*, and American privateers raised havoc with
British commerce, but the main front was Canada, and here
there was little to cheer about. Perry won Lake Erie, but it
was clear by the end of 1813 that the Canadian front was a
bloody stalemate.

Nor did the east coast escape. British warships maintained

an ever-tighter blockade, and during much of 1813 an enemy squadron roamed at will about the Chesapeake Bay. Raiding parties burned Frenchtown and Havre de Grace, pillaged Hampton, and prowled up the Potomac only 50 miles from Washington itself. The President's irrepressible wife Dolley dusted off "the old Tunisian sabre," but she seemed the only one prepared. The militia fluttered helplessly about, and naval defense was virtually nonexistent.

Finally the British sailed away, but by the spring of 1814 a strong squadron was back in the Bay again, harassing the shores as it pleased. Then in May sensational news arrived from France: Napoleon had fallen. His defeat released thousands of Wellington's tough veterans for service elsewhere —presumably across the Atlantic. Reports set the figure as high as 25,000 men; the objective: "unconditional submission."

And so the summer of 1814 found America threatened with national extinction—her people torn by dissension . . . her treasury empty . . . her economy in ruins . . . her coasts blockaded and defenseless . . . her army bogged down . . . her navy bottled up . . . her cities and farms now facing a new, apparently irresistible blow to be delivered at will by the richest, most powerful nation in the world. It would not be surprising if the whole American experiment collapsed under the impact.

Yet within eight months all had changed. America was again at peace, her people unified, her economy mending, her army and navy bursting with pride, her prospects limitless, her position safe in the family of nations. The turning point in this remarkable reversal of fortune is the story of this book. . . .

The Dawn's Early Light

CHAPTER ONE

Sails on the Chesapeake

The guests at the Pleasure House, a popular inn near Cape Henry, Virginia, could hardly believe their eyes. There in the first light of August 16, 1814, the horizon was dotted with sails, standing in from the rolling Atlantic.

By 8:30 they were entering the Chesapeake Bay, and Joseph Middleton—the U.S. Navy's lookout stationed at the hotel—could make them out pretty well: three big ships of the line, a brig, a topsail schooner, several frigates, at least nine transports—some 22 vessels altogether. With a good glass he caught sight of the blue flag of a British admiral flying from the mizzenmast of the leading ship. Middleton jotted down the details, and by 9:45 an express rider was pounding hard for Norfolk. But the ships didn't head that way. They turned north, and with fair wind and tide swept on up the Chesapeake.

Around 1:00 P.M. they passed New Point Comfort . . .

19

3:00, they were off Gwynn's Island . . . 6:00, Lieutenant Colonel John Shewning reported them abreast the Dividing Creeks near Wicomoco Church . . . 7:00, Major Hiram Blackwell picked them up off Smith Point at the mouth of the Potomac. Here they met about a dozen other ships, already in the Bay, and as the two groups joined forces, the evening echoed with the thunder of saluting guns.

Dawn of the 17th, a meticulous lawyer from Washington, D.C., named Thomas Swann took up the watch. Swann was a volunteer military observer for the U.S. Army, stationed at Point Lookout on the northern side of the mouth of the Potomac. His job was especially to keep an eye on ship movements.

This morning he had his hands full. The ships were spread over two miles, and a heavy August haze made the viewing difficult. But he managed to count them up, and during the night the total had grown to 46 sail. Adding three more frigates off St. Georges Island and another two in the Patuxent River, that made 51 altogether.

At 8:15 A.M. they began to head up the Bay again. There was no more time to lose. To Swann, all those transports meant only one thing: invasion. It was the third year of this ugly war with Britain, and now at last the fighting was moving south from the Canadian border to the nation's front door.

Collaring a young man by the name of Carmichael, Swann dashed off a dispatch and started him for Washington 70 miles away. All over the tidewater countryside other riders too were galloping over the rutted clay roads, bound on the same mission. For every vantage point in sight of the Bay, there was some leading citizen or militia officer who, heart in mouth, scribbled down the details and sent word to alert the capital.

Meanwhile Washington lay dozing and unknowing in the

August heat. Few could see any danger. John Armstrong, the stubborn, arrogant New York Democrat who was Madison's Secretary of War, felt the city was perfectly safe. Who on earth would want the place? He never liked the capital here, and every time he looked at the little clusters of buildings scattered around the swamps and meadows, he knew he was right. "This sheep walk," he called it.

James Monroe, the dedicated but ambitious Secretary of State from Virginia, feuded with Armstrong over almost everything; but on the subject of Washington's safety he was inclined to agree. Late in June he had written Minister William Crawford in Paris that any British expedition had "little prospect of success."

Secretary of the Navy William Jones, a modest, hard worker from Philadelphia, felt just as secure. In May, when Madison suggested that he might strengthen the capital's naval posture, Jones had three 12-pounders mounted on carriages at the Navy Yard. The cooks and clerks at Marine headquarters would man them. The rest of the cabinet were equally confident.

Some of these officials, it must be added, had their occasional doubts. When several of His Majesty's ships blockaded Commodore Joshua Barney's flotilla of American gunboats up the Patuxent River in June, Secretary Jones did indeed warn Barney of a possible strike at Washington. But on the whole, nobody expected anything serious, and every alarm was followed by a return to complacency.

There was one exception: the President himself. But James Madison was anything but forceful in driving home his opinions. He had none of that quality that would later be called charisma; he was only five feet, six; always dressed in black with old-fashioned knee britches. Unkindly but not unreasonably, Washington Irving called him "a withered little applejohn."

Yet he had a good head—Jefferson said there was none better—and his good head told him that with Napoleon out of the way, the British would be coming in force. Then, on June 26 a grim letter arrived from England supporting his worst fears. Dated May 6, it came from Albert Gallatin and James Bayard, two of five American peace commissioners sent by Madison at Downing Street's suggestion. They were marking time in London until the site of the conference was set, and what they saw was chilling. England had the troops to spare, "and there can be no doubt that if the war continues, as great a portion of that disposable force as will be competent to the objects of the British government will be employed in America. . . ."

That was enough for Madison. No time to waste trying to wake up Armstrong. Enlisting Monroe's help, the President quickly conjured up his own defense plan. It called for concentrating 2,000 or 3,000 men at some point covering both Baltimore and Washington. They would be in the field, ready to fight. An additional 10,000 to 12,000 militia would be earmarked in neighboring states, ready to assemble and march when called. It would have been better, of course, to put them on active duty, but as usual the problem was money. The government couldn't afford to pay or feed them.

Since the whole mission of this force was to protect the capital, the President also decided to give it special status by setting up a new military district for the area, under a separate, independent command. The new commanding general would be an attractive 39-year-old Brigadier named William Henry Winder.

In peacetime General Winder had been a Baltimore lawyer and politician. He had seen little military service. In his only battle he had been captured on the Canadian front and just recently exchanged. His ideas on tactics were unknown, and his immediate superior, Secretary Armstrong, was against the appointment.

Yet there were good reasons for naming him. First, he was available—often important in the military selection process. Also, the very fact that Armstrong opposed him worked in his favor with Monroe, as the two Secretaries continued their feuding. But most important, Winder's uncle was the Honorable Levin Winder, the Federalist Governor of Maryland. The state was bitterly divided on the war, yet had to supply most of the militia for this particular effort. It was all-important to win the Governor's support. What better way than to make his nephew the commanding general?

July 1, promptly at noon, the cabinet assembled to hear the plan at the President's House on Pennsylvania Avenue. Standing bare on unlandscaped ground, the building had a rather unfinished look; yet it somehow promised great things to come, and along with the Capitol, it was quite the pride of Washington. It was just beginning to be called the White House.

Madison explained the danger, collected some unimpressive defense statistics from Armstrong, then outlined his scheme. The cabinet had no ideas to add, and the meeting adjourned after a large dinner, which the President always hoped in vain would bring his official family closer together.

Now to put the plan into action. July 2, the 10th Military District was officially set up, covering northern Virginia, Maryland and the District of Columbia, with General Winder in command. July 4, a requisition went out to the governors of all 15 states calling for 93,500 militia to be held in readiness.

It took General Winder about a week to discover that his command existed mainly on paper. He had no staff, no transport, no surgeon, no provisions, no rifles, no flints. There

wasn't even a guard at his door. There were few regulars and
no militia. It turned out that Secretary Armstrong had a pet
theory that militia fought best on the spur of the moment. It
dulled their spirit, he felt, to spend time drilling in camp; so
they would be called up only when the British appeared.

Winder did his best to point out that this would be too
late. "What possible chance will there be of collecting a force
after the arrival of the enemy?" he wrote Armstrong on July
9. "He can be in Washington, Baltimore or Annapolis in four
days after entering the Capes."

Armstrong never even answered. Stuck with a plan and a
general he didn't want, he let the whole business slide. He
rarely replied to any of Winder's letters. He failed to stock-
pile military stores, as directed by the President. It took him
six days to get a copy of the militia requisition to the Governor of Maryland, only 23 miles away. He idled ten days before sending Winder authority to call out any of the militia
he had been appointed to command.

Even then, the General was severely limited. Although the
militia pool totaled 93,500 men, Winder was authorized to
draw only on Maryland's quota of 6,000—and these only
"in case of actual or menaced invasion." Later some Pennsyl-
vanians and Virginians were added on the same basis, but he
never had authority to call more than 3,000 Marylanders for
immediate service.

Undismayed, Winder deluged the Secretary with a stream
of suggestions and questions. How to strengthen Annapolis?
Were express riders stationed at observation points along the
Bay? Shouldn't the militia from remote places be drafted first,
since it would take them longer to assemble? Would Armstrong order some necessary tents and supplies? "I have no
knowledge where these articles are. . . . I must pray you
give the necessary orders."

As usual, Armstrong didn't answer.

The Secretary's whole performance seemed incredible to tall, impressive Major General John P. Van Ness, who commanded the District of Columbia Militia. A civic-minded banker deeply involved in the capital's future, he had seen Secretary Armstrong on several occasions, always urging that the city's defenses be strengthened. This July he finally went to James Monroe and asked if the government was deliberately planning to abandon Washington. Not at all, said Monroe; "every inch" would be defended.

More danger signals were coming in. Mid-July a batch of Canadian newspapers arrived, reporting that thousands of British troops were boarding transports in France, bound for America. The stories were uncomfortably specific, even ticking off the regiments. The latest London papers said the same thing.

Van Ness decided to try once again. He went back to Armstrong, this time urging an extension of the earthworks at Fort Washington, a key position 12 miles down the Potomac. The owner of the land wanted too much for it, the Secretary replied, "considering how poor the government was."

In exasperation Van Ness got the local banks to offer the administration a $200,000 loan to build the necessary fortifications. If the government wouldn't put up the money to defend its own capital, the citizens would do it themselves.

No one charged General Winder with such indifference. The commander of the 10th Military District was a whirlwind. Nothing seemed too small to occupy his personal attention. One minute he was mediating a quarrel between Paymaster Clark and Colonel Carberry over the clerical services of Sergeant Rowe . . . the next, he was telling "the non-commissioned officer left at Butler's Mills" to obey his captain . . . the next, he was arranging a corporal's guard to escort two cannon to Washington.

And all the while, he was dashing around the countryside

at a pace suggesting that he equated activity with accomplishment. July 24, he was at Nottingham . . . the 25th, at Fort Washington . . . the 26th, at Port Tobacco . . . the 27th, at Piscataway . . . the 28th, at Upper Marlboro . . . the 30th, back at Washington. He gyrated about so much that one of Armstrong's few letters, mailed on the 17th, took 22 days to catch up with him.

This passion for trivia and movement left little time for the kind of thinking that went into being the commanding general. Weeks rolled by, yet Winder developed no over-all plan for defending his district. The capital had no fortifications, nor did he devise any. Alexandria, the most important city near Washington, was left entirely out of his calculations. He was desperate for men, but did little to get them. He was positively diffident when he wrote Major General Samuel Smith, the tough commander of the 3rd Division of Maryland Militia, asking how much help he might expect. Winder wondered whether the Maryland troops would act under himself or, as he gingerly put it, "whether they expected to act as allies with the troops in the service of the United States but independently of their authority and that of their officers and solely for the defense of Baltimore."

The turnout was predictably poor. Of the 3,000 Maryland Militia called out, Winder got only 250. As July turned to August, the General privately wrote Secretary Armstrong that in his official dispatches he deliberately kept his troop figures vague "to tranquilize the morbid sensibility of the people of the District."

The political situation in Maryland was as touchy as ever. Governor Levin Winder's nephew might be the commanding general, but the Governor himself remained cool to the war. The Federalist-controlled state legislature felt the same, and opinion in some tidewater counties bordered on treason. Still bottled up in the Patuxent, Commodore Barney had a good chance to observe, and he sent a stream of bitter comments to Secretary Jones. The inhabitants at Benedict spiked some of his guns. . . . "Old Major Taney" supplied a British shore party with horses. . . . The local people told the enemy everything. In fairness, most of the inhabitants were at the mercy of the Royal Navy if they didn't cooperate.

The only open contact permitted with the enemy was through John S. Skinner, the exchange officer on prisoners of war. Mid-August he visited the British squadron and returned to report a disquieting remark by the commanding officer, Rear Admiral George Cockburn: "I believe, Mr. Skinner, that Mr. Madison will have to put on his armour and fight it out."

This sparked a flurry of interest, but most Americans considered Cockburn a braggart, and Washington soon lapsed in the doldrums of a smothering heat wave. Congress had adjourned, and the wealthy citizens were away at country places or taking the waters in Virginia or Maryland. On August 13 the Washington Theater, the capital's only gesture to sophisticated living, gave up and closed for the rest of the summer. The few people remaining in town went about their small affairs. Thomas L. McKenney decided to sell one of his drygoods stores; Roger Chew Weightman, the enterprising book dealer on Pennsylvania Avenue, offered a new *Life of Wellington* (despite the war, the British General remained a favorite); and, reminding one that the nation's capital was really a small town after all, a Mr. Doyhar advertised for a red cow that had strayed away from his place on F Street.

The 18th began like just another day. At the plain brick building shared by the State, War and Navy Departments, Secretary of State Monroe glanced over an application from the British prisoner-of-war agent Thomas Barclay, asking permission to come to Washington on personal business. Normally Barclay was confined to Bladensburg, a small village just northeast of the capital. Here he had little opportunity to gather intelligence for His Majesty's government, but apart from professional considerations, Barclay hated the sleepy little place and used any excuse to come to town. This time there seemed no harm. Nothing much was going on . . . few British raiding parties were about . . . Washington itself was dead in the August heat. Monroe issued a pass good through August 20.

Across the hall the War Department's new accountant Tobias Lear hunched over his desk. He busily scratched away at a letter to Colonel William Pratt in New Orleans, pointing out that 7 pairs of hinges at 37½ ¢ cost $2.62½, not the $8.62½ claimed by the Colonel.

Elsewhere in the building Allen McLane, Collector of the Port of Wilmington, Delaware, complained to Secretary Jones about the navy's seizure of some ships and cargoes in his district. Suddenly he was interrupted—an express just in, requiring Jones's immediate attention. Carmichael, the messenger from Point Lookout, had arrived with the momentous news that the British invasion fleet was at hand.

Instantly, McLane forgot all about business. He was a veteran of the Revolution, and he smelled powder again. He knew Secretary of War Armstrong from the old days and rushed to offer his services. Armstrong didn't know what to do with him and bucked him off on General Winder. More or less impulsively the General made him an aide and put him in charge of getting 300 axes to the Wood Yard, a camp site taking shape 12 miles east of Washington. The axes would be vitally needed for blocking the British advance, wherever they landed—an important assignment to give a totally untried stranger who just happened to be in town on a customs problem.

If Winder seemed harassed and preoccupied, it was understandable. With the enemy about to land, he was suddenly faced with the cold reality of his paper army. He didn't have the thousand regulars so firmly promised when he took command . . . he didn't have the 15,000 militia Armstrong authorized "in case of actual or menaced invasion" . . . he didn't even have the 3,000 militia promised right away. Scraping everything together, all he really had was a mixed bag of 330 regulars at Piscataway down the Potomac, 140 cavalry near Georgetown, 240 Maryland Militia at Bladensburg, and 1,400 more militia at Baltimore 40 miles away—about 2,100 scattered men to meet the conquerors of Napoleon.

McLane and the axes were forgotten as the General spent a frantic afternoon churning out appeals for more help. He was staying at McKeowin's Hotel down Pennsylvania Avenue, and without anyone planning it, the place became a sort of unofficial headquarters. Clouds of dust rose from the broad unpaved roadway as couriers, officials and well-meaning amateurs came and went.

Orders flew in all directions. Locally, General Van Ness was told to call up his District of Columbia Militia. In Baltimore, General Samuel Smith was ordered to federalize his whole 3rd Division and hold it ready for active service. In Virginia, Brigadier General John P. Hungerford, 120 miles below, was summoned with his 2,000 veteran militiamen. Special appeals went to the governors of Maryland and Pennsylvania for help in the emergency, and a circular order was sent to every militia brigadier in Maryland, asking each to send 500 men.

And what to do with these men when they came? How to use them? It all depended on where the British planned to strike. . . .

Annapolis, thought Winder. A fine port, easy to defend, a good base for conducting future operations. Supporting his hunch, a British frigate was hovering offshore, and some of the enemy's boats were buoying the nearby South River.

Baltimore, guessed Armstrong. In any case, not Washington. As always, the capital was nothing more than a sheep walk. No one would want it.

James Monroe thought differently. He first heard the news while visiting Madison that morning, and immediately remarked that the most likely target was Washington itself. After all, it was the nation's capital. Madison agreed, tactfully overlooking the point that this was what he had been saying all along to a skeptical cabinet, including Monroe. But Madison had more than a convert in his Secretary of State—he had a rare man of action. During the Revolution James Monroe had been a dashing young cavalry colonel. Although his subsequent career always seemed to lead him to a desk, he never lost his thirst for sheer physical activity. When this new war broke out, he openly yearned for a field command, but Madison told him he was needed in Washington. This appeal to his sense of duty touched another wellspring in his character. Just as some men crave money or power, the idea of public service was an obsession—almost a matter of vanity—with James Monroe.

So it was back to desk work, but always with an eye on the field. He chafed at the string of incompetents who botched up the war in Canada. He suffered as Armstrong dragged his feet this summer in Washington. He fretted as Winder hopelessly floundered around. And now that the British were really here, he could stand it no longer. He turned to Madison and made what was surely a most remarkable request for a Secretary of State of the United States: Could he take a few horsemen, ride out to the "coast," and see what the British were really up to?

The President said yes. The necessary orders were issued, and Captain Thornton of Alexandria was assigned to provide an escort of 25 to 30 local dragoons. There was some delay getting everyone together, but at 1:00 P.M. on August 19 Monroe set out. Behind him lay the chaos of Washington; ahead, the mystery of British intentions.

CHAPTER TWO

"Chastise the Savages"

"Now that the tyrant Bonaparte has been consigned to infamy," declared the London *Times* on April 15, "there is no public feeling in this country stronger than that of indignation against the Americans." And with good reason:

> That a republic boasting of its freedom should have stooped to become the tool of the Monster's ambition; that it should have attempted to plunge the parricidal weapon into the heart of that country from whence its own origin was derived; that it should have chosen the precise moment when it fancied that Russia was overwhelmed, to attempt to consummate the ruin of Britain—all this is conduct so black, so loathsome, so hateful, that it naturally stirs up the indignation that we have described.

Actually, Washington knew nothing about Napoleon's Russian venture at the time war was declared. But the British people weren't interested in chronology. Nor did they care about American grievances. They only knew that Britain had been fighting for freedom—*everybody's* freedom—and for what seemed the most trivial, legalistic reasons, America had made war on her.

"Only two motives can with the least show of plausibility be assigned to Madison's conduct—venality, or malice," declared the *Times*. "It is possible that he may have been in the direct pay of Bonaparte; or it is possible he may have performed the monster's bidding out of pure rancour toward England."

Madison himself was always the villain. The picture of the gentle, ineffectual scholar—all too evident in Washington—never crossed the Atlantic. In London he was a vicious, crafty gnome. "An ambitious madman," the *National Register* called him. "Liar" . . . "serpent" . . . "impostor" . . . "traitor" . . . "wretched tool"—the *Times* labeled him all these in the space of four days.

Americans in general were not so much evil as contemptible, with special scorn reserved for the military. The London press caustically quoted a New York Militia notice begging the men to be "punctual." A correspondent wrote the *United Service Journal* that American officers were "a strange, uncouth set." And describing their appalling taste in one wine mess, he exploded: "Some preferred gin sling! Some rum twist! One gentleman preferred BUTTERMILK!!!"

These buttermilk warriors would be no match for "Wellington's Invincibles." It was just a question of what peace terms to impose. The House of Commons rocked with cheers as Major Barber Beaumont called for a new Canadian frontier; a new Indian boundary; Americans to be excluded from the Canadian fisheries and from trading with the British West Indies; America forbidden to take over Florida; the cession of New Orleans; plus a final and somewhat ambiguous insistence on "the distinct abandonment of the new-fangled American public law."

The *Times* refined all this a little, demanding that the Canadian boundary be at least a hundred miles below the Great Lakes and not less than ten miles from Lake Champlain. It also urged an indemnity and, confusing the American with the British political system, it called for the dismissal of Madison. "Certainly it would be the height of folly in the British government to sheath the sword so long as a faction which is so steeped in hatred of our name retains the reins of power."

But more than any specific terms, what most Britons wanted was to punish America. A century later, war would be far too costly, complex and overwhelming for such an uncomplicated goal, but this spring of 1814 it was very real indeed.

"Chastise" was the word. Gleefully turning around a phrase Madison had used in describing his Indian policy, the *Times* demanded that Britain "not only chastise the savages into present peace, but make a lasting impression on their fears." Major Beaumont picked it up in his rousing speech to Commons, and even the professional military joined the game. "Government have turned their views toward the *chastisement* of *America*," Colonel Henry Torrens, military secretary at the Horse Guards, enthusiastically wrote Lieutenant General Sir Henry Clinton.

Madison's peace commissioner Albert Gallatin, still sitting in London while the British completed arrangements for the coming negotiations, got the point. "To use their own language," he wrote Monroe, "they mean to inflict on America a chastisement that will teach her that war is not to be declared against Great Britain with impunity."

Only Gallatin and his colleagues, many Britons felt, stood in the way. These wily men would be using all their tricks to save the Americans. Let Britain be on her guard. "May no false liberality, no mistaken lenity, no weak or cowardly policy interpose to save them from the blow," warned the *Times*, and once again: "Strike. Chastise the savages. . . ."

There was little need to worry. Feelings were running so high the government couldn't have offered easy terms if it had wanted to. When one member of Commons had the temerity to propose an early peace with America, he was greeted by a storm of hisses and cries of "Off! Off!" His resolution was quickly voted down with tumultuous cheers.

Lost in the boasts and the swagger of this giddy spring were the doubts of a solitary soldier—the Duke of Wellington. The Duke enjoyed these days of triumph as much as anyone—he was quite aware of his own importance—but he also remained as levelheaded as ever. As early as February, while he was still battering at the gates of France, he wrote the Secretary for War and the Colonies Earl Bathurst a sobering assessment of prospects in America. As he saw it, geography was all against Britain. The trackless wastes, the lack of roads, the thin population made large-scale military operations impractical.

> You may go to a certain extent, as far as a navigable river or your means of transport will enable you to subsist, provided your force is sufficiently large compared with that with which the enemy will oppose you. But I do not know where you could carry on such an operation which would be so injurious to the Americans as to force them to sue for peace, which is what one would wish to see. The prospect in regard to America is not consoling.

Nobody else gave it a thought. "The Government have determined to give Jonathan a good drubbing," Colonel Torrens assured Major General Sir George Murray on April 14. That same day official orders were sent to Wellington, earmarking some 13,400 infantry plus small detachments of cavalry and artillery for this laudable purpose. No objective was mentioned; it was simply to be an attack on the American coast.

But even Britain couldn't do everything at once. It turned out that most of the army was needed to keep order in France. Other troops were wanted for Flanders . . . still others for Canada, where Sir George Prevost was to launch a drive of his own. Nor did it help when Wellington refused to let any of the light infantry leave Europe.

All this set back the schedule and cut down the number of men available. Small matter. Jonathan's drubbing wouldn't take much. Mid-May, some of the designated troops were dropped altogether; 6,000 others were syphoned off for Prevost. This left about 2,800 men waiting at Bordeaux and 1,000 others near the Mediterranean. All would go to the British base at Bermuda, where they'd join the marines and naval units already on hand. Operating together, they were "to effect a diversion on the coasts of the United States in favor of the armies employed in the defense of Upper and Lower Canada."

There were still no specific targets. Vice Admiral Sir Alexander Cochrane—the over-all commander waiting at Bermuda—was simply told to use the force "in such operations as may be found best calculated for the advantage of H.M. service, and the annoyance of the enemy."

About May 20, after much juggling, command of the troops was given to Major General Robert Ross, one of Wellington's many competent if somewhat anonymous subordinates. Ross was a 47-year-old Irish country gentleman with bright blue eyes and a ready smile. But behind that pleasant front, he was also the toughest of disciplinarians. Despite this, his men respected him, for like most soldiers, they would put up with almost any qualities in a commander as long as his system paid off. It was enough for them that in the long retreat to Coruña in the Peninsular campaign, Ross's 20th Foot—thanks to all that hard drilling—lost fewer men than any other regiment.

He also had another quality the men admired. Whatever the hardships or danger, Ross was right there with them. He had been wounded twice, and at Pamplona had two horses shot out from under him. Sometimes he almost seemed to be daring death.

Ross's instructions, meticulously drawn up by Earl Bathurst, carefully spelled out his relations with Admiral Cochrane. The Admiral would pick the targets, but Ross should "freely express" his opinion from the military point of view. He also had veto power over the use of his troops, and once ashore had complete control over their operations. He was especially cautioned "not to engage in any extended operation at a distance from the coast."

Bathurst had another caution too. "You will not encourage any disposition which may be manifested by the Negroes to rise upon their masters."

This raised a most sensitive question. What to do about the slaves in any southern states attacked? The first whisperings of nineteenth-century liberalism were already rustling through England. William Wilberforce had persuaded Parliament to stop the slave trade, and universal abolition was in the air. It was a great temptation to turn the invasion into something of a crusade, enlisting the slaves in the British Army in a battle for their own freedom. It was also a way (although less was said about this) to help solve the manpower shortage that had watered down the first joyful plans for chastisement. On the other hand, Britain was a growing colonial power too, and in a different sense the barriers between white and black were becoming ever more firmly cemented into place. To the aristocratic gentlemen planning the attack, it was a squeamish business, turning the slaves loose on "our own kind."

The solution was highly ambivalent. Earl Bathurst's orders were firm against encouraging any insurrection: "The humanity which ever influences His Royal Highness" recoiled against "the atrocities inseparable from commotions of such a description." But if individual Negroes happened to help, that would be quite all right. They could either enlist in a Black Corps or go as free settlers to a British colony . . . the Admiral had full instructions.

The full instructions showed a curiously offhand concept of geography. Northern Negroes were to be sent to Halifax; southern to Trinidad. There was no clue as to what was a "northern" or a "southern" Negro, nor was there any policy for handling either category. It was impossible to say whether a black might be better off "northern" and shivering without a job in Halifax, or "southern" and toiling once again as a field hand in Trinidad.

With the plan finally set, the whole cumbersome machinery of the British government swung into action, grinding out the necessary orders. "Colonel Torrens is directed by the Commander-in-Chief," one typical directive began, "to request Major General Bunbury to move Earl Bathurst to give directions to the Commissioners for the Transport Service to provide a conveyance. . . ."

The sober shuffling of paper at Whitehall offered a curious counterpoint to the tumultuous joy that swept London all spring. Napoleon was really gone. For the moment everyone forgot the harsh realities of life in the Regency—the high prices, the Corn Laws, the dreadful extremes between rich and poor. Angry reformers like William Cobbett scolded "the senseless, noisy joy of England," but nobody listened. The people were lost in euphoria; they wanted only to rejoice and shower their gratitude on the rulers who had brought them through.

This took some doing. The Prime Minister Lord Liverpool was drab and pious. The Tory cabinet, though capable, was utterly colorless. And the Royal Family itself verged on the scandalous. The "old King" George III was hopelessly mad; the Prince Regent was a shrewd but lazy rake; the Duke of York was a nominal Commander-in-Chief whose mistress had been caught peddling army commissions. Indeed, the royal sons were collectively described by Wellington himself as "the damndest millstones about the neck of any government that can be imagined."

Yet none of it mattered this spring, and on June 2 excitement reached a new peak when a *Gazette Extraordinary* announced the signing of peace with France. As if to cap this glorious news, that evening the Queen held a Drawing Room at Buckingham House that proved, according to the press, "the most numerous and splendid assemblage ever before witnessed in this or any other country."

Crowds surged around the carriages rolling toward the scene, and as they recognized Lord Hill, Beresford and other heroes of the Peninsula, great huzzahs went up. On the front lawn the band of the Royal Horse Guards was stationed, with its great silver kettle drums thundering in time to "Rule, Britannia." As the Grand Duchess Oldenburgh of Russia entered the gates, the Tower guns began to fire, saluting the end of the European war.

At just about this time 450 miles to the south, signal flags fluttered from HMS *Royal Oak*, 74 guns, anchored in the Gironde Estuary west of Bordeaux. Then came the rattle of anchor chains, the creaking of block and tackle, and at 5:30 P.M. she glided seaward on a gentle ebb tide. Thirteen other warships and three transports fell in behind her; the British invasion force to chastise the Americans was on the way.

Flying from the *Royal Oak* was the blue flag of the convoy commander, Rear Admiral Poultney Malcolm. He proved a congenial officer who practically never slept and when he did, kept up a stream of conversation which no one understood and he never remembered afterward. But he was a good host, maintaining a lavish table for General Ross and his suite, who were guests on the flagship.

Packed on the vessels that trailed behind were the best units of three regiments: the 4th, 44th and 85th Foot—2,814 men altogether. On the *Diadem* Lieutenant George Robert Gleig of the 85th found himself jammed in a cabin with 40 other junior officers. At that, he was better off than the enlisted men and seamen crowded together below. Hot, damp, dark, smelly—their life was all that and worse. For food, there was usually just salt beef, tough as mahogany; cheese so hard it could be made into buttons; and biscuits so full of insect life that before eating, the men would tap them on the table to shake out the bugs.

But Wellington's Invincibles were above all adaptable. Life soon settled down to the not unpleasant monotony of a seven-week trooping voyage. A newspaper, christened *The Atlantic News*, made its appearance on the *Royal Oak*. Captain Hanchett of the *Diadem* opened his fine library to the officers of the 85th. The men on the *Weser* attempted a production of Sheridan's *The Rivals*, enlivened when a sudden squall sent both performers and audience reeling. On calmer evenings the superb band of the *Menelaus* serenaded the nearby ships, reminding everyone of home.

The social high point of the voyage came one evening when the fleet lay to, and Admiral Malcolm invited officers from all the ships to the *Royal Oak* for a play and grand ball. Cutters and pinnaces streamed to the flagship, and as the visitors came aboard, they found the guns rolled aside and the deck festooned with bunting and lanterns. After a vigorous performance of *The Apprentice*, the grand ball opened with a country dance by Admiral Malcolm and the Honorable Mrs. Thomas Mullins, wife of the Lieutenant Colonel of the 44th Regiment. She, as sometimes happened on long campaigns, had wangled approval to come along on the expedition. There were a few other wives, but for the most part the officers had to dance with one another.

Not invited to the ball and remaining shadowy figures below decks, were other women in the fleet. It was completely against regulations to have them along on an operational voyage, but the captains were practical men, and some looked the other way. Never mentioned officially in the logs or muster rolls, they were occasionally referred to euphemistically as the men's "wives," but most often were called just what they were—"the women on the ship."

The situation briefly surfaced toward the end of June, when typhoid broke out on the *Diadem*, hitting one of the "women" along with some 30 men. But the fleet's main problem was always water—the *Weser* stowed only 90 tons for 538 on board—and on June 21 the convoy stopped at the Azores for more.

June 23, they were on their way again, and on the 26th Admiral Malcolm sent the fast frigate *Pactolus* ahead to give Admiral Cochrane advance word of their coming. The troops were in fine spirits, he reported, "all anxious to punish the Americans for depriving them of the pleasure of returning home after their long and glorious service in the Peninsula. . . ."

At Bermuda, Sir Alexander Cochrane waited impatiently. Just appointed to replace the elderly Admiral John Borlase Warren as commander of the North American Station, Cochrane would hopefully be more aggressive, and he was only too delighted to oblige.

How he hated Americans. It was one of the important

qualities he brought to the job, although actually he had seen very little of them firsthand. Most of his career had been spent in the Mediterranean and West Indies, much of it on administrative work. He had done a stint in Parliament and most recently had been Governor of Guadeloupe. This contact with the political world had greatly sharpened his sensitivities in that direction—he knew all about prize money, the amenities of office, the art of fence-mending, and especially the game of patronage and "interest." He had managed to enter his son Thomas as a "volunteer" on his nephew's ship in his own squadron at the remarkable age of seven. With this kind of maneuvering, the boy was a captain at 17, and one of the Admiral's pet projects was to bring the young man (now an old veteran of 25) back under his protective eye.

He had a thousand schemes. Sir Alexander knew nothing of events in Europe, but he assumed Napoleon was finished, and with 15,000 of Wellington's army, there was nothing he couldn't do. "I am confident," he wrote Lord Melville, First Lord of the Admiralty, on March 10, "that all the country southwest of the Chesapeake might be restored to the dominion of Great Britain, if under the command of enterprising generals."

As a starter, he planned to kidnap political leaders close to the Madison administration. This would have to be done from within, but that could be arranged. "A little money well applied will attain almost any object amongst such a corrupt and depraved race."

By March 25 he had a new idea. Gone was the plan to redeem Virginia and kidnap the Madisonians. Instead, he'd take the army to New Hampshire, destroy the Portsmouth Navy Yard, and send it slashing its way overland to join Prevost in Canada.

This would mean few troops for the south, but he hoped to make up for that by encouraging "the disaffection of the colored population." If he could get the slaves to join the British cause, there was no limit to what might be done. Tangier Island in the Chesapeake Bay would be seized with this end in view: "When fortified it will be a place of refuge for the blacks to fly to."

All this was certainly stretching his orders—they covered only individual Negroes seeking his protection—but he was prepared for that. In forwarding to London a proclamation he planned to distribute to the blacks, he assured Lord Melville, "I keep the Ministers out of sight." As for the Americans, let them howl: "They are a whining, canting race much like the spaniel and require the same treatment—must be drubbed into good manners."

April, he was mainly concerned with the blockade. Originally he had planned to go easy on New England, feeling that a soft policy might encourage secession. Now it was the other way around. His political intelligence expert James Stewart, formerly British Vice Consul at New London, assured him that a tight blockade was the way to get secession; so that was how it would be.

May, his mind turned again to landings on the Chesapeake. On the 27th he wrote Admiral Cockburn in the Bay to start collecting the necessary information. He would pay well, he added vaguely, for "some enterprizing characters who run all risks for money."

Cochrane's chief interest continued to be his scheme to recruit blacks to the British cause. From now on, he wrote Cockburn on July 1, the main purpose of his landings should be to cover the Negroes as they swarmed under British protection. "The great point to be attained is the cordial support of the Black population. With them properly armed and backed with 20,000 British troops, Mr. Maddison will be hurled from his throne."

"The Blacks are all good horsemen," he assured Earl Bathurst on the 14th. "Thousands will join upon their masters' horses, and they will only require to be clothed and accoutered to be as good Cossacks as any in the European army, and I believe more terrific to the Americans than any troops that could be brought forward. I have it much at heart to give them a complete drubbing."

There was little ground for such optimism. At this moment, after three months of the most energetic efforts, Admiral Cockburn had been able to raise only 120 black recruits.

Cockburn unconsciously touched on the heart of the problem in his very first comment on Cochrane's Proclamation:

> If you attach importance to forming a corps of these Blacks to act against their former masters, I think, my dear Sir, your Proclamation should not so distinctly hold out to them the option of being sent as free settlers to British settlements, which they will most certainly all prefer to the danger and fatigue of joining us in arms. In the temptations I now hold out to them, I shall therefore only mention generally our willingness and readiness to receive and protect them. . . .

Yet changing the emphasis meant ending the chance of winning any large number of blacks at all. They were interested mainly in true, not nominal freedom. If they couldn't have that, it made little difference whether they stayed in the fields or served in a Royal regiment. They didn't want to be used by either the Americans or the British.

But Cochrane planned on. When he wasn't dreaming up fanciful intelligence networks or legions of black Cossacks, he was concocting new operations for the troops he daily expected. There were reports of Lord Hill with 15,000 from Bordeaux . . . two regiments more from the Mediterranean . . . others from England. He could see 20,000 altogether.

Mid-June, he felt he might operate in the Chesapeake until

July, then go to Block Island—a good base for attacking New England. July 1, he toyed with the idea of assaulting Philadelphia, Washington or Baltimore—he didn't care which, although he leaned toward Baltimore. July 17, he was planning to take New York by landing on Long Island and bombarding the city from Brooklyn . . . or maybe he'd seize Philadelphia, then move south ultimately to Richmond. July 23, all that was forgotten; now he'd attack either Portsmouth or Rhode Island. "I do not think any attempt should be made south of the Delaware before October."

Whatever he did, he would hit hard. On July 17 a letter arrived from Sir George Prevost complaining of new American atrocities in Canada—specifically the burning of Dover—and calling on Cochrane to assist in retaliating. The Admiral was happy to oblige. Back in January—before leaving London—he had asked Lord Melville for "a quantity of combustible matter made up in packages from 50 to 5 pounds each, not to be extinguished by water. . . ." Now he had his official sanction. July 18, he issued orders to his fleet "to destroy and lay waste such towns and districts upon the coast as you may find assailable."

To this, however, he added a secret memo, authorizing his forces to spare most kinds of property in return for tribute. This opened up the possibility of prize money instead of just ashes as the fruit of retaliation. With evident relief, the Admiral's new fleet captain, Edward Codrington, wrote his wife about the policy, "I hope it will not be the less productive of prize money, of which I begin to expect a bigger share than I had promised myself."

And beyond seizing goods and exacting tribute on the eastern seaboard, Sir Alexander eyed a far more lucrative target to the south. Early in the spring he had sent a mission to the Creek Indians on the Gulf Coast. Long before the mission arrived, Andrew Jackson had virtually wiped out the Creeks at

Horseshoe Bend, but nothing was said about this. Back came reports that thousands would flock to the British colors, and New Orleans lay open for the taking. This would not only divert the Americans from Canada, but yield untold riches in cotton, sugar and other stores that had piled up in New Orleans since the blockade. The total worth was said to be £4,000,000; the Commander-in-Chief's share could come to over £125,000.

June 20, Cochrane wrote the Admiralty urging approval for an expedition. Knowing the government's penchant for cheap operations, he stressed that the Indians and disaffected Creoles would do most of the work; he would need only 3,000 British troops. Writing Earl Bathurst a few days later, he even improved on that: 2,000 troops would be enough. Keeping his fences mended, he sent along with his letter a turtle for the Earl and some arrowroot for Lady Bathurst.

Anticipating approval, Cochrane also dispatched Major Edward Nicolls of the Royal Marines with a detachment of 115 men to work with the Creeks. They took along two guns and a thousand muskets. He would have sent more, he wrote his friend Governor Cameron of the Bahamas, but he needed everything for the momentous events about to break "in the heart of the United States as soon as Lord Hill and the army come."

These high hopes suffered a mild setback on July 21, when the *Pactolus* arrived with word that Admiral Malcolm was approaching. Now for the first time Cochrane learned that his force would be closer to 5,000 than 20,000 men. Still, he could do a lot with that, and there was much rejoicing three days later when the *Royal Oak* led the convoy safely in. As she passed Cochrane's flagship, the 80-gun *Tonnant*, the coral cottages of St. George's echoed to a 15-gun salute. Meeting Malcolm and Ross, Sir Alexander outlined his latest scheme, the proposed attack on Portsmouth or Rhode Island.

All that was changed July 26. This day the sloop *St. Lawrence* arrived from the Chesapeake with the latest dispatches from Rear Admiral Cockburn. Included were detailed answers to a long query from Cochrane on the 1st, fishing for advice on where to strike to hurt the Americans the most.

Self-assured George Cockburn knew exactly what to do: "I feel no hesitation in stating to you that I consider the town of Benedict in the Patuxent, to offer us advantages for this purpose beyond any other spot within the United States. . . . Within forty-eight hours after the arrival in the Patuxent of such a force as you expect, the City of Washington might be possessed without difficulty or opposition of any kind."

He ticked off his reasons—the ease and speed the operation offered, so important in launching the assault . . . the éclat of taking the enemy's capital, "always so great a blow to the government of a country," . . . the relative difficulty of attacking Baltimore or Annapolis first (two of Cochrane's ideas), but the ease of taking them from the rear once Washington was secured. And to his broad strategy, he added the extra touch of a good tactician:

> If Washington (as I strongly recommend) be deemed worthy of our *first* efforts, although our main force should be landed in the Patuxent, yet a tolerably good division should at the same time be sent up the Potowmac with bomb ships etc, which will tend to distract and divide the enemy, amuse Fort Washington, if it does not reduce it, and will most probably offer other advantages. . . .

Everything was ready. The Patuxent had been mapped, soundings taken, a good American guide put on the payroll. Now Cockburn said he was leaving the river, lest the enemy suspect something. Next he would go to the Potomac and do a little charting there too. But again, he wouldn't stay long; he didn't want to give away the show.

This display of total confidence ended Cochrane's vacillation. He would head for the Chesapeake. And by the grapevine that has laced all military operations through all time, the decision—which Sir Alexander considered the darkest of secrets—spread instantly through the fleet. Excitement mounted still further on the 29th, when more sails appeared from out of the east. A new convoy from the Mediterranean brought three more regiments. Two were for Canada, but the third—the 21st Foot—was a splendid-looking outfit that joined up with Ross's force.

Now for last-minute preparations. As always before a troop embarkation, everything was confusion. The *Diadem* leaked. None of the ships had enough provisions. Ross's troops had no maps, no entrenching tools, no medicines. In the chaos, Lieutenant Gleig tried to smuggle a small black boy aboard the transport *Golden Fleece* as a mascot, but he was caught and barely escaped a fine.

August 1, order miraculously began to return. During the morning General Ross and his suite came aboard the *Tonnant*, and shortly before noon, with Admiral Cochrane's red flag flying at the fore, the great flagship weighed anchor. Followed by two frigates, she glided down Whalebone Bay, through the treacherous reefs, and turned westward on the sparkling Atlantic.

"We are on our way to the Chesapeake—mind you don't tell the Yankees," Captain Codrington playfully wrote his wife on the 3rd. That same day Malcolm and the troop convoy followed from Bermuda—24 vessels altogether. Once again life settled down to the usual shipboard days of sunning, fishing, gambling and boredom . . . broken only when someone remembered that the 12th was the first day of grouse-shooting back home, and an impromptu celebration broke out.

Far ahead, the *Tonnant* swept through the Capes on the 11th and started up the Chesapeake. The long sea voyage had given Admiral Cochrane plenty of time for thinking, and by now he wasn't nearly as enthusiastic about this venture. "I cannot at present acquaint their Lordships of what may be my future operations," he wrote the Admiralty, "they will depend much on what information I may receive in this quarter."

August 12 was too hot to decide anything. To men used to an English summer (or at worst, the dry heat of the Peninsula) the fiery furnace of the Chesapeake seemed almost unbearable. At noon Captain Wainwright of the *Tonnant* laid a thermometer down on the quarter-deck and it hit 133°. The top command sat sweltering in their shirtsleeves—Codrington was amazed that even in the wilds of America it had come to that—while Sir Alexander sweated through some paperwork that proved an admiral's life was more than just sailing and fighting: how on earth could the HMS *Majestic* have consumed 3,750 gallons of wine in three weeks?

August 13 and most of the next day they continued up the Bay . . . nothing in sight except the flat, sandy shoreline. Then, around 4:00 P.M. on the 14th they made out several vessels lying at anchor. Closing, they saw that one was the 74-gun *Albion*, and from her mizzen flew the white ensign of Rear Admiral Cockburn.

"It is almost impossible to depict my boyish feelings and transport when I gazed for the first time in my life on the features of that undaunted seaman Rear Admiral George Cockburn, with his sunburnt visage and his rusty gold-laced hat," one of his 15-year-old midshipmen later confessed. And Cockburn was indeed the sort of daring, resourceful leader any 15-year-old could worship. He was one of the curiously many cases where the Royal Navy's system of protection and patronage really brought forward the best men. Under the watchful eyes of Admirals Sir Joshua Rowley and Lord Hood, he got his navigation in the trackless seas of the East Indies, his seamanship on the rough waters of the English Channel, his battle training with Nelson, and his promotions like clockwork. To all this he added verve, aggressiveness and a coarse, humorous candor that was all his own.

Now at 42, Cockburn had been on the North American Station for nearly two years, and it perfectly suited his jaunty, independent temperament. Here was plenty of opportunity for the skirmishes, the unexpected blows, the earthy exchanges with enemy leaders that he enjoyed so much. In a way he was a throwback to Elizabethan times. He fought war with gusto, and he played very, very rough.

"It is quite a mistake to set fire to a house to windward; it should always be fired the leeward side," explained Lieutenant Frederick Chaumier of the *Menelaus*, who gained his experience around the mouth of the Potomac. "The air becoming rarefied by the heat, the wind rushes round the corners, and blows the flames against the house; whereas on the weather side, the wind blows the flames around the angles, one half of their force is lost. . . ."

Such were the lessons learned this summer as Cockburn, personally heading the raiding parties, swept through Nomini, Chaptico and other tidewater communities. If the inhabitants showed no hostility, they might escape with the loss of their livestock at absurdly low prices. If so much as a militia musket was heard, he applied the torch.

Occasionally, he had a point. At Nomini, he charged, some poisoned whiskey was left enticingly on the porch of Mrs. Thompson's house. Even General Hungerford of the Virginia Militia recoiled at this, denying that any of *his* men could have committed such an atrocity. More often, Cockburn didn't bother explaining. It was, in fact, hard to justify stripping a cemetery vault at Chaptico . . . cutting up Mrs. Sally Cox's beds . . . stealing Dr. Bolinbroke's library . . . or chopping down the trees that lined a lane simply because they were *English* walnuts.

There was one thing rarely destroyed—tobacco. Bringing $500 a hogshead on the British market, it was usually loaded on captured schooners and ultimately sent off to be sold by the prize agent in Bermuda. Cockburn was as interested in prize money as the next man, and sometimes his raids seemed mere plundering expeditions to pick clean the Maryland and Virginia shoreline. "I have sent 84 more hogsheads of tobacco down in vessels to go to Halifax and under convoy of the *Dragon*," he wrote Captain Watts of the *Jaseur* on July 18. "There is now no more tobacco than what you have at Tangier, but I have sent the *Swan* in search of some I have had information of. . . ."

Good commander that he was, he also tried to look after his men. Again writing Watts four days later, he had some cheerful news:

> I have been picking a little for you, which as peace is so near may not be unacceptible intelligence. I hope to be able to do a good deal more for you in the same way. The only difficulty I have is how to dispose of the prize goods after we get them. I believe you must convert some of the barracks or other buildings on Tangier into store houses till the Admiral sends us a transport to take away our riches.

Americans compared him to Attila, but George Cockburn bore no hard feelings. Unlike Cochrane, he never hated them; he was just trying to give them a hard time as part of the game. It was a shame about Mrs. Cox's bedding or Dr. Bolinbroke's library, but Jonathan had asked for war and now he was getting it. When there was no fighting, he was quite capable of relaxing in amiable nonsense—like the quiet day up St. Marys River when he amused himself at ninepins.

But if Cockburn didn't hate Americans, he didn't rate them very highly either. He poked gentle fun at Cochrane's early scheme for kidnaping Madisonian leaders—they weren't worth the money it would cost. Nor did he have a high opinion of the American war effort. "The country is in general in a horrible state," he wrote Sir Alexander in June. "It only requires a little firm and steady conduct to have it completely at our mercy." July, he still felt the same: "It is impossible for any country to be in a more unfit state for war than this now is."

Nothing that happened these first days of August changed his mind. On the 4th he led 500 marines in a raid on Kinsale, ten miles inland. Here he burned houses, routed the militia, and returned with five captured schooners loaded with tobacco—all at a cost of only three killed. The countryside lay at his feet. More and more respectable people were actually coming to his aid. James Smith of Jerome's Creek agreed to supply the squadron with livestock. Mr. Hopewell of Drum Point gave Captain Nourse of the *Severn* regular estimates of American troop strength along the Patuxent, the latest news from Washington, and current copies of the *National Intelligencer*. Acting on this information, Nourse advised Cockburn that a small force could easily march into Washington and burn the place.

So the reduced size of Cochrane's force didn't bother Admiral Cockburn as he climbed aboard the *Tonnant* August 14 to pay his respects to the Commander-in-Chief and General Ross. What probably did bother him was whether Sir Alexander would still approve his cherished attack on Washington. Cockburn didn't know Ross, but he knew plenty about Cochrane, whom he treated with the faintly humorous deference a lively junior sometimes shows a stuffy, cautious superior.

Cochrane was predictably wary, and Ross followed along. Sir Alexander was now convinced there just weren't enough men to strike a serious blow at Washington. Better gather everyone together and head instead for Rhode Island.

Numbers were misleading, Cockburn argued. The whole place was defenseless. He had been roaming wherever he liked with only a battalion of marines. Moreover, he had a new angle that would spread the Americans even thinner. The British would go up the Patuxent, landing at Benedict just as planned. But instead of heading straight for Washington, they would first continue up the river—the troops by land, the marines and seamen by boat—and destroy Barney's flotilla. The Americans would think they were just going for Barney, but if all went well, a quick thrust could also take Washington from the rear. If that looked too difficult, they'd at least get the flotilla and could retire back down the Patuxent.

It was just "iffy" enough to win over Sir Alexander. Then, to remove any lingering doubts in Ross's mind, Cockburn took the General along the next morning on another of his jaunts through the tidewater countryside. By now he had these down to a system. As he and most of his men advanced along some rural road, flankers equipped with bugles spread through the woods to the right and left. Whenever they saw anything suspicious, they blew a blast. The rest of the force then closed up and deployed to meet the threat. This day everything worked perfectly. They moved inland several miles from St. Marys River, burned a factory, and returned to the fleet without firing a shot. Ross was sold.

August 16, they beat back down the Potomac, and at 6:00 P.M. that evening, just as they entered the Chesapeake, they sighted a cloud of sail standing up the Bay toward them.

Three hours later, in the last glow of the long summer twilight, the *Royal Oak* glided alongside. Anchor chains rattled down, and her guns roared out their salute, announcing to the Commander-in-Chief that Admiral Malcolm and the troops had safely arrived and were ready for business.

Next morning at 8:00 A.M. the captains of all the ships rowed over to the *Tonnant* to get their final briefing. In the Admiral's paneled quarters they hunched over rolls of bad charts as Sir Alexander explained the plan. By now he had added a couple of embellishments. The main force would go up the Patuxent as decided, but in line with Admiral Cockburn's original proposal, Captain James Alexander Gordon would also lead a small squadron up the Potomac and destroy any fortifications along the river. Hopefully this would both divert the Americans and give the British troops a separate escape route if they were ever cut off from the transports in the Patuxent.

Finally, as a second diversion, Captain Sir Peter Parker would take his frigate *Menelaus* with a couple of schooners and sail up the Chesapeake above Baltimore. Cockburn was sure the people of Maryland so dreaded any cut in their communications with Philadelphia and New York, they would fall for even a small thrust in this direction.

Sir Peter Parker seemed the perfect choice for the job. The son, grandson and great-grandson of admirals, he was loaded with cocky self-assurance. He too had known nothing but favoritism in the Royal Navy—lieutenant at 16, captain at 20. He was now a very senior 29, immensely spoiled and a merciless disciplinarian, but he had great dash, resourcefulness, and took to independent command.

By 9:00 the briefing was over, and 15 minutes later Captain Gordon was on his way up the Potomac. He led in his frigate *Seahorse*, followed by the frigate *Euryalus*, a rocket ship, four bomb vessels and a dispatch schooner—a small but powerful squadron perfectly suited for its mission of bombardment.

The main part of the fleet was soon under way too, heading on up the Chesapeake. From time to time signals fluttered from the *Tonnant:* prepare three days' rations for troops landing . . . watch out for poisoned spirits. Sunset, and they were off the Patuxent, where the *Menelaus* left on her special assignment. The rest of the ships anchored for a restless night of worrying about the tricky passage up the river tomorrow.

It proved a superb demonstration of British seamanship. With the *Severn* leading the way—her Captain Nourse had sketched the only map—they headed into the Patuxent shortly after dawn on the 18th. Both wind and tide were against them, and as they tacked back and forth, constantly crisscrossing each other, the whole effect was like a peacetime regatta.

At Point Patience, a long sandspit about four miles upstream, the wind and tide proved too much even for British seamanship. The whole fleet anchored to wait for a change, and Admiral Cochrane used the delay to shift the troops from the heavier to the lighter vessels. He himself transferred to the frigate *Iphigenia* in order, as Captain Codrington put it, "to give the general every personal proof of his desire to assist him."

Late afternoon, they were on their way again, twisting and turning even more as the river narrowed and became more shallow. The heaviest ships dropped out; the frigates, brigs and schooners crawled on. The high east bank was thick with magnificent trees, and as he looked back, Ross's assistant adjutant Captain Harry Smith got the curious impression of a fleet not sailing on water, but stalking through some primeval forest. It was dusk when they finally anchored, the lead ships just short of Benedict, the rest strung out for ten miles downstream.

Tomorrow, word passed, they would be landing at dawn. The troops—now loaded down with arms, ammunition, blanket, knapsack, canteen, 3 pounds of pork and 2½ pounds of biscuit—peered hard at the dark, silent shoreline and wondered what awaited them. The most amazing thing so far, everyone agreed, was the complete lack of opposition. More than that, the complete absence of any human beings. The park-like meadows that ran right down to the river bank, the white cottages that dotted the shore—everything seemed absolutely deserted. Writing his wife, Captain Codrington felt it was extraordinary that the enemy had completely ignored them, "although the cliffs which occasionally arise on either bank offer facilities apparently irresistible to a people so disposed to hatred and so especially hostile to the Navy of England." What on earth were the Americans doing?

CHAPTER THREE

Face to Face

The British were *in* the Patuxent, Commodore Barney hurriedly wrote Secretary of the Navy Jones at 9:00 A.M., Friday, the 19th. More than that, the Commodore's lookout reported an intriguing tidbit, apparently picked up from one of those county squires on such good terms with Cockburn. The Admiral, it was said, planned to destroy Barney's flotilla and "dine in Washington on Sunday."

By 2:00 P.M. the capital knew. Secretary Jones ordered Barney to take the flotilla as high upstream as possible, burn it if the British approached, and fall back with his men on the city. General Winder galloped up Pennsylvania Avenue to confer with Secretary of War Armstrong. A courier rushed off to overtake Monroe, the reconnoitering Secretary of State, who planned to start his scouting at Annapolis: forget that, head for Benedict.

Washington boiled with excitement, yet no one really believed Cockburn's boast that he'd soon be dining there. Winder's favorite enemy objective remained Annapolis. Jones warned Barney, "It may be a feint, to mask a real design on Baltimore." Armstrong felt sure that was just what it was. When John P. Van Ness—still trying to get some action on the capital's defenses—predicted a really serious blow, the Secretary replied, "Oh yes! By God, they would not come with such a fleet without meaning to strike somewhere, but they certainly will not come here—what the Devil will they do here?"

Van Ness offered some thoughts on this, but Armstrong brushed him off: "No, no! Baltimore is the place, Sir; that is of so much more consequence."

Wherever the British went, men were needed more desperately than ever. Bad news had just arrived from Pennsylvania. Winder learned that he couldn't count on any of the 5,000 men he expected from that state. The old militia law had expired, and the new one wasn't in effect yet. He issued a ringing appeal, calling on all volunteers to "rally around the standard of their country."

Meanwhile expresses galloped off with new orders for Sam Smith's command in Baltimore. Brigadier General Tobias Stansbury was told to head for Washington with his two mobilized regiments of county militia; Brigadier General John Stricker was ordered to send down his elite 5th Regiment of city volunteers, his rifle battalion and "two of your most active companies of artillery." Suspecting that Stricker might hold back a little, Winder assured him that the British weren't heading for Baltimore—quite a promise, considering the commanding general's own uncertainty on the point.

Secretary of the Navy Jones pitched in with calls to Commodore John Rodgers in Philadelphia to hurry south with 300 seamen . . . to Commodore David Porter in New York to come with as many men as he could collect . . . to the

Marine commandant Lieutenant Colonel Franklin Wharton in Washington to send "as many Marines as can possibly be spared from Headquarters" to join Barney's flotillamen.

But the most immediate source of help was the District's own militia. Already called out twice this summer, they were again ordered to report on the evening of the 19th. Squeezing into their tight trousers, jamming on their shakos, they assembled at the foot of Capitol Hill.

Perhaps it was due to haste, but they were never in worse shape. Some had no shoes; others lacked weapons. Captain John J. Stull's company of riflemen had not a rifle among them. General Winder looked at the slipshod ranks. He needed men right away—but *these?* After a quick inspection, they were dismissed with orders to report back fully equipped in the morning.

At 9:00 A.M. on the 20th Colonel William Brent's 2d Regiment reassembled on the Capitol grounds, and around noon Colonel George Magruder's 1st Regiment joined up—but this time they lacked a commander. General Van Ness knew he was smarter than Winder and thought he outranked him too. After all, he was a major general in the militia and Winder only a brigadier in the regulars. When Armstrong and Madison overruled him on a technicality, Van Ness resigned in disgust.

Brigadier General Walter Smith took over, and the men waited another two hours while the high command decided the next move. A new message had just arrived from Barney, giving first word of actual British landings. They had been coming ashore at Benedict since noon the previous day, but there was no sign of further movements. Lacking more precise information, it seemed best simply to head east for the Wood Yard and let the enemy make the next move.

As the men waited and gossiped, news suddenly spread of a great victory in Canada—a bloody repulse of the British at

Fort Erie. Major George Peter's artillery fired a salute, and infantry muskets exploded in a noisy *feu de joi*. Spirits soared even higher as a special Proclamation from General Winder was read to all. Full of stirring words, it assured them that thousands of volunteers were on the way to "teach our haughty foe that freemen are never unprepared to expel from their soil the insolent foot of the invader."

Three mighty cheers, and at 2:00 P.M. the ranks formed and started off—Captain John Davidson's Union Light Infantry with its cheerful band . . . Captain Benjamin Burch and his Irish artillerymen . . . Captain Stull's riflemen, still without rifles . . . some 1,070 men altogether. They didn't look very professional; but there was a quality, nevertheless, that caught the independent American spirit. The very ideal of the citizen soldier seemed embodied in amateurs like Sergeant John Kearney, a prosperous grocer, or Lieutenant Christian Hines, who ran an up-and-coming bakery with his brother.

Moving east from Capitol Hill, they marched down Pennsylvania Avenue to the Eastern Branch of the Potomac River. Here they crossed the lower of the two bridges that led toward the Maryland countryside. Taking the road to the Wood Yard, they continued another four miles, then halted for the night. At this point all trace of glory vanished, and confusion once more took over. There was no sign of their tents or camp equipment, and most of these clerks and tradesmen had to sleep in an open field. A thousand flints were meant to be on hand for distribution, but only 200 turned up . . . meaning 800 men couldn't fire their guns.

Back in Washington, General Winder's volunteer aide Colonel McLane tried to trace the 300 axes his "pioneers" were meant to use to block roads and bridges as the British advanced. The Quartermaster kept putting him off, until finally McLane gave up. He announced he was off to the Wood

Yard and told the Quartermaster to send along the axes as
soon as they turned up. Ultimately they were sent to Bladensburg by mistake.

Thirty-five miles east of Washington, James Monroe, the
Secretary of State-turned-scout, was having an equally frus-
trating day. He had neglected to bring a spyglass. Reaching a
hill three miles from Benedict around 10:00 A.M., he studied
the Patuxent and squinted in vain at the jumble of masts and
sails. He could neither count the ships nor estimate the number of men swarming ashore. At 1:00 P.M. he sent a letter to
the President full of vague observations. "The general idea,"
he summed up, "is that Washington is their object, but of this
I can form no opinion at this time."

Lieutenants Burrell, Codd and Gleig of the 85th Foot were
just starting a lunch of pig with goose and a couple of fowl,
when the bugles sounded assembly all over the British camp
at Benedict. It was always that way. For the better part of
two days they had been completely idle—getting the feel
of grass again, listening to the crickets at night, staring in
wonder at the blaze of stars and fireflies. During the morning
they gingerly ventured forth . . . rounded up their meal
from the neighboring barnyards . . . and now, just as they
were about to enjoy it, they had to get moving again.

Slowly the men fell in, forming a column of three brigades.
The first consisted of the lightly equipped 85th Foot and the
light companies of the other regiments; the second, of the 4th
and 44th Foot; and the third, of the 21st Foot and the Royal
Marines. Adding some drivers, artillerymen and miscellaneous units, they totaled perhaps 4,500 men.

Once formed, the column swung onto a sandy road leading
north and halted for further orders. At this point there was a
commotion to the rear and General Ross rode up with his

aides and staff. No signals—nothing planned—but a
great cheer went up, rolling along the ranks. Surprised and
pleased, the General doffed his hat and bowed to his soldiers.
Then the command to march, and at 4 P.M., Saturday, August 20, the column began moving north toward Nottingham, about 20 miles upstream.

It was, in fact, a two-pronged advance. The road ran parallel to the Patuxent, and as Ross led his men along, Admiral
Cockburn kept pace up the river with a miniature fleet of
armed boats, tenders and other small craft. These were
loaded with seamen and marines from most of the ships at
Benedict. Nothing official was said about the objective, but
by now nearly everyone in the British force knew that Barney was supposed to be at Nottingham. Excitement rose at
the prospect of early action.

So far, there was still no sign of the enemy at all. It seemed
almost incredible that they had landed, camped for two days,
and now were pushing into the heart of the country—all
without a shot fired. There was no sign of American troops;
in fact, little sign of anybody. Occasionally a gentleman
farmer would welcome them, or some old crone would stare
at them from a cottage door. More often the houses were
empty . . . some with white sheets hanging from the windows, limp in the August heat.

Perhaps it was just as well. In some ways the British were
completely unprepared for their adventure. Admiral Cochrane had sent orders ahead to collect as many horses as possible, but Cockburn had been so engrossed in his raids and
prize goods that he completely neglected to do so. Now there
were only three or four personal mounts brought along by
the staff from Europe.

This meant no cavalry at all for scouting purposes—
easily fatal if they met serious opposition. Nor were there
any horses for the artillery. Except for two 3-pounders and

two little howitzers that could be drawn by hand, all the other guns had to be left behind—that too could be fatal on meeting a resolute enemy.

To ensure at least some warning, Ross deployed skirmishers far ahead and to the right and left of his marching column. Just ahead went an advance guard of three companies. Then came the main column of three brigades, and finally a rear guard and more skirmishers. As it crawled up the road, the force looked rather like some longish bug full of feelers and antennae.

It was hard, hot work. The skirmishers crashed through thickets and tangles of underbrush. The main column choked through a cloud of stifling dust. The sailors who drew the cannon sweated and cursed the fate that brought them to this. No one had light clothing; packs weighed a ton; the day was stifling; and everyone was soft from the weeks they had spent cooped up on the transports. Stragglers fell out by the score, breaking into houses and lapping up water, cider, whiskey —anything—despite warnings that all of it might be poisoned. After six miles Ross decided to camp for the night.

Now they faced a new ordeal. Toward midnight great thunderheads blacked out the stars, lightning streaked across the sky, and the rain fell in torrents. It was the men's introduction to the full violence of an American thunderstorm. Fascinated, they almost forgot their discomfort.

Dawn, August 21, they were on their way again. Soon the scenery changed from the farms and open fields of the first day's march to thick, trackless woods that seemed to stretch forever. The men were used to the neatly defined landscapes of Europe; the sheer space of America was overwhelming.

There was still no sign of enemy troops, but certain of the country people quietly warned Ross to watch out for an ambush. Hearing there was an American rifle company ahead, Lieutenant Gleig rushed with a party of men to the spot.

Too late, but he did catch a glint of metal a little deeper in the woods. Deploying his force, he closed in . . . and found sitting under a tree two men in black coats, armed with muskets and bayonets. They started up; then seeing they were surrounded, one quickly turned to the other and said innocently, "Stop, John, till the gentlemen pass."

Gleig couldn't help laughing, but the men played it straight, insisting they were simple country folk out to shoot squirrels. The Lieutenant asked whether their bayonets were for charging the squirrels. Then he hustled them off—the British army's first prisoners of war.

That afternoon the column had another brush, interrupting a pause for a meal. Captain Charles Grey of the 85th was happily contemplating a boiled hare, when shots were heard up forward. Everyone rushed to the scene, caught a glimpse of some American riflemen scattering through the woods. It was a situation made for cavalry, and in their frustration three or four mounted officers, led by General Ross himself, made a brief dash in futile pursuit. A rash thing to do, but the General was always putting himself in dangerous situations —it was a mark of his leadership.

About 5:00 P.M. they reached Nottingham, only to find Barney was gone. He had moved his flotilla farther up the river. The town itself, a neat village of clapboard houses, was completely empty—so recently evacuated, bread was still baking in the ovens. But as Cockburn's boats approached, they did have one small brush with the enemy. Some American cavalrymen appeared, fired a few shots, then rode off. Ross's infantry rushed to the scene just too late.

James Monroe galloped out of Nottingham just in time— but at last he had found the British troops. Until this moment the Secretary of State's brief career as a scout had been anything but productive. Unable to do much without a spyglass on the afternoon of the 20th, he had gone to Charlotte Hall for the night. This was a small place below Benedict, and the net effect was to put the British between himself and Washington—perhaps the worst thing a scout could do.

He recognized this early on the 21st, when he went back to the river—still below Benedict—and saw no enemy troops at all. His original idea had been to continue south to the Potomac and see what was doing there, but now all thought of that was gone. Fearing the British were already on the direct road from Benedict to Washington, he raced to a point that would intercept them. But again, no sign of anybody. Next, cross-country to Nottingham to see if they might be there. But again, no one at all.

Actually, he had ridden completely around them, which became clear late in the afternoon when he saw the first British barges rowing up the Patuxent. There were only three in sight, and he excitedly scribbled a message to Winder to send 500 to 600 men. "If you could not save the town, you may perhaps cut off their retreat or rear."

But he wrote too soon. In a few minutes the river was alive with barges, boats and tenders. At 5:30 P.M. he added a hasty postscript that 30 or 40 were in view. His cavalry escort began firing at them, but they swept ever closer, and now a column of troops could be seen marching along the bank too. No time to wait any longer. The little group of American horsemen wheeled and galloped off.

Riding west a few miles, Monroe learned that Winder was at the Wood Yard, seven miles farther on, still collecting the army. He hurried there and clomped into the General's quarters shortly after 8:00. He was soon followed by Colonel William D. Beall, a Maryland Militia officer who had also been watching the enemy. But it turned out the two couldn't agree on the size of the enemy force: Monroe thought 6,000, Beall 4,000.

At this point the Secretary of State, exhausted by a long day in the saddle, lay down to rest; Beall went off to his command at Annapolis; and Winder was left to contemplate the quality of his intelligence system. No one had dared take a really good look—generally just a quick peek through the bushes, then a scramble from danger. Estimates varied wildly from Beall's 4,000 to 12,000 or more claimed by some of the local people.

Fortunately, Winder's own force was building up: 240 Maryland Militia from their camp at Bladensburg . . . 300 regulars up from Piscataway . . . Lieutenant Colonel Jacint Laval's 125 dragoons down from Carlisle, Pennsylvania . . . Captain Samuel Miller's 120 Marines and five heavy guns from Washington during the afternoon. Counting the District of Columbia Militia, the General now had over 1,800 men, some cavalry, 20 pieces of artillery—maybe enough to do something.

But what? So much depended on where the British were going. Through most of the day Baltimore remained a strong possibility. Winder even sent a message to General Stansbury and Lieutenant Colonel Joseph Sterett, hurrying south with separate contingents of Maryland Militia: hold at some halfway point so as not to leave the city exposed. But after learning the British were at Nottingham, the General had a new fear: they would strike directly west to the Potomac, attack Fort Washington from the rear, and join their squadron coming up the river. Then the combined force would move on the capital, leaving him completely out of position.

At 10 P.M. Winder fired off a new set of instructions to Stansbury and Sterett: forget the orders to hold; keep coming as far as Bladensburg. Here they would leave Baltimore more exposed, but be in a far better position to defend Washington. If only he knew what the British general really planned to do . . .

General Ross just couldn't make up his mind, as the British force passed the night of August 21 at Nottingham. Handling an independent command for the first time, he had come this far only with Admiral Cockburn's prodding. It was the Admiral who said it would be easy to get Barney; who talked up the idea of a quick blow at Washington. Ross had followed along, but he was quite aware of Earl Bathurst's orders, which strictly enjoined him "not to engage in any extended operations at a distance from the coast."

Now he was 20 miles from the fleet, 40 miles from the Bay—and still he hadn't caught up with Barney. His orders also authorized him to steer clear of any operation which might discredit his troops with failure or "expose them to loss disproportionate to the advantage which it may be the object of the attack to attain." With no cavalry, little artillery and uncertain intelligence—with signs of the enemy increasing —might not that moment be at hand?

Coming ashore from the boats anchored off Nottingham, Cockburn learned of the General's doubts and quickly went to work on him. With Barney practically in their grasp, the Admiral argued, they couldn't turn back now. He was always a good persuader; early on the morning of the 22nd the wavering Ross came back into line.

At 2 A.M. on the 22nd the drums beat reveille in the American camp at the Wood Yard. Not knowing where the British would go next, General Winder had decided to seek them out. The men sleepily fell in, and after one of those long army waits, the General formed an advance corps of the regulars, Colonel Laval's cavalry, and 300 of the best militia under Major George Peter. With the rest of the army following in support, they set off at sunrise down the road toward Nottingham and the enemy.

Ahead of everyone rode General Winder with James Monroe. Five miles and they stopped at the ample farmhouse of Benjamin Oden, a loyal Madisonian who had actually given his cattle to Winder rather than hold them for selling to the British. Just ahead lay a fork in the road. Here the route from the Wood Yard, Washington and the west joined another from Upper Marlboro and the north to form a single road into Nottingham.

It was an important junction to control. Winder sent out cavalry scouts and waited for his advance to arrive. Twenty minutes, and he knew he was too late. The British were coming up the road from Nottingham and would certainly reach the fork before his own force. After that, it all depended on which road they took. If they turned right to Upper Marlboro, they were going for Barney and maybe on north. If left, they were heading for the Wood Yard and the west—including Fort Washington and the capital itself.

As General Ross's men tramped toward the fork, the mood was almost festive. After a very slow start, they had left Nottingham about 7:00 A.M. and marched north through a shady woods, laughing and joking as occasional soldiers slipped out of ranks to chase a stray pig or turkey. The road gradually slanted away from the river; so they were now out of touch with Cockburn's boats, but it didn't seem to matter. As usual, there was no opposition.

It was 8:30 when the advance reached the fork and suddenly spotted some American horsemen lurking in the woods ahead and to the left. It looked like action at last. The officers gave their orders, and the column quickly swung left onto the Wood Yard road. But with this, the Americans faded away.

Ross waited briefly, then reversed course and took the right-hand fork, continuing on toward Upper Marlboro. Here he would again be near Cockburn's boats in the chase after Barney's flotilla. The troops were still marching north around 11:00, when the men were startled by several distant explosions. Word spread that Cockburn had caught up with the flotilla.

He had indeed. Moving up the Patuxent, the Admiral's boats had finally reached Pig Point, where the river narrowed to little more than a stream. And there, rising from behind the point, the British sailors could see the tips of many masts. Putting the marines ashore to attack by land, Cockburn himself led the boats on a final dash. Now the whole American flotilla came in view: Barney's sloop *Scorpion*, flying his pendant . . . 16 gunboats strung in a line . . . 13 trading schooners taking shelter behind them.

But already the Admiral was too late. Smoke suddenly poured from the *Scorpion*, and she exploded in a blast that sent spars, rigging and pendant flying. Then the gunboats began blowing up too—the ammunition boat with an ear-cracking roar and a great mushroom cloud of smoke. Only one was taken, saved when a British sailor scrambled aboard and stamped out a lighted fuse. The rest had been scuttled in line with Washington's orders.

The British scoured the shore, searching for Barney's flotillamen. Cockburn landed his aide, Lieutenant James Scott, to help out and continued hovering offshore in his gig. As Scott worked his way up the steep river bank, a shot whizzed by his ear from behind a bush.

"He's below you, Scott, he's below you," the Admiral yelled in excitement. The Lieutenant jumped down and found himself face to face with an American seaman. Scott grabbed the man before he could fire again, but other shots came from the underbrush, and there was a brief, lively skirmish before a handful of the flotillamen were caught. The rest were gone, including the elusive Commodore.

High drama was nothing new to Joshua Barney, a swashbuckling old salt whose past adventures even included a kiss from Marie Antoinette. The Commodore had removed most of his flotillamen the night before the British attack, leaving only skeleton crews to scuttle the boats. By the time those heavy explosions shook the Maryland countryside, he and 400 of his men were well on their way to join Winder's army at the Wood Yard. They arrived around noon to find the bulk of the American force just returning from its march toward Nottingham.

Watching from the Oden farmhouse, General Winder and James Monroe never saw the British reverse tracks and take the right-hand fork to Upper Marlboro. They only saw the enemy start up the Wood Yard road toward them. That seemed evidence enough: Ross's army must be heading for the capital—either by Fort Washington or by the two bridges over the Eastern Branch. In either case, there weren't enough Americans to meet them. Winder ordered his troops to fall back toward the city, and at 9:00 A.M. Monroe dashed off a dispatch to the President:

> The enemy are advanced six miles on the road to the Wood
> Yard, and our troops retiring. Our troops were on the

march to meet them, but in too small a body to engage. General Winder proposes to retire till he can collect them in a body. The enemy are in full march for Washington. Have the materials prepared to destroy the bridges.

Then he added a somber afterthought: "You had better remove the records."

Washington didn't need to be told. The capital already had a bad case of the jitters. "All look with confidence to the capacity and vigilance of the commanding general," the *National Intelligencer* proclaimed that morning, but the people were looking harder at the refugees streaming in from Maryland . . . at the 200 sturdy citizens who set out under Colonel Decius Wadsworth to dig entrenchments at Bladensburg . . . at the wagons rattling out of town loaded with furniture, bedding and government records.

At the State Department, clerk Stephen Pleasanton stuffed books and papers into coarse linen bags especially sewn for the emergency. The documents included some of the government's most cherished possessions: George Washington's commission . . . the papers of the Revolutionary Government . . . the secret Journals of Congress . . . the Declaration of Independence.

As Pleasanton struggled with the sacks outside of his office, Secretary of War Armstrong passed by on the way to his own room across the hall. Armstrong paused long enough to observe that it all seemed an unnecessary alarm. Once again he explained to anyone who would listen that the leaders of the British force couldn't seriously be planning to come to Washington.

Pleasanton politely replied that he thought differently— anyhow, he was doing the prudent thing, whatever the danger. He went on with the job . . . loaded up some carts waiting outside . . . and secretly stored his treasures in Edgar

Patterson's empty grist mill across the Potomac and two miles above Georgetown.

Across town Mordecai Booth, clerk of the Navy Yard, searched for wagons to carry away the gunpowder stored at the naval arsenal. Pickings were slim, and even slimmer when Secretary Jones told him to get additional teams to take supplies to Barney's men, wherever they might now be. Everyone seemed to have a good excuse not to go. Booth finally rounded up five wagons, including John Anderson's fine rig, which had already been hired by the Renner & Heath ropewalk. Daniel Renner's younger brother flew into a rage, but the old man proved a good sport. "You are doing your duty," he told Booth. "I cannot say anything against it— you must take the wagon—private considerations must give way to the public good."

Others weren't as graceful. Two drivers ran away when Booth tried to impress them; another promised to head for the Navy Yard, only to vanish. The driver for the Riggs & Badon store flatly refused to comply at all—government orders or not—and he was backed by Mr. Riggs himself, using "such language as was degrading to gentlemen."

Profiteers soon appeared on the scene. John Hare made a nice deal renting his hack to the navy at $6 a day—a skilled man's wages for a week. William O'Neill, the enterprising innkeeper, saw his $50 nag seized by the army—and later filed a claim for $750.

Even at top prices, no one could find decent transportation to move the mountain of books and records at the Capitol. Clerk of the House Patrick Magruder was away taking the waters in Virginia, and his two underlings, Samuel Burch and J. T. Frost, didn't realize the danger until noon on the 22nd. By then it was too late. Frost looked all over town in vain, finally went to the country and found a single cart and four oxen. Late that night they creaked off with their first load to the hiding place they had selected nine miles away. With an 18-mile round trip and depending entirely on one oxcart, saving the records of Congress was clearly going to be a challenging task.

As fears increased, the most popular people in town suddenly became French Minister Louis Serurier and his wife. He was charming, suave and agile—the only French diplomat to make the leap from Napoleon to Louis XVIII without missing a beat. She was exotic, beautiful and surrounded by an aura of romance and adventure. As a child of seven, it was said, she had saved her parents during the slave insurrection in Haiti. A fascinating couple, but what made them irresistible right now was their unique status: they were the only people in Washington with diplomatic immunity.

Mrs. Joel Barlow, widow of the capital's most prominent literary figure, wondered whether she might store some things with the Seruriers. A discreet note from their mutual friend Mrs. William Thornton brought a gracious response, and more:

> Mrs. Serurier has the honor to receive Mrs. Thornton's note. She has given orders to admit into the house Mrs. Barlow's furniture. In case Mrs. Thornton has anything belonging to her that she would wish to place in her asylum (although she is in hopes that it will be no occasion for it) Mrs. Serurier would be happy to be of some service. . . .

Colonel John Tayloe, the gentleman horse-breeder, tried the Seruriers' amiability even further. His splendid brick mansion Octagon House lay just west of the President's House—surely in the path of any British invaders. Would Monsieur Serurier consent to move in for the duration? The Minister proved most understanding, and Colonel Tayloe's roof soon displayed a large white sheet on a pole—a makeshift flag of the Bourbons, telling the world that Octagon House was under the French King's protection.

But these early fears were nothing compared to the panic that erupted when Monroe's warning arrived on the afternoon of the 22nd. "The enemy are in full march for Washington," it said; and the effect was electric. People piled into hacks, carriages, anything on wheels to get out of town. Some struggled with bedding and furniture; most simply slammed their doors and fled. "The distress here and in Georgetown is beyond description," a correspondent wrote the firm of Cox & Montaudevert in New York, "women and children running in every direction."

And no wonder. The redcoats were bad enough, but rumors soon spread of a stab in the back as well. By now everyone knew about those Tories in southern Maryland who treated the British to food and information—how many of them were mixed with the refugees streaming through the capital? Washington Boyd, Marshal of the District, worked to clear the city of "all persons of suspicious character or irregular conduct." Mayor James Blake enforced a 10:00 P.M. curfew and urged the citizens "to be vigilant and take up all suspected persons."

Even more terrifying were the rumors of slave insurrection. No matter how hard the proponents of slavery defended the institution—both the masters' "benevolence" and the blacks' "loyalty"—a gnawing fear of revolt always arose in times of crisis. It was never stronger than now. Stories circulated of a dangerous conspiracy uncovered at Frederick 40 miles to the west, with several leaders already arrested. With British encouragement, was the whole countryside about to erupt?

Actually, the blacks were never more steadfast. Despite all Admiral Cochrane's inducements, only a handful of slaves joined him, even after the landings. And the free blacks—

far from siding with the British—worked with everyone else, digging the few entrenchments that were finally thrown up to protect the city.

But nobody knew this Monday evening, August 22. Some fresh danger seemed to ride with every murky lantern bobbing through the streets. Perhaps the only people more worried than the frightened citizens still in town were the government wives who had already found safety . . . and then thought of the men they left behind. "Take care of yourself, my dearest husband," Mrs. Richard Rush wrote the Attorney General from Piney Grove. "Remember that the happiness of your wife and helpless little boys are bound up in you, and do not expose yourself unless impervious duty demands it. I am all anxiety to hear from you, really think of nothing else. God bless you. . . ."

At the President's House, James Madison could no longer bear the suspense of this harrowing evening. He might not be able to do much, but he simply had to be with his troops at a time like this. He explained his feelings to Dolley and asked whether she had the courage, the firmness, to remain home until he returned. He needn't have asked. The indomitable First Lady was up to any crisis. She assured him she had no fear, but for him and the success of the army. Urging her to take care of herself, and to look after the cabinet papers, the President then recruited William Jones, Richard Rush, two or three aides and headed for the army.

Around 9:00 P.M. they reached Long Old Fields, a crossroads eight miles east of Washington. Here they found Winder already encamped with the troops. It had been a trying day for the General. Even after he learned the British were heading not for the Wood Yard and Washington, but for Upper Marlboro, he still felt overextended and undermanned. He continued to retire, finally choosing Long Old Fields as a new base that covered about equally well every possible enemy target—Fort Washington, Alexandria, Bladensburg and the capital itself.

But in pulling back, Winder did not seem to realize he was missing a golden chance to fall on the British rear. His intelligence, of course, was wretched, but even his staff surgeon noticed that the enemy had no cavalry; and Benjamin Oden, the patriotic farmer, had carefully calculated the length of Ross's column, coming up with a remarkably good estimate on the actual numbers involved. Nor was Winder any longer at such a numerical disadvantage. During the day Barney joined up with his 400 flotillamen, and other units were coming. He now had over 3,000 men, 425 cavalry and 20 guns.

None of it made any difference. As night fell on the American camp, the General retired to his quarters, spent several hours over the paperwork he loved so well. At some point after midnight Rush came in to report that the President was on hand, staying at the Williams farm about a mile behind the camp. Winder sent over a captain's guard and went back to his paperwork. Finally, after listening to a few last words of advice from the amateur strategists that constantly barged in, he lay down to snatch a moment's rest.

He had little chance. About 2:00 A.M. on the 23rd the alarm gun sounded as the sentries heard a thrashing in the darkness. It turned out to be some cattle the commissary had driven into camp, but no one knew it at the time. Muskets began going off, and the night echoed with shouts and cursing as the sleepy troops stumbled into position to meet the expected attack.

Colonel Allen McLane was appalled at the sight. Apparently giving up his search for axes, he had spent the day conducting a distant and very safe reconnaissance; now he was returning at the height of the confusion. The whole camp was "as open as a race ground"; fires blazed up, silhouetting every detail; men were shouting the countersign without a thought of security. Going to Winder's quarters, he said to himself, "If General Ross does not rout us this night, it will not be our fault."

Eight miles away at Upper Marlboro, General Ross was passing a quiet and thoroughly comfortable night. He was staying at the home of Dr. William Beanes, the only local resident still in town when the British entered about two o'clock that afternoon. At 65, Beanes was far more than the community's leading physician. He was its most prominent citizen: major landholder, proprietor of the local grist mill, owner of the best house in town. When he offered it to Ross as a headquarters, the General was glad to accept. It was not only a pleasant place, but the host was a friendly man. Ross even got the impression that the doctor's Federalist leanings amounted to actual sympathy for the British cause.

But the General gave the matter little thought, for he was once again beset with doubts about the whole operation. Barney's flotilla—the primary target—was now destroyed; should the British carry on with the attack on Washington, so close to Admiral Cockburn's heart? They were now nearly 30 miles from the fleet, still without any decent artillery or cavalry (although 40 of the artillerymen were now mounted on farm horses), and without any real idea of what the enemy was doing.

The lack of intelligence was particularly irritating. Despite Admiral Cochrane's long-standing orders to develop a network of agents, this was another thing neglected by Cockburn in his hit-and-run raids and chasing after tobacco. Occasional friendly inhabitants were all very well—they gave one a good feel for the Americans' apathy and dissension— but they didn't take the place of hard intelligence on enemy troop movements. For this Ross depended mainly on a single man named Calder, a miserable wretch with a dreadful skin disease, who had come into camp apparently hoping to supply information in exchange for medical treatment.

Most of the staff disagreed with Ross. His Deputy Quartermaster General, Lieutenant George de Lacy Evans, an enterprising young officer who at 23 had already served in India, Persia and the Peninsula, thought it was absurd to turn back. They were now only 16 miles from Washington, and the enemy had yet to show any mettle. If only Cockburn were here to steel the General's resolve. . . .

And why couldn't he be? It was only four miles to Mount Calvert, where the Admiral was resting on the tender *Resolution* after the day's excitement. Quietly, two members of Ross's staff slipped down the road and visited Cockburn. They explained the problem, stressed their own desire to push ahead, and invited the Admiral to come back with them to throw his weight on the scales. They had even brought along an extra horse.

They knew their man. Early in the morning of August 23 Cockburn mounted the saddle and rode back to Ross's quarters with his aide Lieutenant Scott and the two self-appointed emissaries.

The Admiral proved as persuasive as ever. Even if they had accomplished their primary mission—even if the orders restricted their movements—no one in London, or with the fleet, could have conceived the opportunity that now lay open. Washington was there for the taking.

Ross swung back into line, and to steel his resolve, Cockburn quickly sent orders to Captain Harrison, whose Marine Artillery were with the rear guard left at Pig Point: bring his men and guns to Upper Marlboro and join the army. Other orders went to Captain Wainwright to hurry over with the seamen from the armed boats and barges. Finally, the Admiral sent Lieutenant Scott back to Admiral Cochrane, waiting at Benedict, to report what had been accomplished and, even more important, what was about to be done.

At 2:00 P.M. everything was in hand. The bugles blew . . . the troops fell in . . . and the British force moved out from Upper Marlboro, taking the road west toward Long Old Fields, Washington, and their next adventure.

At 2:00 P.M. James Madison headed back to Washington from his visit to the American camp at Long Old Fields, reasonably sure that the British would not be leaving Upper Marlboro any time soon.

He was now confident that the capital was safe—that the enemy would probably return direct to their ships. Best of all, there was finally an American counterblow in the making. Things had come a long way since those dark hours last night when the panicky troops were firing at their own livestock.

Madison's day had begun at 6:00 A.M., when General Winder arrived at the Williams estate to pay his respects. After the usual amenities Secretary Armstrong asked for a military briefing, and the General stressed the lack of enemy cavalry and artillery. He concluded that the British would remain in Upper Marlboro until their squadron on the Potomac reached Fort Washington. Falling back on a pet theory, he felt Ross's troops would then go down and join in a combined assault on that stronghold. Once taken, the two forces would together move on the capital.

Armstrong had little comment, except to say once again that whatever the British did, there would be no serious attack on Washington. At most, there might be what he called a "Cossack hurrah"—a quick hit-and-run strike. The best way to meet this, he added, was to hole up in the Capitol Building; then, the minute the enemy momentum seemed spent, the Americans should emerge in an all-out charge. "On the success of this plan," Armstrong declared somewhat grandly, "I would pledge both life and reputation."

Perhaps because in Madison's eyes he now had very little reputation to lose, nothing more was said. The meeting broke up indecisively, and at 8:00 A.M. the President went to the camp to review the troops. They were drawn up in three or four long straggling lines, but were remarkably cheerful, considering their harrowing night of false alarms.

Right after the review a scout galloped up with a report that gave an entirely new twist to the situation: the British were leaving Upper Marlboro, bound for Annapolis. This fitted another favorite theory of Winder's—the Maryland capital was always high on his list of possible targets—and for the time being he cast aside his picture of a link-up on the Potomac. He sent Captain Luffborough and 20 troopers to report on the latest development.

Annapolis was still on everybody's mind when Thomas L. McKenney, the Georgetown drygoods dealer serving as aide and scout, rode into camp a little later. McKenney had been watching the British all morning. He knew they were still in Marlboro, but noted some activity and predicted they would attack Winder's camp within 24 hours.

"They can have no such intention," Secretary Armstrong broke in. "They are foraging, I suppose; and if an attack is meditated by them upon any place, it is Annapolis."

Attention turned to two deserters brought in by McKenney—perhaps they would have the answer. Madison himself led the interrogation, but the results were disappointing. They didn't know their destination, their strength or even who commanded them. Finally, McKenney asked them to look at the American force and see whether theirs was equal to it.

"We think it is," they answered with a smile.

At noon Captain Luffborough sent a message confirming
that the British were still at Upper Marlboro. Winder
quickly swung back to his old theory: Ross's troops would
join the Potomac squadron in a day or two. Meanwhile he
saw a golden opportunity. He now had 3,000 men at Long
Old Fields; Stansbury had 1,400 at Bladensburg; Sterett
would soon arrive there with another 800; Colonel Beall had
still another 800 near Annapolis. Altogether they added up to
some 6,000 men within 20 miles of each other. Winder decided to concentrate them all and attack tomorrow before the
British left Upper Marlboro. He even pictured a simultaneous
assault, launched from different directions, from the heights
around the town.

He quickly outlined his ideas to Madison and the cabinet.
The President apparently differed only in the matter of British intentions. He doubted whether they had the power for
any extended operations at all. With Barney's flotilla destroyed, they would probably return straight to their ships.

In any event Madison was satisfied that the situation was
now under control. He went back to the Williams place,
where he penciled a note to Dolley. He reassured her that
"the last & probably truest information" indicated that the
British were not very strong, "and of course that they are not
in a condition to strike at Washington." Unless some new development kept him away, he concluded, "I hope I shall be
with you in the course tho' perhaps later in the evening."

Nothing had happened by 2:00 P.M.; so now—in company with Jones, Armstrong and several aides—he mounted
his saddle and headed home.

Meanwhile Winder put his victory plan into effect—
orders to Stansbury at Bladensburg to advance toward
Upper Marlboro, stopping at a crossroads about four miles
away . . . orders to Sterett, not yet at Bladensburg, to follow
along. No one knew where Beall was at the moment, but as

soon as located, he was to close in from the north, joining the
ring that would encircle the enemy. To keep a "fix" on the
British—to watch them closely and contain them as much
as possible—Major Peter was again sent forward with the
same advance force he had led yesterday near Nottingham.

Shortly after 12:00 all was in motion, and Winder headed
up toward Bladensburg with a few cavalrymen, hoping to
meet Stansbury coming down. Reaching the Bladensburg–
Upper Marlboro road, he halted and pushed a patrol toward
Marlboro. Soon two prisoners were brought in; they confirmed that the British wouldn't be marching that day. So it
was just as he thought: if they hadn't moved by now, they
wouldn't move at all, and by tomorrow they would be too
late—he'd hit them from all sides.

Some time after 2:00 these pleasant thoughts were jarred
by the sound of gunfire. Winder decided that Peter's detachment must have made contact with the enemy at Upper
Marlboro.

He was right. Approaching the town, Peter had sent some
scouts ahead, and they soon came under fire. But it was not
just some enemy pickets guarding the camp; it was the whole
British Army. Contrary to all expectations, Ross was on the
march. Worse than that, he was heading along the road directly toward Peter's detachment . . . toward the American
camp at Long Old Fields . . . and ultimately toward Washington itself.

Peter cautiously pulled back from his position on a high
hill overlooking the road. Almost immediately a handful of
British officers, bright with red coats and gold lace, appeared
on the crest he had just left. Captain Stull's riflemen fired a
volley, missed, and cursed the day they had been issued muskets instead of their rifles. But the "red-coat gentlemen" (as
Peter liked to call them) did seem shaken and quickly retired
behind the brow of the hill.

The British advance now edged over the summit. Stull's men fired two or three more ineffectual volleys and slowly fell back. Enemy troops were soon pouring down the hill after them, and there was a frantic moment when Sergeant Nicolls collapsed of sunstroke. Somehow he was pulled to safety, and Peter gained extra time by turning a couple of his 6-pounders on the British. They fired two or three rounds —misses but close. Incredibly, this was the first American artillery to fire on the enemy in five days.

But Peter was no match for "Wellington's Invincibles," now beginning to work their way skillfully around him. At one point he tried persuading Colonel Laval to use his cavalry detachment to cover the American flanks. After all, they were regulars, they were supposed to do that sort of thing. Sorry, said Laval, his horses were "not trained" and he could do nothing to help.

On a nearby ridge James Monroe sat on his roan horse watching the British advance. The Secretary of State had been in the saddle for nearly a week, but he still relished this life of action, infinitely preferring it to the confused strategy sessions he perhaps should be attending. He was still at it when Thomas McKenney, the scouting drygoods dealer, rode up and joined him. As they watched together, the British advance halted at an estate called Melwood. To McKenney, they were clearly going into bivouac, slinging their kettles, and so forth.

Monroe now took the road toward Bladensburg, while McKenney himself rushed back to Long Old Fields and breathlessly reported that the enemy were "within a mile." Actually, the distance was three miles, and he certainly didn't make it clear that the British had gone into camp. To Brigadier General Walter Smith, the militia officer left in charge by Winder, the enemy were upon him and his own commanding general was nowhere around.

Making the best of it, Smith quickly formed a line of battle across the road and waited for the British attack. Then, remarking that he didn't like taking the responsibility for a fight if Winder could be located, he rushed McKenney off again on a frantic search. The commanding general was found about eight miles away, trotting north on the Marlboro-Bladensburg road, looking forward to his meeting with General Stansbury, the union of his two main forces, and the coming all-out assault on the enemy.

McKenney's message changed everything. In a heart-stopping instant all plans for the great American counterblow vanished. Winder dashed off new orders to General Stansbury: turn around . . . return to Bladensburg . . . if attacked, resist as long as possible, then retreat toward Washington. He himself spurred his horse and raced back to Long Old Fields. Arriving around 5:00, he glanced with approval at General Smith's battle line, grimly expecting the British at any minute.

"It is all well arranged," he complimented Smith, "but the manifest object of the enemy is to attack us in the night. We have not the material for a night fight."

This was a new thought. There was no evidence that the British contemplated a night fight. The countryside was totally strange to them; they had never moved at night so far; and McKenney was right there to say they were going into camp when he last saw them. Never mind. A good commander must think of everything, and Winder shuddered at the idea of a British assault in the dark. The Americans' biggest advantage lay in their artillery, and this would be lost in a night fight. Then it would be just his raw militia against the trained British regulars—hopeless odds. He must break up this battle line and move his army at once.

But where? If he marched to Bladensburg and joined

Stansbury, that would combine his two main forces, giving him a concentration of 4,400 men right away . . . 6,000 when Sterett and Beall arrived.

But the military textbook said for every plus there's a minus, and the minuses here began to haunt him. Concentrating at Bladensburg would leave wide open the road to Fort Washington and the Potomac squadron (that old nightmare) . . . it would be useless if the British went to Annapolis (that other old nightmare) . . . and added to all this, a new nightmare suddenly occurred to him. Going to Bladensburg would also leave open the road to Long Old Fields and direct to Washington—the one he was now on. True, there was the Eastern Branch to cross, half a mile wide at this point. But suppose no one carried out his orders to destroy the two bridges if the British approached? The enemy could walk unopposed into the heart of the city while he sat at Bladensburg!

There was only one thing to do: return to Washington at once. It never seemed to occur to Winder that all necessary precautions could be taken by one trusted lieutenant . . . that it wasn't necessary to use his whole army to make sure the bridges were burned.

At sundown the troops began to pull back, covered at first by Captain Benjamin Burch and his Washington Artillery Company. But in half an hour a courier rode up, told Burch to join the rest, and as night fell the whole army was reeling back in a single, dispirited mass. To John Law, one of Burch's artillerymen, the retreat turned into "a run of eight miles." Shortly after 8 o'clock they reached the Eastern Branch, swarmed across the two bridges, tumbled into the city, and sank exhausted in a field near the Navy Yard.

The sight of these weary heaps of men, lying motionless in the open field, expelled any lingering thoughts of optimism in the minds of those left in the capital. "I cannot find language to express the situation of the women and children, who are running the streets in a state bordering on distraction," one of Winder's footsore militiamen wrote a friend in Philadelphia late that night. "Some are trying to remove their bedding, clothes and furniture, while others are determined to stay by their homes until they are burnt around them."

Official Washington tried its best to put on a brave front, but here, too, the air was heavy with foreboding. "In the present state of alarm and bustle of preparation for the worst that may happen, I imagine it will be more convenient to dispense with the enjoyment of your hospitality today," Eleanor Jones, wife of the Secretary of the Navy, tactfully wrote Dolley Madison, begging off from an engagement that evening at the President's House.

The First Lady was only too glad to excuse her. Much had happened since that hopeful note from her husband early in the afternoon, assuring her that all was well. Toward evening a second note arrived that was anything but cheering. By then the home-bound President had been advised of the new British advance; now he told her to be ready "at a moment's warning" to get her carriage and leave the city . . . the enemy seemed stronger than first reported . . . they might reach Washington and destroy it.

She jammed fistfuls of cabinet papers into as many trunks as her carriage would hold; then marked time—determined not to go until she was sure Madison was safe. It was a nerve-racking wait, not helped when Jean Pierre Sioussa, her faithful and indispensable major-domo, offered to spike the cannon at the gates and lay a train of powder which would explode as the British entered the house. Dolley's Quaker training, though often dormant, rebelled at this. She told him that even in war some things weren't done. Then

she firmly sat back and continued waiting for some sign of
the President . . . or the British.

At Melwood, General Ross and Admiral Cockburn lay on
their cloaks, sound asleep in the small shed that served as their
headquarters. Outside, the last of the seamen and marines, ordered from the boats to join the army, bedded down for the
night. Nearby, Lieutenant Gleig put in some anxious hours
on picket duty, half-convinced that the Americans would attack him. At Upper Marlboro, Captain Robyns of the Royal
Marines relaxed after a long day spent loading prize tobacco
for transport down the river. At Benedict, Admiral Cochrane's fleet lay silently at anchor in the black, quiet waters of
the Patuxent.

Despite all the American jitters, there was not a hostile
move on the night of August 23. In fact, practically the only
Englishman in motion was on quite a different mission. Dispatched to Admiral Cochrane to report the destruction of
Barney's flotilla and the planned descent on Washington, Admiral Cockburn's aide Lieutenant Scott was now hurrying
from Benedict to the British camp with orders emphatically
disapproving any attack on the American capital.

The project was much too rash, Fleet Captain Codrington
had argued, and finally new orders were drafted. Techni-
cally addressed to Cockburn but clearly meant for Ross as
well, they said that the Rear Admiral had already accomplished more than England could have expected with such a
small force; that he was on no account to proceed any farther; that the army was instead to return immediately to Benedict and re-embark; that it would be risking the success of
future operations to make any attempt on Washington with
such inadequate means.

Handing the letter containing all this to Scott, Cochrane told him to memorize it. Then, if he was in danger of capture on the way back, he was to eat it—do anything, in fact, to keep it from falling into the hands of the enemy. If he was lucky enough to reach the camp after all, he was to give the message verbally to Cockburn.

It was late that night before Scott got back to Upper Marlboro; then still more hours while he and Captain Robyns rode through the dark, searching for Melwood. At last, however, the bivouac fires came in sight, and Scott galloped ahead, still clutching the orders that would—if obeyed—change the fate of the expedition and save the American capital.

CHAPTER FOUR

Sleepless Hours

It all seemed utterly unreal to Colonel George Minor of the
10th Virginia Militia. Ordered from Falls Church to Washington on the afternoon of the 23rd, his regiment had rushed
to the city so fast that few of the 700 men came armed. Arriving at sunset, they found the whole army still off in Maryland; there was nobody even to report to.

In a quandary, Minor looked up his old friend Dr. James
Ewell—perhaps Washington's best-known physician—who
lived in a big brick house facing the Capitol. He knew everybody, and with no military superior in sight, Minor asked the
doctor to take him to the President.

Ewell, a rather expansive name-dropper, was delighted to
oblige. In fact, he used the opportunity to invite along Minor's regimental surgeon Dr. Peake, apparently hoping to do

a fellow physician a good turn. They reached the President's House by dark and found Madison inside, just back from his long day in the field.

Minor quickly outlined the arms and ammunition he needed, but the President interrupted, saying all this was Armstrong's business—he was the man to see. Finding the Secretary at his boardinghouse farther up Pennsylvania Avenue, Minor again ran through his list of needs. Fine, said Armstrong, Colonel Henry Carberry would supply everything in the morning. When Minor begged for the weapons right away, the Secretary shook his head. This was out of the question; it was late, and there would be plenty of time tomorrow. Meanwhile, he added helpfully, the men might put in shape the few arms they brought. That would make it easier for Colonel Carberry in the morning.

Minor and Ewell headed back toward the Capitol empty-handed. As they rode along, the Colonel sputtered with indignation, saying that this kind of indifference could only lead to losing the city. Still grumbling, he spent the night at Dr. Ewell's house; his regiment, with no billeting arrangements whatsoever, moved into the Capitol and slept amid the Corinthian columns and red baize curtains of the House Chamber.

Outside, the last of General Winder's troops were across the Eastern Branch and back in the city. With his army safe, the General headed up Pennsylvania Avenue to pay a visit of his own to the President. He made a full report, describing the retreat from Long Old Fields and the present position of the army, camped near the Navy Yard. Twenty minutes later he rode slowly back Pennsylvania Avenue, stopping at McKeowin's Hotel to leave the borrowed horse he was riding. It was the third one that had broken down under him this long, hard day.

He continued on foot, trudging past the gaunt poplars that

lined the avenue . . . on around Capitol Hill . . . and finally down Virginia Avenue to the dark field where his weary men lay. Everything seemed all right, so he headed for the Eastern Branch to check the preparations for destroying the two bridges that led into Maryland. As he feared, little had been done. At the lower bridge—the main one—30 men stood around with axes (where had they been all week?), but there was no powder, no pitch or kindling.

The situation was even worse at the upper crossing, or Stoddert's Bridge as it was sometimes called. Though old and rickety, it was perfectly usable, and nobody was on guard at all. It lay there for the taking, with the British maybe lunging toward it at this very moment.

Midnight, Winder was back in camp, trying to do something about the situation. He gave orders to burn the upper bridge immediately; he posted a party of infantry across the river to keep the lower bridge from being taken by surprise . . . he searched for someone reliable enough to blow it up when the final moment came.

It was well after 12:00 when the General came to the tent of Captain Benjamin Burch, whose Washington Artillery had performed so coolly during the retreat to the city. As the Captain sleepily pulled himself together, Winder spoke in an emotion-packed voice that suggested he might now be close to the breaking point. He knew how tired the men were, he said, but in all probability this night would mark one of the last good deeds Burch could ever do for his country. Would he take 30 of his men, with three guns, and defend the passage of the lower bridge? There was reason to believe the British would try to storm it before morning.

Winder added that he had told the Navy Yard to send a boat to the bridge loaded with explosives, but nobody paid any attention to his orders. Now he would try once more —he wouldn't rest until he had that boat in hand.

Then he was off into the night again, as Burch roused his men and started for the river. Winder himself, still on foot, went next to the Navy Yard. But it was dark—the streets were strange—and he was tired, dead tired. As he stumbled along, he plunged into a ditch, badly wrenching his right arm and ankle.

One o'clock, and he was banging on the door of Captain Thomas Tingey, in charge of the Yard. Roused from his bed, the Captain appeared with Commodore Barney, who had chosen this out-of-the-way spot in the hope that here, at least, he might get a little rest.

Don't worry, Tingey assured Winder. Several casks of powder were packed in boats, ready to be sent to the bridge "when necessary." The General was exasperated. Why couldn't the man see? It was necessary *right now*. The British might come any minute. He begged Tingey to increase the amount of powder and get it there at once. The Captain said he would, and this time he really did.

Winder limped off. Now it was back to the bridge . . . a quick check on Burch's guard . . . then to camp again, where shortly after 3:00 A.M. he stumbled into the tent of Major George Peter. Here was a trained soldier—one of the few around—but if Winder was looking for professional sympathy tonight, he had the wrong man. Peter was as tired as anybody else, and when the General lay down beside him and began complaining about everyone, it was more than the Major could handle. He fell asleep, and by the time he awoke, the commanding general had wandered off again.

Meanwhile Winder had become the subject of an interesting conversation at the other end of town. Secretary of the Treasury George W. Campbell shared the same boardinghouse with Secretary of War Armstrong in the block called "The Seven Buildings," and Campbell used the opportunity to say some things that had been bothering him. He couldn't

help feeling surprised that the British had advanced for five
days without serious opposition. Now they were at the gates
of the city and all seemed to depend on one battle—a single
throw of the dice—wasn't that too big a gamble, considering the inexperience of the American militia?

Armstrong seemed to agree.

Then, asked Campbell, had any of this been done with
Armstrong's advice and approval? And would the army have
the benefit of his advice in its future movements?

He had nothing to do with it, the Secretary replied. Winder was in charge of the District and the army assigned to defend it. The General presumably had his plans, and any inter-
ference by himself might be considered "indelicate." Of
course, if the President specifically asked for his advice and
help, that would be different.

To Campbell this was incredible. Things had come to a
point where the government needed all the military experience it could get. The Secretary of War had a lot, and this
was no time to hold back out of feelings of "delicacy." He
told Armstrong so, and made a mental note to speak to the
President in the morning.

At the President's House James Madison listened to all
sorts of last-minute suggestions, as well-meaning visitors came
and went. Everyone now seemed convinced that the fum-
bling of the past would continue, and the British would soon
be in the city. Someone (probably the banker Jacob Barker)
volunteered to blow up the Capitol with his own hands—
all he needed was a corporal's guard, a few miners and a little gunpowder. No, said Madison, it would do more to
arouse the nation if the enemy did it themselves.

Outside, the streets were nearly empty. Enjoying his diplomatic immunity in the Octagon House, Minister Serurier of
France decided that this was the only inhabited residence left
in Washington. Gallic overstatement perhaps—a number

of families were still hanging on—but it was indeed a desperate night. To some, daylight seemed long overdue when finally, between 3:00 and 4:00 A.M., a pink glow appeared in the east. But it wasn't dawn yet—it was the upper bridge, now being burned under Winder's orders.

The glow in the sky meant only one thing to General Stansbury's Maryland Militia at Bladensburg. If Winder was burning his bridges, the British attack would be coming their way, for the Bladensburg bridge was the next crossing up the Eastern Branch. A depressing thought, capping a depressing night. Stansbury's 2,200 troops were still footsore from the long march from Baltimore. Some 800 of them had just come in that afternoon with Colonel Sterett. Everybody was hungry—the salt beef was spoiled, the flour musty—and adding to the general discouragement, a rumor swept camp around 8:00 P.M. that Winder had been captured and the army was leaderless. About 11:00 James Monroe—in from one of his scouting sweeps—didn't help by suggesting the troops fall on the British rear in the dead of night. They had orders to remain here, Stansbury answered coolly; and besides, the men were in no condition to march. The Secretary of State accepted the rebuff and rode off again into the darkness.

Around midnight the sentries began firing at imaginary British grenadiers. The troops fell in, and it was 2:00 A.M. before they were dismissed. At 3:00 they were called out again. A message had arrived from Winder, breaking the news that his force was back in Washington. This left Stansbury uncovered—he was out there all alone—and after a hasty council of war, he decided to move closer to the city. At 3:30 the troops began to pull back, and it was at this point that the sky turned red with the flames of the upper bridge, adding to everyone's sense of gloom and frustration.

After a mile or so, a second message arrived from Winder emphasizing that they were to stand at Bladensburg—the place they had just left. Another council of war, but the decision was not to return as directed; it was to continue toward Washington. Now a third message from Winder, insisting on the point, and at last Stansbury reluctantly turned around and marched back to Bladensburg. But this time, instead of crossing the bridge and digging in on the east side of the river as before, he stayed on the west side. If nothing else, he was determined to have at least the river between himself and the British.

Private John P. Kennedy really didn't care. Through most of this backing and filling, he was dead tired and wanted only to lie down and sleep. Ironically, he was wearing his dancing pumps, brought along from Baltimore with the vague idea he'd need them at the Victory Ball in the President's House. During the night alarm he had put them on by mistake; right now, as he struggled along with feet of lead, that Victory Ball seemed far away indeed.

General Ross and Admiral Cockburn lay peacefully asleep in their shed at Melwood. Then, around 2:00 A.M., there was a small commotion outside—a low, quick exchange with the guard—and Lieutenant James Scott broke in on their slumbers. Back from his mission to Admiral Cochrane and the fleet, he handed Cockburn the letter from the Commander-in-Chief, disapproving the attack on Washington and ordering the force to return at once.

Cockburn silently digested the contents, passed it over to Ross. The General studied it a moment, then looked up and announced there was nothing left to do but return.

"No," said the Admiral, "we can't do that. We are too far

advanced to talk of retreat. Let's take a turn outside and talk the matter over."

Leaving the shed, the two officers walked to and fro under the August stars, deep in earnest conversation. Lieutenant Scott followed at a respectful distance with Ross's aide Tom Falls and the Deputy Quartermaster General, Lieutenant Evans. Occasionally they caught snatches of what was said.

Cockburn was going all-out. This was the fourth time his project had nearly been abandoned; he had saved it three times; he wasn't going to give up now. He tried every approach. If they went ahead, he said, he pledged "everything that is dear to me as an officer" that they would succeed. If they turned back without striking a blow, it would be worse than a defeat, it would be dishonor . . . "a stain upon our arms."

Ross wavered.

"I know their force," the Admiral persisted, with perhaps just a touch of exasperation. "The militia, however great their numbers, will not—cannot—stand against your disciplined troops. It is too late—we ought not to have advanced—there is now no choice left us. We must go on."

As the minutes ticked on, the sky to the west gradually reddened with the glow of the upper bridge burning. Finally, just as dawn was breaking, Ross suddenly struck his hand against his forehead and exclaimed, "Well, be it so, we will proceed."

No more time to lose. Both Ross and Cockburn assumed that Winder would burn the bridges over the Eastern Branch at Washington itself. So they would go by way of Bladensburg, five miles upstream. There, even if the bridge was gone, they could ford the river anyhow.

Aides rushed off with orders to the various unit commanders . . . the drums began to roll . . . the men fell in. It had been rumored that the army planned to retire; now, as word spread of the decision to advance, a murmur of excitement swept the ranks. The columns formed up, and at 5:00 A.M., August 24, the troops swung onto the road, in full march for the capital of the United States.

CHAPTER FIVE

Time Runs Out

"We feel assured that the number and bravery of our men will afford complete protection to the city," the eternally optimistic *National Intelligencer* told its readers on the morning of August 24. "It is highly improbable that . . . the enemy would advance nearer to the capital," echoed the Georgetown *Federal Republican*.

For the past week the press had maintained an almost eerie cheerfulness, oblivious of the mounting confusion, the scurrying citizens, the overloaded wagons rattling out of town. Now there were few left to read the good news. Down New Jersey Avenue, William A. Bradley, cashier of the Bank of Washington, piled the bank's assets into a cart and joined the tail end of the exodus. At his house on F Street, the Superintendent of Patents, William Thornton, had his horses harnessed and ready to go. Near Capitol Hill the Reverend Andrew Hunter and his wife Mary held a last-minute family conference: it was decided that Dr. Hunter would take the children to safety in the country; Mrs. Hunter, a formidable lady, would remain with the housekeeper and a servant, standing guard on their property. An unusual quiet settled over the city, as the clear morning sky promised another hot day.

General Winder, who ended his hectic night on a cot lent by one of General Smith's aides, got up at sunrise . . . rode to McKeowin's for a hasty breakfast . . . and returned to camp, where he established his headquarters at the Griffith Coombs house near the lower bridge. Here he listened to more conflicting reports from his array of amateur scouts, then wrote a troubled note to Secretary Armstrong. He briefly outlined his situation, adding that the news "up the river" was very alarming. But he must have meant "down the river," for he next suggested putting Barney's men at the batteries on Greenleaf's Point and the Navy Yard—a move that made sense only if he thought the British squadron on the Potomac was practically in sight. In any case, he was clearly at his wit's end and finished with an almost pathetic plea for advice: "I should be glad of the assistance of counsel from yourself and the government. If more convenient, I should make an exertion to go to you the first opportunity."

James Madison took one look at the note—it had been delivered to the President by mistake—and rushed to Winder's headquarters. Arriving around 7:00, he was soon joined by James Monroe, who had only returned from Bladensburg at 2:00 A.M. but was already champing for a new assignment. Then William Jones came in his gig from his house near Georgetown, fretting about the Navy Yard and the enormous amount of material stored there.

New reports continued to pour in—the latest a rumor that the British were heading for Bladensburg. Winder was inclined to discount it—Annapolis, Fort Washington, the lower bridge, any place made more sense than that—but Monroe was extremely impressed. Could he go back and make sure Stansbury knew? Madison and Winder approved, and so, in the Secretary's words, "I lost not a moment in complying with their desire."

Across town Attorney General Rush, also back in the saddle after a long night scouting, rode over to the Seven Buildings around 9:00 A.M. to ask Secretary Armstrong if there was any late news. Only a note from Winder, said the Secretary, showing him the message that had now been relayed by Madison. The Secretary saw no reason to hurry, but Rush caught the General's tone of despair, and hurried to headquarters.

By now Monroe had gone, but a growing crowd milled in and out of the house—Commodore Barney, Captain Tingey of the Navy Yard, miscellaneous officers, even occasional civilians whom nobody knew. Inside, it was all a babble of voices as first one "expert," then another, tried to be heard. The reports were as conflicting as ever, but the consensus still favored an enemy advance toward the lower bridge. Some said the British were only two and a half miles away.

Hanson Catlett knew better than that. Winder's staff surgeon had been out all night, apparently feeling that in this army of amateurs a physician could be as good a scout as anyone. He had slept near the abandoned American camp at Long Old Fields, had sent a man over at daylight to see what was doing there. No enemy in sight. He then came back to Washington, returning by the very road the British were said to be on. So he knew firsthand they weren't coming that way.

Nobody listened. The calm, quiet doctor was forgotten as far more exciting news came in. A message arrived from down the Potomac indicating that the British were pressing hard on the city. A dragoon pounded across the lower bridge dramatically announcing, "The enemy are in force at the Old Fields—coming on!"

Winder rushed Major Peter's artillery to join Burch's men already covering the bridge. They frantically pulled down the tollhouse to make kindling for burning it. Lieutenant Forrest of the navy took the boat sent by Captain Tingey—piled high with eight barrels of powder—and lined it up under the arch next to the draw.

By now Winder felt even stronger measures were necessary. About 9:30 he sent Commodore Barney to take over defending the bridge. The Commodore had fresher men and heavier guns. Those 400 tough flotillamen ought to give even a British grenadier reason to pause.

Shortly before 10:00 Secretary of the Treasury Campbell joined the crowd at headquarters. He and Secretary Armstrong had left their boardinghouse together, but Armstrong —still in no hurry—stopped to talk with some people along the way. Campbell went on alone, and was soon as bewildered as the rest.

Suddenly one more messenger burst in. The British, he said, were definitely heading for Bladensburg—yes, Bladensburg—and this time Winder immediately considered the information "decisive."

At last. But what finally swayed the General remains unclear. Attorney General Rush later said the message was direct from General Stansbury on the scene. General James Wilkinson—not present, not always trustworthy, but extremely knowledgeable—said the word came from one of those hospitable southern Marylanders, who had entertained Ross and Cockburn the previous evening. Others have attributed the report to a reliable scout who actually saw the British feint toward Washington and the Potomac, then turn right on the road to Bladensburg—which indeed they did.

Whatever the source, it must have been good, for until

now General Winder had resisted every temptation to look
toward the little Maryland town just northeast of the District. Annapolis, Baltimore, Alexandria, Fort Washington, the
upper and lower bridges—he had considered them all—
but Bladensburg never, although it had the only bridge
across the Eastern Branch above the city itself.

But all that was over. Now he rushed to put his army on
the road. Laval's cavalry . . . Peter's and Burch's artillery
. . . the District Militia . . . Scott's regulars . . . Stull's riflemen, still without rifles—all were ordered to proceed immediately to Bladensburg. No time for delay—the British
already had a good head start. By 11:00 the first units were
moving out.

Only Barney was left behind. Whether Winder forgot, or
felt he didn't have the authority, or once again succumbed to
his underlying fear for the safety of the lower bridge, no one
ever knew. The fact remained that the toughest element in
the whole defense force—the Commodore's 400 flotillamen, together with Captain Samuel Miller's 120 Marines and
their five splendid guns—were left all alone, still guarding
the half-mile expanse of the Eastern Branch.

Good soldier that he was, Winder himself planned to join
his men in battle. He was just leaving when Secretary Armstrong came riding up—first to be sought, last to appear.
Little was said between them. By now their relations were
beyond words. With Armstrong, it was a case of utter contempt: "I took it for granted that he had received the *counsel*
he required; for to me he neither stated doubt nor difficulty,
nor plan of attack or of defense."

With Winder, it was more a matter of utter despair. For
weeks this administration had denied him everything it
promised—everything he needed. Now, on the spur of the
moment, he was expected to achieve a miracle. When his aide
Major George Biscoe turned to him with some question

about the march to Bladensburg, the General violently pulled his hair and blurted, "Major Biscoe, I am but nominal commander. The President and the Secretary of War have interfered with my intended operations, and I greatly fear for the success of the day."

Their frigid exchange over, Winder galloped off for Bladensburg, and Armstrong entered the house that served as headquarters. The meeting was just breaking up, and the President acidly expressed surprise at his Secretary of War's delay in getting there. He quickly brought Armstrong up to date and asked if he had any advice to offer. None, replied the Secretary, adding that as the coming battle would be between militia and regulars, the militia would be beaten.

George Campbell could bear it no longer. As the group streamed from the house and mounted their horses, he rode over to Madison and confided how distressed he was at Armstrong's attitude. He reported their conversation the night before—how the Secretary had said the defense of Washington was none of his business; that it would be "indelicate" to intrude; but that, if Madison gave his express approval, he'd be happy to assist. Now Campbell begged the President to intervene.

Madison was stunned. He said he could scarcely believe that Armstrong could have so misconceived his duties as Secretary of War. It went without saying that any proper directions would carry Presidential approval. He was sure Winder would listen to any advice or suggestions.

All very well, replied Campbell, but unless the President did something, he still felt that the Secretary would take no further part in the business of the day.

Madison now turned his horse to Armstrong. He said how worried he was about the Secretary's attitude. He urged him to use his full powers to help, stressing that it was especially important to go to Bladensburg and give Winder all the advice and assistance he could. If any conflict over authority arose, Madison added, he himself would be there to resolve it.

To Armstrong, the President was really telling him to take charge of the army, and that he would be on hand to back him up. Satisfied at last, the Secretary prepared to head for Bladensburg and put some life in the fight.

But before setting out, he joined Madison and the cabinet for a brief inspection of Barney's position at the lower bridge. The Commodore fairly exploded at them. What did they mean, he raged, by leaving him here to blow up a bridge miles from the scene of action? Why should he be "kept with five hundred of the precious few fighting men around to do what any damned corporal can better do with five?"

He won his point. Madison told him to head for Bladensburg at once with all the flotillamen, Marines and guns. Captain John O. Creighton of the navy and a "corporal's guard" would stay behind and destroy the bridge if the enemy approached.

That settled, the group split up. Armstrong left for Bladensburg . . . Madison, Rush and a few aides prepared to follow . . . Jones headed for the Marine Barracks to check the situation there. Only Campbell would remain inactive. He was in wretched health, and there seemed little a Secretary of the Treasury could do on a battlefield. It was an emotional moment for them all as Madison called out that if the city were lost, they'd meet again at Frederick, Maryland. On an impulse, Campbell unbuckled his pair of great dueling pistols and handed them to the President. Madison strapped them on, looking less like the nation's Commander-in-Chief than a small child dressed up to play war.

By 11:30 they were all on the road—a long, thin straggling column of men, strung out over most of the five miles between the lower bridge and Bladensburg. In the lead was Colonel Laval's 125 cavalrymen . . . then General Smith with the District Militia and Colonel Scott's regulars . . . then General Winder, galloping after them . . . then Secretary Armstrong traveling alone, the way he liked it . . . then Madison, Rush and several aides . . . and finally Commodore Barney with his flotillamen, Captain Miller's Marines, and their five heavy guns.

Back in Washington 700 seething, infuriated men remained. All morning Colonel George Minor had tried to get arms and ammunition for his Virginia Militia; all morning he had met one frustration after another. Resuming his search for the elusive Colonel Carberry, he was told that the Colonel had gone to his "seat in the country." Finally Minor went to the armory to requisition personally the weapons he needed.

But here the Colonel met a new frustration. He came up against a conscientious young clerk, who insisted on counting out the flints one by one. When Minor's own officers tried to speed up the process, the young man was not satisfied. He counted them out all over again.

Finally the men had their flints, along with everything else, and marched off to the Capitol, while Minor stayed behind to sign a blizzard of receipts.

At this point Colonel Carberry arrived, exchanged his compliments and apologized for the delay. He later denied that he had gone to his "seat in the country"; rather he was at Mr. Semmes's hotel in Georgetown—which nevertheless was about as far away as a person could get and still be in the District of Columbia.

At Bladensburg, General Stansbury—unaware of the reinforcements rushing up—struggled to get his lines in order. By 11:00 A.M. the last of his troops were back from their abortive march toward Washington. Now they waited in a large field, shaped rather like a slice of pie, just west of the village and the Eastern Branch. Looking east, the left side of the "pie" was the road from Georgetown; the right side,

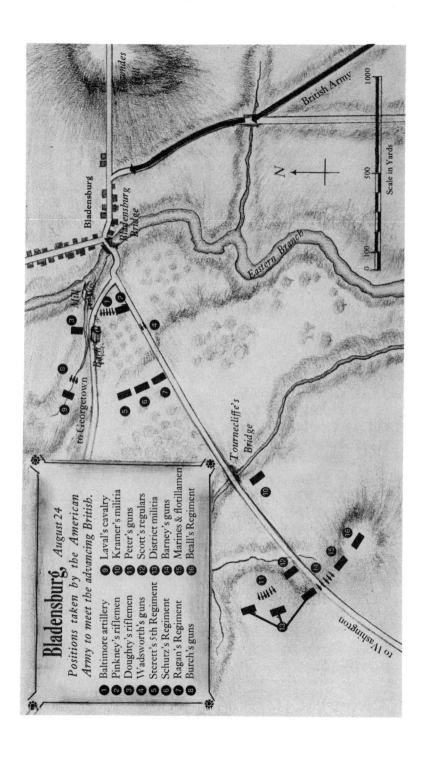

Bladensburg, *August 24*

*Positions taken by the American
Army to meet the advancing British.*

1. Baltimore artillery
2. Pinkney's riflemen
3. Doughty's riflemen
4. Wadsworth's guns
5. Scerer's 5th Regiment
6. Schutz's Regiment
7. Ragan's Regiment
8. Burch's guns
9. Laval's cavalry
10. Kramer's militia
11. Peter's guns
12. Scott's regulars
13. District militia
14. Barney's guns
15. Marines & flotillamen
16. Beall's Regiment

the turnpike from Washington. The two gradually converged till they met almost at the bridge which crossed the river into town. There the road branched out again—this time in three directions. To the north ran the turnpike to Baltimore; to the east, the direct route to Upper Marlboro; to the south, another road that generally followed the river. It too had numerous turnoffs, one of them a more circuitous route to Upper Marlboro.

The general convergence of roads at the bridge explained the existence of Bladensburg, but the place was anything but a hub of the universe. Once a flourishing tobacco town, all that was over. The trade had moved farther south, and now its pleasant brick houses languished in polite decay.

The focal point of the place was, of course, the bridge, a narrow wooden affair about 90 feet long standing on stone abutments. Above here, the Eastern Branch quickly dwindled to a small stream, easily fordable. But the country to the north and west was largely a tangle of woods, and with the river a barrier to the south, Bladensburg did function as a sort of funnel through which anyone bound for Washington from the east might very well go.

Nearly everyone except General Winder saw this clearly. It was where General Van Ness and Mayor Blake wanted entrenchments—and where Colonel Wadsworth dug them. It was where James Monroe told Minister Serurier that the decisive battle would "most likely" occur. It was where Secretary Jones wrote Commodore Rodgers, racing down from Philadelphia, that the British would probably go.

General Stansbury saw it too. That was why he had retired on Washington during the night . . . why he twice disobeyed Winder's orders to return to the town . . . why, when he finally did come back, he halted on the "safe" side of the river. He had only 2,200 raw militia, and he felt sure the whole British Army would be heading straight for him.

Even now Colonel Sterett and two other key officers were for disobeying Winder a third time and again falling back. No, said Stansbury, the orders were positive—they must make a stand. James Monroe, arriving from Washington shortly after 11:00, supplied some additional backbone.

The strongest spot was clearly the earthwork thrown up in the field by Colonel Wadsworth and his civilian volunteers. It lay facing the river and about 350 yards from the bridge into town. An ambitious work planned for heavy cannon, it was much too high for Stansbury's 6-pounders, but the Baltimore artillerymen cheerfully clawed away at the dirt, making embrasures for their six light guns.

To the left of this earthwork Stansbury put two companies of militia; and to the right, Major William Pinkney's battalion of riflemen. The earthwork stopped well short of these groups, but they were somewhat protected on the left by a tobacco barn and on the right by a rail fence. Taken together, the guns and supporting troops formed a line that covered both the bridge and the roads fanning out from it.

About 50 yards behind this line, in a pleasant apple orchard that took up the center of the pie-shaped field, Stansbury stationed his supporting troops. On the left flank were Colonel Jonathan Schutz's and Colonel John Ragan's regiments of drafted militia; on the right, Colonel Sterett's 5th Regiment, which included many of Baltimore's most fashionable young blades. All volunteers, they were there for the love of it— men who regularly drank and occasionally drilled together. Though nearly as inexperienced as the rest, they were considered Stansbury's best unit.

The General was especially pleased with his idea of putting these regiments in the orchard. Here they were near enough to support the front line, yet protected by the apple trees, which would offer excellent cover whenever the British appeared. Meanwhile the men could rest in the shade until needed. Satisfied, Stansbury returned to the earthwork to check his artillery.

Moments later James Monroe passed along the line, took one look at the troops in the orchard . . . and felt he could do better. He had been aching for active duty the whole war—the past week of scouting just whetted his appetite —now he had his real chance. Without saying a word to Stansbury, he ordered Schutz's and Ragan's regiments to leave the orchard and occupy a hill farther to the rear. The Secretary of State wasn't in anybody's chain of command— hadn't been in the army for 30 years—but he was very, very important. The two regiments promptly obeyed his orders.

The new position was more than 500 yards behind the first line—well beyond supporting range. It was also clear of the orchard and its friendly cover. The men suddenly began to feel very naked and very much alone out there on the bare hillside—easy targets whenever the British appeared. Worse, there just weren't enough men to defend the hill; a large gap appeared on the left.

Monroe knew how to fix that. Again without telling Stansbury, he yanked Colonel Sterett's 5th Regiment out of the orchard, and sent them too back to the hill. This left no one at all supporting the guns at the earthwork or the infantry alongside them.

Then came still another opportunity for the Secretary of State to try his hand at tactics. A great cloud of dust appeared on the eastern horizon above the road from Upper Marlboro. At first everyone assumed it was the British, but it turned out to be Colonel Beall's 800 militia rushing over from Annapolis. Stansbury had been expecting them all morning . . . planned to put them on the left of his line, covering his flank and a ford upstream. Before the General even knew of their arrival, Monroe had them placed not on the left but on the right—up another high hill, this one over a mile from the first line.

Stansbury discovered what was happening in the midst of these various shifts. He raced up the hill behind the orchard to find who was responsible, but was diverted when he learned for the first time that help was on the way from Washington, that General Winder himself was already on the ground. He also met General Walter Smith, who had ridden ahead of his District Militia and was now poking around in search of a good position. Sensing one more disaster in coordination, Stansbury briefly squabbled with him over seniority, then dashed off to get Winder—maybe he could solve all these problems.

Winder meanwhile was looking for Stansbury. Like Smith, the over-all commander had galloped ahead of his men. Approaching the field just before 12:00, he met Francis Scott Key, a poetically-inclined, somewhat daydreaming Georgetown lawyer who was serving as volunteer aide to General Smith. Buttonholing Winder, Key poured out suggestions on where the Washington troops might be placed. The bewildered General finally turned him over to Smith, who by this time had ridden up.

Continuing on, Winder rode to the earthwork . . . to the bridge . . . back to the earthwork again . . . and ultimately to a mill near the extreme left of the American position. Here he finally met Stansbury, who by this time was with Monroe again. The Maryland Militia General rushed up, but before he could say much, Monroe remarked smoothly that he had been "aiding" Stansbury in posting his command, and asked Winder to inspect the line to see if he approved.

But time had run out. Even as they talked, another cloud of dust appeared on the horizon—this time to the south and above the river road. Any hope that it might mean still more reinforcements vanished as the men caught glimpses of polished metal, red tunics, glittering bayonets moving in the distance. The British Army had arrived.

It was too late for a formal inspection, too late even to chop down the bridge. There was only time for a couple of last-minute adjustments. The Baltimore artillery seemed dreadfully exposed—Winder shifted Captain John Doughty's company and some of Pinkney's riflemen to strengthen the left. The orchard looked vulnerable—he decided to borrow some of the artillery coming from Washington to help out here. With this in mind, he sent frantic orders to Captain Burch, hurrying from the capital with five guns: report with three of them at once.

Burch got the order as his guns rattled along the road toward the Bladensburg bridge. Taking three 6-pounders, he raced ahead as directed, then couldn't find Winder anywhere to learn where to put them. It was one of Burch's young lieutenants, John Law, who finally located the General and got the necessary orders. The guns were to be placed on the far left of Stansbury's line, in position to rake the orchard. "When you retreat," Winder added pessimistically, "take notice you must retreat by the Georgetown road."

Burch's other two guns were borrowed by Colonel Wadsworth and planted on the turnpike just to the rear of the Baltimore artillery. They were completely exposed, but the Colonel was a professional and made sure the field of fire was good.

The Washington troops were now pouring in. As Major Peter hurried along his battery of six guns, he was stopped by Francis Scott Key, about a mile short of the bridge. Still acting as General Smith's aide, Key showed him a position off to the left. It was on a high bluff that commanded the road, but was isolated by a stream on one side and a ravine on the other. Once stuck there, Peter decided, he could never maneuver again. He picked another spot farther back but with better access.

General Smith liked the first position better—it was closer to Stansbury's line—but there was no time to argue. With the British in sight, the troops from Washington had to be put somewhere right away. As fast as they arrived, he did the best he could: Lieutenant Colonel Kramer's Maryland Militia, off the road to the right . . . Scott's regulars, off the road to the left . . . Magruder's regiment, 100 yards farther back . . . the rest of the District Militia, on the ridge to the left to support Peter's guns. There was one hectic moment when Smith discovered that Scott's regulars lay directly in Peter's line of fire. He pulled them back, and Magruder's men too.

Far off to the right, about 250 yards away, Colonel Beall's 800 Annapolis militiamen moved onto their isolated hill. They weren't under Smith, or any longer under Stansbury. Monroe had sent them there, but beyond that they had no orders. Now they watched the confusion along the road and wondered what to do.

Between them and the road there was still a gap, but here, for once, there was agreement. Winder, Smith, everybody hoped that Barney's men would fill it. But would they be in time? The British column was in plain sight now, and the Commodore hadn't reached the District Line.

In contrast, the cavalry were on hand, but nobody had any plans for them. Reaching Bladensburg just as the enemy appeared, Colonel Laval led his 125 men all the way to the bridge looking for General Stansbury. Failing to find him, he decided to water his horses, then realized the British were much too close for that. Turning back, he ran into James Monroe and asked whether he had any suggestions.

Once again the Secretary of State turned tactician. He

pointed to a ravine in the rear and far to the left of Stansbury's line. Going there, Laval found himself in a gully—so deep he couldn't even see out of it. Gradually other horsemen arrived too, until there were over 380 altogether—none able to witness, much the less join, any action that might develop.

John Armstrong was the next of the administration leaders to arrive. The Secretary of War had ridden out rather relishing the President's decision (as he thought) to put him in charge of the battle. Now that he was here, he wasn't so sure. For better or for worse, the lines were already set.

Moving off the road to the left, still assessing the troops' position, Armstrong didn't see the next arrivals from Washington. The President's party was pounding in. Past the Washington contingent . . . past Stansbury's line . . . past the earthwork . . . right up to the bridge itself they galloped. And they would have crossed it too, and plunged into the midst of the British advance, if William Simmons—a lone, self-appointed American scout—hadn't stopped them just in time.

Ironically, Simmons had recently been fired as the War Department accountant—the climax of a feud with Secretary Armstrong. He hated the administration and spent much of his new leisure attacking it in venomous public letters. But he rallied around in the crisis, and having a fresh horse, volunteered that morning to reconnoiter the Bladensburg side of the river. Riding up Lowndes Hill behind the village, he watched the British steadily advance. When they reached the edge of town, he knew that for him it was now or never. Racing down the hill, he darted back across the bridge— and headlong into the Presidential party.

"Mr. Madison!" he shouted. "The enemy are now in Bladensburg!"

"The enemy in Bladensburg!" the President echoed; the

group spun around and dashed back for the American lines. As Simmons later told the story, their flight had almost farcical overtones, with Rush losing his hat in the process. Whatever the details, the embittered accountant almost certainly saved the President from capture.

Back to the earthwork again. Here, on the extreme right, Madison's party unexpectedly met Winder and Monroe consulting with John Armstrong, who had just come up himself a moment earlier.

Joining the Secretary of War, Madison quietly asked if he had spoken to General Winder as planned, offering his advice and views. No, said Armstrong, he had not. Time was short, the President urged, yet maybe he could still do some good. Armstrong now rode over to the commanding general, but their brief conversation was lost as Madison's horse began bucking wildly.

By the time the President regained control, the exchange was over. Madison again rode up to Armstrong and again asked if he had offered the General any suggestions. The Secretary again said no: under the circumstances things were about as good as they could be.

With this shaky endorsement, the little army nervously waited. If Barney ever came, they'd be 6,000 strong, but the figure was misleading. None of Stansbury's men even knew that Winder's troops were on the field. Major Pinkney's riflemen, to the right of the earthwork, felt they were 180 men against the whole British Army. They couldn't see the corresponding companies on the left. They saw the three supporting regiments in the orchard transferred to the rear. They felt very, very much alone.

Major Pinkney—once Madison's Attorney General— tried to cheer them up with a heavy joke. He boasted that he had once theoretically, and now would practically, show the British how he felt about Anglo-American relations.

Others also tried their hand at last-second morale-building. Congressman Alexander McKim of Baltimore raced up and down Stansbury's line on one of his fast trotters, explaining that he had voted for war; now he'd stand by the men who must fight it.

Perhaps the most painful moment came when Richard Rush impulsively harangued one of the same regiments: "You are fine fellows . . . a glorious day for Baltimore . . . you will act like men . . . one of you is equal to two Englishmen."

At this point an officer looked sternly at Rush; said his men wanted no praise; and if any words were needed, he as commanding officer would speak them. The Attorney General apologized and retired.

General Winder had perhaps the best idea. About the time the enemy was sighted, someone rode up and reported a smashing victory in Canada . . . a thousand British killed, many prisoners taken. Actually, there was nothing to it, but nobody knew that at the time. Winder ordered the troops to be told, and as the good news was announced, a rising cheer spread through the ranks.

"Let's see what you'll say when we've been at it half an hour or so," scoffed one of Ross's old-timers as the yells drifted across the Eastern Branch. Lieutenant Furlong of the 21st also felt the cheering was a case of misplaced American bravado, but Lieutenant Gleig of the 85th saw more to it than that. What a contrast this raucous demonstration made to the disciplined silence of the British regulars, broken only by the perfect cadence of their marching feet. To Gleig, it somehow showed the rabble-like quality of the whole American military effort.

And if anyone wanted further proof, there was the very

appearance of these Yankee-Doodles. Here and there a few companies sported military dress, but most of the troops had no uniforms at all. Some were in blue coats, some in black, some in ordinary shooting jackets. Some even wore plain frock suits. They looked, Gleig decided, like "country people" who should have been going about their daily tasks, rather than standing with muskets on the brow of a bare green hill.

Not that the British wanted a hard fight. The day had been exhausting enough already. Leaving Melwood about 5:00 A.M., Ross's army tramped west for five miles, feinted toward the Eastern Branch bridge and Alexandria, then doubled back and headed north on the road to Bladensburg. At first the march had been in the shade—along a beguiling lane thick with branches overhead—but the last part was all in the broiling sun. The bugles played a lively tune, but the men needed more than that. Still soft from three weeks at sea and sweltering in their heavy woolen uniforms, dozens fell by the wayside. Captain Tom Falls, Ross's devoted aide, went delirious with sunstroke.

Some time before 10:00 they halted an hour, then pushed on again. Choking with dust, eyes smarting with sweat, but stepping with the precision that Gleig so admired, they finally reached Bladensburg around noon after a march of 15 miles.

There was no sign of life in the cluster of neat brick buildings directly ahead. The yards and the L-shaped main street were silent and empty. Yet Ross didn't dare move in just yet. It seemed inconceivable that anybody—even the Americans—would abandon the town. Those sturdy houses were so perfect for sharpshooters. An aide hustled over to Major George Brown with orders to take the advance guard and feel out the place.

The rest of the column then peeled off to the right and up

Lowndes Hill directly behind the town. Here they halted, waiting for Brown's report. And the delay was just as well, for despite Lieutenant Gleig's pride in the troops' professional polish, the long morning march had taken its toll. Some of the men were in a state of collapse, and the whole army was badly strung out. The lightly equipped 1st Brigade had drawn far ahead of the 2nd and 3rd, still trudging along through the dust.

Soon Major Brown sent word that Bladensburg was indeed empty, but by now there was another cause for delay. Ross and his staff had gone to the nearby Bowie house, which offered an excellent view of the countryside, and what they saw was anything but encouraging to the General. The hills across the river swarmed with Americans; the earthwork bristled with guns; the uniforms worn by a few units suggested that their regulars had come.

All the old doubts returned. How could his little force cope with such enormous numbers? And if stopped, how could it ever get back to the ships? The best reply turned out to be another question. "What will be said of us in England if we stop now?" asked an unidentified officer who sounds suspiciously like Admiral Cockburn.

So they must go on, but there was yet another disagreement. Colonel Thornton, the impetuous leader of the 1st Brigade, wanted to attack right away. His 1,100 men would make up in élan what they lacked in numbers. Captain Harry Smith—trained by thoughtful, thorough Sir John Colborne in the Peninsula—wanted to hold off a little . . . feint up the river . . . wait for the 2nd and 3rd Brigades to come up.

Thornton won. Whatever the uniforms, he argued, most of the Americans must be militia. They were not known for standing. An unflinching assault, backed by rockets and the British bayonet, should be enough.

On the reverse slope of Lowndes Hill, beyond the sight of

prying American eyes, the bugles and drums began sounding. Quickly the men fell in . . . the column formed . . . and the advance moved over the crest of the hill. Now they were in plain sight, and as the column swung down the street into Bladensburg, a sparkle of gun flashes rippled along the earthwork across the river.

CHAPTER SIX

Bladensburg

William Simmons turned and watched the first American shots plow into the streets of Bladensburg. It struck him that the guns were firing too soon . . . that if they held off a few minutes, they could give much more trouble. He galloped up the hill to Stansbury's line, looking for someone to issue the necessary orders.

Finding General Winder seated on a horse behind Colonel Sterett's 5th Regiment, Simmons poured out his advice. The gunners, he said, were just "heaving their fire away." He made as much impression as a discharged accountant playing artillery observer could reasonably expect. Winder ignored him.

The firing continued, and as the British column drew closer to the bridge, the shots began to hit home. Here and there a red-coated figure crumpled, and the steady, even ranks seemed to waver. Soon a sharp-eyed observer could also see a burst of activity down by the river bank. Little knots of British marines were setting up contraptions of some sort near a warehouse to the right of the bridge. Five minutes passed. Then a sudden series of whooshes, and streaks of smoke and flame snaked across the sky . . . not far above the heads of the startled militiamen.

Rockets. A brand-new experience for the raw American troops. Most of them barely knew the sound of cannon, much the less this terrifying new weapon. Winder dashed along Stansbury's line, calling out not to be afraid . . . the things were perfectly harmless. A few of the men perhaps half-believed him.

The General also took a moment to ride over to Madison, watching from the center of the line with Secretary Armstrong and the rest. Winder quietly suggested that the President's party move farther back.

It must have been a traumatic moment for James Madison. He had come to Bladensburg with the idea that he'd really be the Commander-in-Chief, as the Constitution said. He would be just behind the lines with his cabinet, weighing the pros and cons—supporting Armstrong here, Winder there— generally presiding over the battle. But it didn't work out that way at all. The troop positions were already set; the guns roaring; the rockets flying. The fight now had a momentum of its own far beyond the power of the President, with the collective wisdom of his cabinet, to guide and direct. Turning to his party, Madison remarked that military matters should be handled by military men. "Come, General Armstrong; come, Colonel Monroe, let us go and leave it to the commanding general."

They now rode to the rear, with Armstrong smoldering in disgust. He felt that the President had completely reversed himself. Madison had persuaded him to come to Bladensburg only by promising that he could advise Winder, and that this advice would be sanctioned by Presidential authority right on the spot. Now the man was taking it all back.

Yet Armstrong himself was no less ambivalent. Only a few minutes earlier, when Madison asked him if he had any advice, he said none—it was too late. Perhaps the explanation is the human one. In his basic resentment at having Winder in command, the Secretary was dragging his feet—consciously or unconsciously—whatever Madison proposed. In any event, there was no doubt about his attitude now. He went into an angry sulk and refused to have anything further to do with the battle. As he later put it, "I now became, of course, a mere spectator of the combat."

But even the most critical spectator had little to complain about so far. Down at the earthwork the Baltimore artillery kept up a lively fire. To the right, on the turnpike itself, Colonel Wadsworth's two "borrowed" guns hammered away. Together they scored several more hits, as the British column advanced right to the foot of the bridge. Then the enemy troops suddenly halted, and before the almost unbelieving eyes of the militiamen, "Wellington's Invincibles" scattered behind the nearby houses for shelter. Stansbury's gunners let out a surprised whoop of triumph.

"Wait a wee bit, wait a wee, with your skirling!" muttered a wounded Scotsman in the 85th Foot, as he sat on a doorstep holding his mangled arm. Nearby Lieutenants Gleig, Codd and several enlisted men crouched behind a brick wall. A cannon ball crashed into their midst, clipping the leg off a young private. Too numb yet to feel any pain, the boy gave Gleig a quizzical look, as though asking how he should behave.

Down the street, near the warehouse by the bridge, Lieutenant John Lawrence fired his rockets at the American lines across the river. Invented by a British artillery officer named Sir William Congreve, they were wildly inaccurate, yet they did have their advantages. They were simple—briefly, just metal tubes filled with powder and capped by a warhead. They were easy to carry—one man could handle three of the 12-pounders brought along by Ross's force. They were easy to fire—a common tube and tripod arrangement did the trick. But above all, they terrified anybody on the receiving end who didn't know how erratic they really were.

Today the Congreve rockets were especially useful, for the sailors dragging the force's four guns had lagged far behind. At the moment there was nothing else to serve as artillery. So Lieutenant Lawrence's men stuffed the missiles into the launchers as fast as they could, while Jeremiah McDaniel, master's mate of the *Tonnant*, kept new supplies coming.

A few more minutes, and Colonel Thornton decided that the time had come to charge the bridge. Flashing out from cover on his gray horse, he drew his sword and called to his brigade to follow. Then, throwing himself full-length on the horse, he clattered onto the wooden span. The artillery across the river was waiting. It crashed out a salvo . . . knocked down eight or nine of Thornton's men as they started after the Colonel. Miraculously, Thornton himself emerged through the smoke unscathed. With his bugler now sounding the attack, the men continued pouring across the bridge, and before Stansbury's artillery could load to fire again, they were fanning out in the bushes and thickets on the American side of the river.

Colonel Wadsworth's two 6-pounders hammered away at the advancing British. In their excitement the crew of one gun stuffed in the wadding before the powder. The men frantically tried to get it out by depressing the muzzle. They pushed it down too far and the whole gun toppled over into the ditch. No time to pull it back—the enemy was practically on top of them. The cry went up to leave it, and the other gun too.

Everyone except a gunner named Barry Parsons took to his heels. Parsons, coat off and sleeves rolled up, felt he had to get off one last shot. Somehow he managed to load, point and fire the gun all by himself. Then, in the smoke of his last discharge, he too scrambled to safety.

He was one in a hundred who stayed. Most needed no orders to run. There was something utterly unnerving about those British regulars—their pace . . . their precision . . . their teamwork . . . and, above all, their bayonets, which glittered so brightly in the sun. A company of Stansbury's skirmishers, stationed to the right of Pinkney's riflemen, broke first. Next, Pinkney noticed the Baltimore artillery limbering up at a speed never matched on the parade ground. Then, without any orders whatsoever, his own men began to vanish, streaming back to the left of the orchard toward Stansbury's line up the hill.

Still standing on the hill behind Sterett's 5th Regiment, General Winder saw them coming. It was his first clue that his front had collapsed. Until this moment his view had been blocked; for in shifting Stansbury's infantry out of the orchard to the hill in the rear, Monroe had not only exposed his own troops but screened any view of the enemy advance. All was now hidden by a tangle of apple trees.

It still wasn't clear whether the whole earthwork was gone, and hoping to salvage something, Winder quickly ordered Sterett to advance down the hill in support of the Baltimore artillery. Schutz's and Ragan's regiments remained in place to cover the 5th's right flank from any British attack through the orchard or along the turnpike.

As Sterrett's men swept forward, a new flight of Congreve rockets streaked across the sky. Until now they had been aimed too high, but this new batch was right on target. Schutz's and Ragan's troops ducked in fright as the rockets whistled past their ears. That was enough. The two regiments didn't fall back or melt away: they simply dissolved. One minute they were there, covering the 5th's right flank; the next instant they were gone, running for the rear, disbanded as if by some prearranged signal.

Aghast, Winder ordered Sterrett's men to halt, and he galloped to the scene of the panic—shouting, threatening, pleading. Many of the men stopped and seemed to reconsider. Encouraged, the General returned to his original position, but on looking back, he saw to his dismay that they were gone again.

This time there was no stopping them. General Stansbury cried in vain to "cut down the cowards," but most of the men he was yelling at were themselves part of the flight. Colonel Ragan fell off his horse and lost the last vestige of any commanding presence. Here and there a few men rallied— Captain Showers's and Captain Gallway's companies, most of Captain Randall's outfit. But they were the exceptions. Out of 1,350 men, nearly 1,300 were gone for good.

Meanwhile the 5th Regiment remained stationary— somewhat in advance of its original position but still short of the orchard. With its right flank uncovered, Winder didn't dare push it farther. But he didn't want to pull it back either. He now hoped to use it, along with Burch's artillery all the way to the left, to keep the British Army from advancing into the orchard.

It was too late for that. Shots were already whining out of the trees—a growing ordeal for Sterrett's men, who were highly visible themselves but couldn't see the enemy among the trees. They fired away anyhow, and were soon joined by

Captain Burch's guns all the way to the left. These concentrated on the tobacco barn down the hill, where British troops seemed to be forming. More help came from Major Pinkney's retreating riflemen. Somewhat ashamed of their hasty flight from the earthwork, they now reformed with Sterett and continued to fight.

But the unseen enemy kept firing. Pinkney himself caught a musket ball in the right arm and had to leave the field. Winder nervously ordered Sterett to fall back . . . then immediately countermanded the order. More shots—some from the turnpike too, indicating that on the right the British had advanced beyond the orchard. Again Winder ordered Sterett to fall back.

The confusion of orders proved too much. Sterett's 5th Regiment boasted the elite of Baltimore, but even gentlemen warriors have their limits. These men had taken the fire of a foe they couldn't see; they had watched while Stansbury's other troops fled in panic; they seemed to be the victims of bewildered indecision. Now as they started back again, they quickly lost all semblance of order. Like Schutz's and Ragan's regiments before them, Sterett's men ran pell-mell for the rear.

No one had any objective, except to get away. Private Henry Fulford started for a friendly woods, but there were too many bullets flying around; so he settled for a swamp that was nearer. Captain Burch's artillery rattled off so fast that the Captain, already exhausted by his work in the field, couldn't keep up with the guns. He fainted unnoticed by the side of the road.

Here and there a man paused long enough to help a comrade. Private Kennedy, still in his dancing pumps, stopped to aid his wounded friend James McCulloch. Kennedy kept tripping over his musket, so he gave it away. Weapons were the last thing a soldier needed at a time like this.

The various infantry and artillery units were soon jumbled together in a single tidal wave of retreat. Anything it touched, it carried along. Most of Colonel Laval's cavalry were still in their ravine as the wave approached, but one company lay in its path. Suddenly the troopers were engulfed in a plunging mass of men, guns and horses. Laval himself barely escaped breaking his leg as a caisson careened against him. He soon found himself left with only 55 men. None of them had any taste for a Thermopylae; so with the Colonel leading, they too ran off.

Stopping the rout was hopeless. Winder felt his only chance was to channel the fleeing men toward the troops from Washington, still coming up about a mile to the rear. These might offer a rallying point for another stand. But it was useless. Even now, Stansbury's men didn't know there were any Washington troops. In running off, they looked only for the easiest way, and this was the Georgetown road, veering off in a different direction.

Lost in the scramble for safety was the President's party. After moving back at the start of the battle, Madison and his group were already well to the rear when the rout began. But they were near enough to see, and a scribbled warning from Winder ended any lingering hope. Each of them reacted in his own way: the energetic Monroe hurried over and tried to rally the troops; the sullen Armstrong drifted off by himself; Madison and Rush gloomily rode to the turnpike and started back for Washington. It was still only two o'clock and hard to believe that such a disaster could have happened in half an hour.

Leaving the scene, the President met a familiar figure just getting ready to fight. Commodore Joshua Barney had arrived only minutes earlier with his 520 flotillamen, Marines and five big guns. Last to start, they were still back in the District when the firing began. With a great spurt of effort they came on at a trot, churning up the dust; now they were taking their place in what became known as the "second line," manned almost entirely by the troops from Washington.

To the left, Colonel Scott's regulars, Peter's artillery, and most of the District Militia were already in place. A little to the right (and too far in advance to be a real part of the line) stood Lieutenant Colonel Kramer's battalion of Maryland Militia. All the way to the right, Colonel Beall's Annapolis contingent waited on their hill. Because of those five big guns, Barney had the honor of holding the center: the turnpike and a field just to the right. He quickly planted his two 18-pounders right in the middle of the road. In the field he put the three 12-pounders with Captain Miller and a company of Marines. The rest of the Marines and flotillamen would act as supporting infantry. This was a new role for his collection of sailors, but they were an adaptable, picturesque lot. Charles Ball, for instance, was an escaped slave with a highly independent streak. He did not take the easy way and go to the British for protection; rather he posed as a freedman and joined the flotilla as a cook.

At the moment there was little any of them could do. The line, which ran along the highest ridge on the Washington side of the Eastern Branch, was an admirable position . . . except that the battle was being fought somewhere else. As matters stood, the men from the District were both too far to the rear and too far to the right to help Stansbury's troops. The best they could do was watch and listen, and it soon became obvious that things were going badly. Although most of Stansbury's men fled down the Georgetown road, enough of them came along the turnpike to describe what had happened. By the time the President rode by, everyone already knew the worst.

The gunfire, the screech of the rockets died down up

front. Ten . . . fifteen minutes went by and nothing happened. Stansbury's line had evaporated so suddenly, it took time to fill the vacuum. But around 2:30 the second line caught its first glimpse of those red tunics—those gleaming bayonets—coming up the road.

Soon the British advance approached a shallow ravine about 500 yards in front of the line. It was spanned by some wooden planking pretentiously called Tournecliffe's Bridge, and as the enemy reached the crossing, Colonel Kramer's militia opened fire from the opposite side. A sharp return fire, and Kramer's men took flight, joining Colonel Beall on his hill. The British pushed on across the bridge—it looked like another rout in the making. But at this point Major Peter's guns opened up from the left, and Barney fired one of his 18-pounders straight down the road. Caught in the crossfire, the British recoiled . . . then came on again. A second hail of fire; once more the enemy stopped, then came on again. A third blast, and this time Ross's troops left the road completely, moving into a field on the American right.

Now it was Captain Miller's turn. His 12-pounders roared into action raking the field with grape and canister. In the smoke it was hard to know what was happening, but Barney decided that this was the moment to strike a blow of his own. He called to his "infantry" to charge.

In a great surge, the motley array of flotillamen, sailing masters, boatswains and Marines swept forward. Through the smoke they could see that most of the British had taken cover behind a rail fence. There was something familiar about that. With cutlasses raised, they swarmed over the rails shouting, "Board 'em!"

The men of the 85th Foot reeled back under the impact. Most scrambled for cover in the ravine . . . a few went as far as the thickets near the bank of the Eastern Branch. But on the whole Lieutenant Gleig was proud of the way the troops handled themselves, retiring "slowly and indignantly, halting from time to time, firing with effect." He was relieved, too, that the Americans didn't press their advantage. Instead, having thrown the British off balance, the sailors retired back up the hill to the guns.

But the attack had taken its toll. Colonel Thornton himself was down, shot in the thigh. At one point in the charge he escaped capture only by rolling down the slope and out of the way. Lieutenant Colonel William Wood took over— then he too was hit. By now, in fact, the 85th had few officers left. Major Brown was gone . . . so was bright, young Captain Hamilton . . . and Gleig's friend Lieutenant Codd, killed by a musket ball in his windpipe. Toting up the carnage, Captain John James Knox decided the only bright spot was the opportunity it gave for battlefield promotions. "By the time the action is over," he said to himself, "the devil is in it if I am not either a walking major or a dead captain."

The whole business was an eye-opening shock for General Ross and Admiral Cockburn. They had watched the battle begin from the Bowie house porch, high behind Bladensburg. It was an unusual vantage point for them both, for they could normally be found where the action was thickest. Perhaps they were hanging back to make sure the 2nd and 3rd Brigades arrived in good order. In any case, there seemed at first no cause for concern: once across the river, Thornton's right easily routed the Americans at the earthwork and behind the orchard; while the Colonel's left met no opposition as it headed across the fields parallel to the turnpike. No one seemed to take seriously the second American line running along the ridge over a mile west of the river.

Then the distant crackling of musket fire and the renewed roar of artillery told them there was more to come. Both

Ross and Cockburn raced to the scene with their aides. Taking in the 85th's troubles at a glance, Ross told Captain Harry Smith to bring up the rest of the army as fast as possible. The 2nd Brigade—some 1,460 men from the 4th and 44th Regiments under Colonel Arthur Brooke—was just entering town, and Smith hustled them across the bridge to the front. Ross told Brooke to take the 4th and work around the American left; he himself would lead the 44th and what was left of the 1st Brigade around the enemy's right.

Galloping to the front—the spot he loved best—the General called on the men to follow him. A moment later his horse was shot—a fine Arabian he had used all over the Peninsula. No time to think about that; he jumped on another and led on.

If anyone made a better target, it was Admiral Cockburn. Prancing about on a white charger—his gold-laced hat and epaulets flashing in the sun—he was trying to plant his rocket men about 140 yards in front of the American line. Lieutenant Scott urged him to be more careful, suggesting he work from a quarry beside the road that might offer a little protection.

"Nonsense!" was the only reply.

The rockets began going off. At first they seemed as effective as ever, but then a hail of return fire cut down Lieutenant Lawrence and Master's Mate McDaniel, the two men in charge, and this put an end to the business. As Cockburn hovered by, a musket ball tore off his stirrup, without touching him or the horse. Then a round shot flew over the saddle, killing a marine trying to make repairs. Through it all, the Admiral remained impervious and immune.

With Ross still leading, the British reinforcements were now hammering the American right, and at last Lieutenant Gleig could feel the tide turning. He watched as one enemy soldier tried to stop the rest by stepping to the front and waving a flag. It was useless, and the man himself was soon gone, dropping his flag in the process. Gleig rushed forward and retrieved it—his own trophy of battle.

At such close quarters war could become very personal indeed. Gleig noticed one man in a black coat who seemed to have taken a particular dislike to him. Three times the man methodically loaded, aimed and fired at him. Twice he missed, but the third time he winged Gleig in the leg.

For Joshua Barney the war had taken a personal turn too. Standing behind the big 18-pounders on the turnpike, he saw one British soldier carefully pile up some stones, then lie down behind them and take aim. "Oh," said Barney to himself, "you are a crack shot, I suppose, but I'll bank you." Personally pointing one of his guns, he let fly a round. When the smoke cleared away, the parapet was in ruins and the sharpshooter gone. Oddly enough, Barney found himself hoping that the man got away.

To the left of the turnpike Major Peter's guns hammered away—all the harder with the British obviously trying to flank them. Seeing the threat, Colonel Scott's regulars changed front, extending the line farther left, trying to block the enemy advance. Some skirmishers were within pistol range now, and Scott's men waited impatiently for orders to fire.

They never came. Instead, General Winder suddenly appeared through the smoke and peremptorily ordered the entire line to retreat. Fresh from Stansbury's rout, the General knew all too well that the American left was now one huge gap. The troops manning this second line could never fill it by spreading themselves thinner. His one idea was to save them before the British rolled them up. Scott's men knew nothing about all that; they only knew they were told to retreat without firing a shot. Raging with indignation, they began pulling back.

It was the same with the District Militia on their right. A howl of anger went up—some men actually wept—as the orders to retreat were passed along. None was more bitter than George Washington Custis, grandson of Martha Washington, serving in Peter's battery. Like any other Federalist, he detested the war; nor did he need to go, for one hand was crippled by arthritis. Yet he was a Washington, and at the start of the campaign he offered his services to Madison. Turned down—more because of his politics than his arthritis—he joined the ranks as an ordinary cannoneer. Now, as his battery retired, he used his good hand to help fire one last shot of defiance.

Young T. P. Andrews couldn't bear to go at all. An adventuresome schoolboy, he had originally run away from home and joined Barney's flotilla in June. Collared by his parents, he returned home only to go off again, this time with the District Militia when it marched to meet Ross. Now, as his regiment headed back for Washington, he slipped away and rejoined Barney.

The Commodore fought on. Winder didn't feel he had any authority over navy people and never even sent word of his own retreat. The net effect was to concentrate a lot more British fire on the flotillamen. Sailing Master John Webster had a close shave when his horse was shot through the head . . . and an even closer one when his hat was shot through the crown.

All the way to the right, at the top of their hill, Colonel Beall's men watched nervously as the British left wing approached. To Captain Jenifer Sprigg, the troops stared as if

they were looking at ghosts. Trying to get them into position, he and the other officers "bawled at them until we were
hoarse." A ragged line finally took shape, but small parties of
the men kept slipping away into the woods.

Just as the firing began, Winder's aide John Eager Howard,
Jr. rode up with the General's order to retreat. Beall seems to
have been almost numb at this point—afterward he never
even remembered Winder's message—but Sprigg gave a
very professional order for the regiment to wheel from the
rear. It proved too great a temptation; half the 2nd Battalion
wheeled and ran off into the woods. In minutes two-thirds of
the regiment were gone. "Every man shifted for himself,"
Sprigg wrote a friend the next day, "and I couldn't stop
them."

The British now took over the hill and poured their fire
down on Barney's men. The Commodore's horse was killed
. . . then his own thigh was hit. In a tight spot like this he
decided it was best to keep the wound secret; he said nothing
and went on fighting. Enemy sharpshooters were creeping
closer too, and Marine Captain Miller found himself locked in
a private duel with one of Ross's infantrymen. Each fired at
the other and missed. Both reloaded, but while Miller was
fixing his flint, the Englishman fired again, this time shattering
the Captain's arm.

Sailing Masters Warner and Martin went down . . . then
several more good men. But the crusher was the loss of the
ammunition wagons. In the custom of the day, Barney's drivers were civilians under contract—but they had never con-
tracted for this and drove off in a panic.

With no ammunition, flanked on the right and deserted on
the left, the Commodore knew that the end had come. He ordered the guns spiked, the men to retreat, and he started to
follow himself. Anyone could see he was wounded now, and

three of his officers tried to support him. They struggled along a few yards, but it was no use. Faint from loss of blood, he sank to the ground.

But there was still one last chance of escape. At this moment Barney's aide George W. Wilson came riding by on a horse furnished by the Commodore himself. Since a sound man could easily get away on foot (thousands proved that at Bladensburg), Barney called to him two or three times for help, but Wilson just rode on. Finally an officer dashed off in pursuit, but it was hopeless. Spurring his horse, Wilson disappeared down the road.

No time for harsh words—those would come later—Barney now told the men supporting him to leave. At first they refused, but he made it an order, and only Lieutenant Jesse Huffington remained by his side as he lay grimly waiting for the British.

It was a corporal in the 85th Foot who first found him. Barney, always a stickler for rank, told the man to get an officer so he could surrender. The corporal brought back Captain Wainwright of the *Tonnant*, who looked so young Barney thought he was a mere midshipman. That straightened out, all went smoothly. Wainwright rushed off and soon returned with both Admiral Cockburn and General Ross. Introducing the Admiral, Wainwright gave his name the English pronunciation, "Coburn."

"Oh," said Barney, " 'Cock-burn' is what you are called hereabouts." And on this cozy note the proceedings continued. All three officers proved fully up to that infinite courtesy that so often marked exchanges between opposing commanders before the twentieth century. . . .

"Well, Admiral, you have got hold of me at last."

"Do not let us speak of that subject, Commodore: I regret to see you in this state."

After a brief huddle with Cockburn, Ross then told Barney

he was paroled on the spot and asked where he wished to be taken. Barney picked a tavern near Bladensburg. The General gave the necessary orders, called a surgeon to dress the Commodore's wounds, and told off a party of soldiers to act as stretcher-bearers. Not to be outdone, Cockburn detached Captain Wainwright to go along and see that every attention was paid to the Commodore. The two British commanders then politely took their leave and went back to the business of war.

So far the profits were enormous. With two-thirds of his force, some 2,600 men, Ross had routed an American army of 6,000. He had taken 10 guns, 220 muskets, 120 prisoners. He had also inflicted about 150 casualties—not very impressive but, as Cockburn put it, the victors were too weary and the vanquished too swift.

Yet the triumph had its price. Ross lost some 250 killed and wounded, including 18 of his best junior officers. At that, he was lucky; for despite the victory, the General had not fought a good battle. He needlessly hurried his men into action; he used them piecemeal; he stormed over the bridge in a dangerous frontal assault, when a little reconnaissance would have revealed the fords upstream. "Heavens! If Colborne was to see this!" groaned Captain Harry Smith, thinking of his old commander's finesse.

In the end it was not British skill but American ineptitude that settled matters. The catalogue of failures seemed endless: the failure to use the sturdy houses of Bladensburg itself . . . the failure to chop down the bridge . . . the failure to support the earthwork . . . the failure to put the second line near enough to the first . . . the failure to make use of the cavalry . . . the failure to fix a rallying point in case of retreat . . . the failure to bring on Colonel Minor's regiment —or General Robert Young's brigade, idle down the Potomac. And overriding everything else was the failure of judgment—the decision to risk everything on a single, formal battle between raw militia and polished professionals.

In the years to come there would be efforts to salvage a little pride. There would be myths of gallant stands and counterattacks. In the English tradition of good sportsmanship, Ross's veterans would say they had never known such firing. Future scholars would claim that all was going well until the British made a flank attack across the ford on Stansbury's left.

The Americans there knew better. To one witness, writing in the Norfolk *Herald*, the British "moved as steadily and undismayed as though there were no opposition." To another, in a letter to the Philadelphia *General Advertiser*, "Our militia were dispersed like a flock of birds assailed by a load of mustard seed shot." Not being one of the hunting set, Barney's flotillaman Charles Ball put it in earthier terms: "The militia ran like sheep, chased by dogs." It remained for Colonel Sterett to sum it up best in his unusually candid official report: "We were outflanked and defeated in as short a time as such an operation could well be performed."

And the flight from the battlefield was just the start. Most of Stansbury's troops instinctively headed for Baltimore. All through the night they streamed, grimy and exhausted, into the frightened city. The men from the District had a shorter way to go, but they were just as disorganized. No one knew what to do next.

Weapons and equipment were hopelessly scattered. The army's baggage wagons rumbled across the Potomac bridge and vanished into the Virginia countryside. For weeks afterward the *National Intelligencer*'s lost-and-found columns made eloquent reading: "LOST, on battlefield near Bladensburg, the 24th, a small Bay Mare" . . . "FOUND, August 25th, between Georgetown and Montgomery Court House, a small pocketbook" . . . "LOST, a rifle placed in the watch house at

Georgetown night of August 24, now missing and seems to have been carried to Baltimore for safety."

Scores fell by the wayside. Major Morgan of Winchester collapsed on the road and died of exhaustion. Several hundred men swarmed around Clover Hill, Dr. Phineas T. Bradley's country home. Most of the family had fled, but Mrs. Bradley—normally a quiet, timid woman—rose to the occasion. She seemed everywhere at once, filling canteens and bathing wounds. Choking with dust as they fled down the turnpike, Captain Jenifer Sprigg and several of Barney's sailors came across a trough of muddy water. While they lapped it up, Sprigg's horse pushed his way among them, and all drank quietly together.

Lieutenant Gleig lay beside a puddle of muddy water about a mile from the battlefield. The fighting was over, the excitement gone, and now that musket ball in his thigh had caught up with him. His leg burned with pain, and the water—filthy though it was—tasted sweeter than any he had ever known before.

Looking around, he saw three British soldiers. They sat with him while he recovered a little strength. Then they helped him back to his regiment, now posted on the ridge where the District Militia had been stationed such a short time before.

With the American Army dispersed, General Ross decided to rest his weary troops a couple of hours before proceeding on to Washington. Most of the men lay sleeping, or sat swapping stories of the fight. To Gleig, their talk and laughter seemed unnaturally loud as they worked off the hours of tension.

Here and there parties moved about the field, destroying

captured guns, trying to help the wounded. Commodore Barney groaned in agony as the four soldiers carrying his litter made some clumsy move. Captain Wainwright of the *Tonnant*—still looking after the Commodore's comfort —abruptly dismissed them, muttering that they didn't know how to handle a man. He then recruited a gang of sailors and all went well. Barney, who rarely missed a chance to contrast army bumbling with navy skill, added the incident to his long list of illustrations.

Other groups of soldiers rummaged through the houses around the battlefield, and bursting into one place, they came up against the unlikely presence of Father Edward Dominic Fenwick, a Catholic priest and missionary visiting from Kentucky. Unlike the militia, Father Fenwick wasn't in the least cowed by the redcoats and vigorously assailed their conduct. Apparently on the assumption that no real clergyman could use such emphatic language, he was hauled off under arrest.

At one house, however, the British received the warmest of welcomes. Thomas Barclay, His Majesty's Commissioner on Prisoner Exchanges, had remained in Bladensburg during the entire British advance, despite every effort by his American counterpart, General John Mason, to move him to Hagerstown.

In a masterpiece of delaying action Barclay successively pleaded that Mason's orders were lost in the mail . . . that he couldn't get a carriage . . . that Bladensburg was so much more convenient . . . that if he really had to move, he'd prefer Philadelphia . . . that the routing was poor; he'd rather come to Washington and travel by the regular stagecoach.

On the morning of the 24th, he was still at Bladensburg and Mason was frantic. The General himself finally sent a carriage, ordering Barclay to leave instantly. By 11:00— two hours before the fighting began—he was on his way, but his assistant George Barton remained behind to protect the files and was there the whole battle.

Now the place was a bit of home to the weary victors. A sentry stood by the door, as Ross's officers streamed in and out, enjoying Barton's hospitality and whatever information he could offer on the next objective—the American capital.

CHAPTER SEVEN

Ordeal by Fire

From a third-floor window in his handsome house on Capitol Hill, Dr. James Ewell studied the horizon, searching for some clue to the course of battle at Bladensburg. Occasionally he could see a puff of smoke, or hear the distant rumble of guns, but that was all. It was impossible to guess what was going on, or what to tell his wife and two daughters standing at his side.

Gradually the smoke and rumble died away, and for a while there was just silence. Then for the first time the doctor noticed a cloud of dust over the outskirts of the city—a cloud that grew steadily thicker and nearer. Soon soldiers began running by—at first in twos and threes, then swarms of them. At one point Ewell caught a glimpse of Secretary of War Armstrong himself, almost lost in the mob. A horseman rode by, shouting warnings of redcoats and rape. The doctor's daughters began screaming and Mrs. Ewell sobbed over and over, "What shall we do? What shall we do?"

On the other side of the city the Superintendent of Patents William Thornton and his wife also scanned the horizon from their house on F Street. They knew the troops were engaged, but they lived farther away than the Ewells and could hear nothing. At last they saw a man riding hard up Pennsylvania Avenue toward the President's House—clearly a messenger bringing news of some sort.

At the President's House a servant boy named Paul Jennings was busy getting dinner ready. Madison had indicated that most of the cabinet and a few "military gentlemen" would be coming, so Jennings carefully set the table, brought up the ale, wine and cider, and placed the bottles in coolers. He was just about finished when, around 3 o'clock, Madison's freedman servant Jim Smith galloped up to the house, waving his hat and shouting, "Clear out, clear out! General Armstrong has ordered a retreat!"

Mrs. Madison had been waiting all day for some word from her husband. Twice Mayor Blake turned up, urging her to leave, but she hung on, hoping for the best, spending much of her time at an upper window turning a spyglass in every direction. She saw little then, but Jim Smith's spectacular arrival made everything all too clear. As if his excited cries weren't enough, he brought another of Madison's hastily penciled notes. This one said the battle was lost . . . fly at once.

But above all, Dolley Madison was a woman of composure, and she wasn't about to leave without first attending to a few important details. By now her sister and brother-in-law, Mr. and Mrs. Richard Cutts, were on hand—also the New York banker Jacob Barker, Charles Carroll of Bellevue, and one or two other gallants—and she turned to them for help. Together they all went to work, trying to save what they could on the spur of the moment. The First Lady even managed to jot down a brief running account for the benefit of another sister, Lucy Washington Todd.

Somebody found a wagon, and they quickly loaded it with most of the silver, some papers, a few books, a small clock, the red velvet curtains from the drawing room. In minutes the load was on its way to the Bank of Maryland safely beyond the city.

What took time was the full-length portrait of George Washington hanging on the west wall of the dining room. Attributed to Gilbert Stuart, it was the showpiece of the mansion, and all agreed that it would be a crowning disgrace if the picture fell into British hands. Only the previous day the President had assured George Washington Custis that it would be taken care of in any emergency. Now the First Lady considered it her special responsibility.

Trouble was, nobody could get it down. The Madisons' versatile French doorkeeper Jean Pierre Sioussa and the gardener Tom Magraw tugged and twisted, but it was screwed too tightly to the wall. Charles Carroll and Jacob Barker tried their hand, but had no better luck.

Minutes ticked by, and Carroll grew impatient. Forget the picture, he scolded Mrs. Madison, she must leave right away. Otherwise she was bound to be trapped among the retreating troops already pouring by the house.

She wasn't ready to give up yet. Magraw worked on, teetering at the top of a ladder, while Sioussa rushed off to get an ax. Finally they chopped the frame apart . . . took out the canvas, still on its stretcher . . . and laid it on the dining room floor. By now Carroll was gone—off to rejoin the President—so Mrs. Madison turned to Barker and Robert G. L. de Peyster, another New Yorker standing by.

"Save that picture," she said. "Save that picture if possible. If not possible, destroy it. Under no circumstances allow it to fall into the hands of the British." At the same time she begged them to rescue the ornamental eagles in the drawing room and four remaining boxes of the President's papers.

Now, at last, she felt free to go. Stuffing a few more pieces of silverware into her netted reticule, she hurried out the door and into a waiting carriage. Her personal maid Sukey jumped in beside her, and with coachman Joe Bolin at the reins, they rolled onto Pennsylvania Avenue and headed for Georgetown. About the same time another carriage left with the Cuttses, and the President's coachee brought up the rear. Madison always considered this a most unsatisfactory vehicle, but his butler John Freeman was only too glad to have it now. Piling in his family, he drove off with a feather bed lashed to the rear.

While Dolley Madison sped westward for safety, the President was caught in the maelstrom of defeat, swirling back from Bladensburg. High and low—the statesmen, the generals, the soldiers and sailors, the "private gentlemen"—they all reeled back together, as General Winder did his frantic best to stem the tide.

At first he had hopes of forming a new line about 500 yards behind the original position. When that failed, he tried again just west of the turnpike gate. He had better luck here, partly because Colonel Minor's 700 Virginians—armed at last—turned up to bolster the effort.

But Winder still felt he wasn't strong enough to make a real stand. At best he had maybe 1,200 men left. Leaving General Walter Smith in charge of these, he himself hurried on another mile and a half to the Capitol grounds. Here he hoped to find a nucleus of Stansbury's force, which he could then incorporate into his own.

This was a masterpiece of wishful thinking: by now Stansbury's men were well on their way to Baltimore. Finding no one, Winder sent word to Smith to fall back again. It was the third call for retreat in an hour, and the men were more discouraged than ever as they streamed down Maryland Avenue and spread out on the rough stubble of the Capitol grounds.

Secretaries Monroe and Armstrong, arriving separately, joined Winder; and while everyone watched and waited, the three huddled over what to do next. Armstrong favored the idea of turning the Capitol into a citadel and holding out indefinitely. He liked those strong limestone walls; he didn't mind the big windows or the fact that the place was really two separate buildings. At this stage in its construction, only the House and Senate wings were finished, connected by a vulnerable wooden passageway. To him it was safe enough, and he pointed out that the British didn't have the artillery to conduct a serious siege.

Winder would have none of it. He had too small a force. The men were too exhausted. The Capitol was too isolated. He could be starved out in 24 hours. Even if he managed to hold the place, the British would be free to roam at will through the rest of Washington. His only hope was to retreat again, this time to the heights behind Georgetown. Here at last he'd be safe. Probably Stansbury's men would come there too (Winder couldn't get over this forlorn hope), and he would have a real chance to collect and reorganize the shattered army.

Monroe backed him up. In fact, he added a point. During the retreat the Secretary of State thought he detected a powerful British column moving to the west. He feared that if the Americans delayed at the Capitol any longer, they might be driven into a cul-de-sac between the Eastern Branch and the Potomac.

Outvoted and half-convinced, Armstrong concurred.

So it was retreat again. And now the last semblance of discipline vanished. Many of the men had stood by this long

only because they were from the District. Their sole purpose
had been to save their homes and families. Falling back to
Georgetown was no way to do that. A few raged—even
wept—but most simply scattered to look after their own
interests.

The rest streamed up Pennsylvania Avenue in no order
whatsoever. Francis Scott Key rode by—his horse steaming, his uniform soaked with sweat. Armstrong tried to dodge
an angry citizen named Thomas Ewell, who rushed up shouting that the Secretary was to blame for everything. At
Hughes's grocery near 7th Street, the crowd swarmed
around the pump. Some were content with the water; others
preferred a barrel of whiskey thoughtfully provided by John
P. Van Ness.

Two visitors—unexpectedly detained in Washington
—watched from the nearby McKeowin's Hotel. A Dr.
Judah of New York and a Mr. Johnson of North Carolina
had been passengers on the southern stage that day. Heading
down from Baltimore, it had almost run into the battle at
Bladensburg, but managed to cross the bridge just ahead of
the British. The turnpike was clogged with troops, but it finally reached the city by various back roads as the passengers
listened nervously to the cannonade behind them. Now
Messrs. Judah and Johnson found themselves trapped—no
coach service south and Pennsylvania Avenue a mass of retreating soldiers. As they pondered their plight, a ripple of
excitement ran through the crowd. A voice cried, "There
goes the President!"

It was true. Back from the shambles of Bladensburg, James
Madison had transferred to a carriage and was now rolling
through the crowd on Pennsylvania Avenue. Ultimately he
arrived at the President's House around 4:30—about half
an hour after his wife had left—accompanied by Rush,
Mason, Carroll and several other aides who had been with

him most of the day. Entering, they found Jacob Barker and Robert de Peyster collecting a few final valuables, and for more than an hour the group sat around exchanging experiences. It was an odd interlude, with the British just over the horizon and the city clearly doomed, and can best be explained by the 63-year-old President's desperate need for rest after his full day in the saddle hounded by disaster.

The conversation was appropriately serious. Madison was especially awed by the superb discipline of the British Army. Like most Jeffersonians, he had relished the theory that the free democratic yeoman fighting for his home was always a match for the mere paid hireling of a foreign foe. Now he knew better. "I could never have believed," he told Barker, "that so great a difference existed between regular troops and a militia force, if I had not witnessed the scenes of this day."

In contrast to this quiet post-mortem, the scene outside was increasingly raucous. The collapse of all discipline, the knowledge that the city was lost, and perhaps a little of John P. Van Ness's whiskey did their work. The fleeing soldiers and civilians began rummaging through the government offices taking what they wanted. At the President's House the guards stationed at the door had long since run off, and stragglers roamed at will through the mansion. Someone even took George Campbell's dueling pistols, which the weary President had taken from their holsters and left on a front hall table.

Clearly it was time to go. The plan had been for the Madison and Jones families to join forces at the Georgetown home of Charles Carroll of Bellevue, but now that was out. It would be simpler and quicker to meet at Foxhall's Foundry by the river, and an aide was sent ahead to alert everyone. But no sooner was he gone than this plan was changed too. Probably it was felt that the sooner the President got across the river, the safer he would be.

Another aide rushed to Foxhall's to say Madison was crossing at Mason's Ferry; he would meet Dolley and the others at
Salona, the estate of the Reverend John Maffitt on the Virginia side. It was sunset when the Presidential party finally
rode across the meadow behind the executive mansion, took a
boat over to Analostan Island, and then went by the cause-
way to the Virginia shore.

Barker and de Peyster remained at the President's House,
continuing their last-minute effort to save a few more things.
At one point a group of exhausted soldiers stopped by, and
Barker took time out to break open some of Madison's
brandy. The big portrait of George Washington still lay attached to its stretcher on the dining room floor.

The time had now come to do something about it. Dolley
Madison had said not to roll it up, and they would follow her
instructions. Recruiting two blacks, the four of them carefully lifted the whole framework, carried it through the front
door, and loaded it on a cart that had miraculously been
found. Tossing in some large silver urns and a few other odds
and ends, they set off up Pennsylvania Avenue in the midst of
the fleeing crowd.

All sorts of people were still flowing by. The William
Thorntons had tried a quick dinner, couldn't swallow it, and
were now in their carriage riding along behind Barker's cart.
William Simmons, who had kept Madison from riding into
the British lines, stopped by the President's House to see if he
could be of further service. He found nobody there except
doorkeeper Sioussa, who said politely that Madison had
"gone out of the city."

Two 6-pounders stood by the door, deserted by their
crews, and the thought occurred to Simmons that he might
save them. Stopping some of the soldiers pouring by, he
called to Sioussa for some of the Presidential brandy and
plied the men liberally with it. Thus encouraged, they said

they would move the guns, and his good deed done, Simmons went on to Georgetown. The men did save one of the cannon, but the other they abandoned and ran on up the avenue.

In the President's House Sioussa went about the last duties of a good doorkeeper. Known to everyone as "French John," he was a truly remarkable character. Born in Paris shortly before the Revolution, he had studied for the priesthood, run away to sea, deserted ship, and drifted to Washington during Jefferson's time. Catching on as a servant to the British Minister Anthony Merry, he picked up a smattering of protocol, and ultimately landed with the Madisons. He was up to unexpected situations, and the quality came in handy now.

Looking around, he carefully hid some gold and silver Algerian pistols that looked like they might make good loot. Next, he put out buckets of water and some bottles of wine for any more thirsty soldiers who might happen by. Then he picked up the mansion's pet makaw—a great favorite of Dolley Madison's—and took it a few blocks to Colonel Tayloe's Octagon House. Here he entrusted it to the French Minister's chef.

Now back to the President's House for a final look around. Everything seemed in order; so he carefully closed all the windows and doors. Then he departed for the last time, leaving the front-door key at the house of the Russian Minister Daschkoff, who had wisely gone to Philadelphia.

The tail end of the retreat was now passing the mansion. Sailing Master John Webster and a handful of flotillamen drifted by, spied the remaining 6-pounder deserted by the gate. They quickly hitched it to four other guns they had saved at the Capitol and rumbled on to Georgetown.

Then came Colonel Laval and his calvalrymen. They had arrived back at the Capitol after the rest of the army had resumed its retreat. There were no orders from Winder; so they just hung around for half an hour. Next, hearing that the troops were reforming at the President's House, they hurried there but found nobody at all. Another long wait; then word that the troops were above Georgetown. With only vague directions to "follow the army," they too moved on.

Some 250 to 300 of Barney's men were still at the Capitol, also without orders. Winder never considered them part of his own command, and with the Commodore wounded and a prisoner, there was really nobody to tell them what to do. While the men lay exhausted in the square, Captain Bacon of the Marines and Captain Gohegan of the flotilla wrangled over who had command.

Captain Tingey at the Navy Yard was another officer Winder left in the dark. Here it was not a question of command—Tingey clearly came under naval authority— but close coordination was all-important so that he would know if and when to carry out his demolition plans. The General never sent a word.

Secretary Armstrong learned of the lapse just before setting out himself for Frederick, where the government was supposed to reconvene once the British had taken the city. There wasn't time to do much, but he did send Major John Bell to Tingey with a verbal message that was crystal-clear in its brevity: "The Navy Yard cannot be covered."

This announcement was punctuated a few moments later by a loud explosion. Captain Creighton had blown up the section of the lower bridge nearest the draw. Then a great cloud of smoke rose, as the rest of the bridge began burning.

Tingey quickly warned the families still living in the neighborhood that the Navy Yard would go next . . . the fires might spread . . . better save what they could. A delegation of "the most respectable women" turned up, begging him to reconsider. Impossible, explained Tingey; he had his orders from Secretary of the Navy William Jones. Unless these were countermanded, he had to obey, and Jones had now gone off to join his family in Georgetown.

The "responsible women" continued to plead, and Tingey grew irritated. If they kept this up, he scolded, he'd blow up the place at once. However, if they left him in peace, he would delay as long as possible. Knowing his temperamental quirks, the ladies wisely left him alone.

Quiet slowly settled over the city. Here and there a few people still scurried about on last-minute missions. At the Capitol, clerk J. T. Frost toiled away in a belated effort to save the records of the House Ways and Means Committee. He made trip after trip, lugging the files to a big brick mansion across the street. It was one of two houses built by George Washington as a mark of his faith in the capital's future.

Nearby, Dr. James Ewell led his wife and two daughters from their house on A Street down a few blocks to the home of his patient Mrs. Orr. Here, the doctor hoped, his family would be safe. Mrs. Orr was so sick he felt even the British wouldn't disturb her.

At McKeowin's Hotel stagecoach passengers Judah and Johnson decided that time had run out. They abandoned their luggage, trudged to the Potomac, and walked across the long bridge to Virginia. They found themselves constantly dodging wagons, still fleeing with the army's baggage and wounded.

At Georgetown Benjamin Homans, chief clerk of the Navy Department, led his own and two other families down the hill to the canal. He had previously loaded two barges with navy records, and brought them this far for safety. Now they looked like a good personal refuge as well. Tagging along was the Homans's house guest, a 15-year-old girl from

New England, known today only as "Miss Brown." Resplendent in her best white satin bonnet, trimmed with pink, she was determined to evacuate in style.

The mood was more somber at Francis Scott Key's house on Bridge Street. Key had arrived home exhausted and was now begging his wife and children to leave. He himself felt duty-bound to stay, but it was no place for them. Polly Key would have none of it. The most Key could do was pack their things. Then he bolted all the windows, and the family sat in the stifling heat, half-expecting the British to come any minute.

Where were they anyhow? At the time the battle ended there wasn't a fleeing American who didn't feel that some redcoat was personally following him. Yet four hours had passed, and not an enemy soldier in sight. In the silence of the August twilight, the jitters steadily grew. Mrs. William Thornton, riding north out of Georgetown, was warned to turn back—the British were purposely herding the American troops that way and planned to fall on them. A delegation of leading Georgetown citizens headed out to obtain the best terms possible, but could find no one to surrender to.

Another rumor had the British approaching by the race track, out 14th Street, but there was no one here either. According to a third story, they were down by the Marine Barracks on the other side of town—"the whistling of the balls had been distinctly heard"—but again, there was nothing to it. Still another account put them at the Capitol . . . in full force. A young officer arrived at the Navy Yard saying it was true. If so, this was getting dangerously close, and Captain Tingey made ready to light his fuses.

His chief clerk Mordecai Booth exploded in indignation, using language quite out of character for this faithful but docile underling. He had just been to the Capitol on a reconnaissance of his own, and he *knew* the British weren't there.

It would be a crime to destroy the Yard on such false information. In fact, he felt it would be a crime to destroy it anyhow; it could so easily be defended by recruiting some of the leaderless flotillamen and using the numerous guns on hand.

Booth offered to ride out and find where the British really were, if only Tingey would hold off his demolitions a little longer. Very well, said the Captain, adding that the intelligence had better be good . . . his whole career was resting on it.

That settled, Booth quickly rode to the turnpike gate and studied the rolling country in the direction of Bladensburg. Nothing in sight. Then a lone horseman suddenly came in view, racing down the turnpike toward him. It was a Georgetown butcher named Thomas Miller. He had been looking for the British too, found exactly where they were, and would be happy to show them to Booth. The two rode to the top of a nearby hill, and Miller pointed out a long column of troops slowly advancing toward them. They wore the dark blue of British seamen, but Booth knew nothing about that. Like most Americans, he assumed every hostile Englishman invariably dressed in red, and he now argued that these must be a Georgetown rifle company still in the field. A shot whizzed by his ears, ending the discussion.

Galloping back to the Navy Yard, he informed Captain Tingey. Momentarily, at least, the news took a little pressure off the Captain: the British were not as close as he feared. Perhaps he could still save the Yard, if he only knew where the American troops were. Except for Armstrong's terse warning, nobody had told him anything.

Once again Booth rode out, this time to the President's House. He supposed that Madison was still there, and if anybody knew where the army was, it ought to be the nation's Commander-in-Chief. Arriving at the mansion, he found only an agitated cavalry colonel standing by the steps. In the gathering dark, the officer assumed Booth was the advance guard of the enemy and pulled his pistol. It was all Booth could do to persuade him they were both on the same side.

Now they banged on the door; they pulled at the bell; and the colonel—who clearly knew his way around—shouted again and again for "French John." It was all in vain. There was nobody there. To Booth, that dark empty house, standing alone in the dusk, said far more than a bundle of intelligence reports. For the first time he fully realized that the capital of his country had been completely abandoned.

By the time he reached Capitol Hill again, several stray horsemen had joined up. These included a trooper named Walter Cox and Captain Creighton, who had also been sent out by Tingey to gather information. It was now quite dark, and as the party approached Long's Hotel on A Street, Northeast, Cox leaned far forward in his saddle. He was clearly trying to make something out. Only cows, Booth remarked. Yes, Cox replied, he saw the cows, but he also saw *men* . . . right there, rising out of that hollow.

They were there all right. British regulars within 40 yards. The little group wheeled and scattered wildly for safety. Booth and Creighton dashed for the Navy Yard to warn Captain Tingey.

Lieutenant James Scott decided that all resistance was over as he rode through the gathering darkness with the British advance guard, led by General Ross himself. Leaving Bladensburg at twilight after a three-hour rest, they found the Americans had disappeared completely. Only an occasional observer lurked in the dusk.

And now Washington lay at their feet, the climax of the week's campaign. It was a soldier's dream of triumph—the capture of the enemy capital—yet there was no trace of

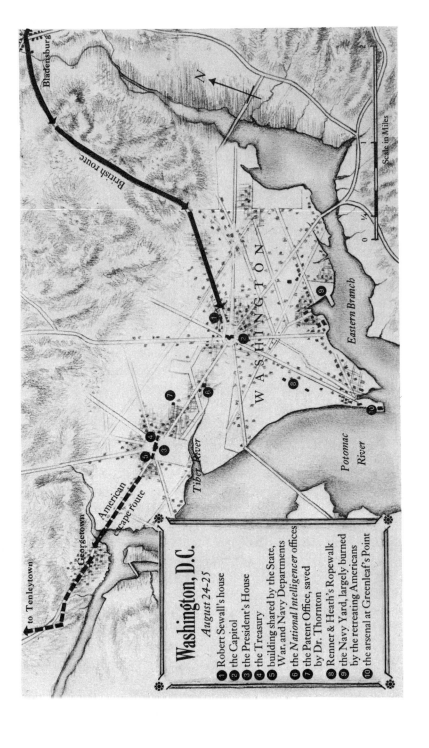

Washington, D.C.
August 24-25

1. Robert Sewall's house
2. the Capitol
3. the President's House
4. the Treasury
5. building shared by the State, War, and Navy Departments
6. the *National Intelligencer* offices
7. the Patent Office, saved by Dr. Thornton
8. Renner & Heath's Ropewalk
9. the Navy Yard, largely burned by the retreating Americans
10. the arsenal at Greenleaf's Point

to Tenleytown

Georgetown

American escape route

Bladensburg

British route

WASHINGTON

Tiber River

Potomac River

Eastern Branch

N

Scale in Miles

martial glory: no bands, no banners, no grand entrance, no conquered boulevards lined with a sullen, beaten populace. The city lay dark and empty, its sprinkling of houses and buildings looking (in the words of a contemporary visitor) "as if some giant had scattered a box of child's toys upon the ground."

Only the 3rd Brigade was making the march. Consisting of the seamen, marines and most of the 21st Foot—some 1,460 men altogether—they had seen little action and were fresh and rested. The other brigades would follow along later, after reorganization. Entering the city, most of the troops halted just inside the turnpike gate. Only Ross, Admiral Cockburn and a small advance guard continued forward. Moving down Maryland Avenue, they headed directly for the Capitol, looming big despite the darkness.

At some point the two commanders had decided to lay the city under contribution as the price of sparing it. Now a drum rolled loud and long, sounding the call for a parley. If any American heard, he either didn't understand this military refinement or chose to ignore it, for there was no answer whatsoever.

The little British party rode on, halting at a point perhaps 200 yards short of the Capitol. Directly to their right stood the large brick house owned by Robert Sewall and, until recently, rented by Albert Gallatin. Other buildings loomed in the darkness. Not a light or a sound came from any of them.

The Admiral and the General conferred, wondering what to do next. A few more seconds . . . then a volley of musket fire shattered the night. Four men were hit—one killed— and Ross's horse was shot from under him. It was hard to see where the firing came from—but certainly Robert Sewall's house, and possibly other buildings too.

Splinters flew as Lieutenant Scott led the party that broke

through Sewall's front door. But it took several minutes, and
by the time the men got in, the house was completely empty.
No one ever knew who fired the shots. Later most accounts
attributed it to a few die-hards led by a local barber named
Dixon, but it seems more likely that some of Barney's flotillamen were responsible. They never considered themselves
bound by Winder's orders to retreat, and many of them had
remained on the Capitol grounds long after the army was
gone.

Whoever they were, British reaction was swift. Cockburn
raced back to get the light companies of the 21st Foot,
and Michael Shiner—a local black, hence left alone—
watched with fascination as the troops fired their Congreve
rockets into the house. Beams and rafters went flying in all
directions.

But no one looked at the blaze very long. Already the glare
of a far bigger fire was creeping across the sky to the south.
Soon billows of flame and smoke were gushing upward. Deep
explosions shook the ground, and embers shot like comets
through the blackness of the night.

Captain Tingey was burning his Navy Yard. For the
colorful, headstrong commandant, it was a bitter moment indeed. Head of the Yard since its founding in 1800, he had
made it the finest in the country. By now he regarded it as
practically his own—so much so that he had even included
the commandant's house in his will.

Yet orders were orders, and it had to go. Alerted by Mordecai Booth and Captain Creighton that the enemy were deep
in the city, he finally gave the signal at 8:20 P.M. The matches
were struck and the powder trains lit, leading to the storehouses and the sail loft. Kindled by the carpet of chips and
pitch that covered the ground, the flames raced along, leaping
from building to building—the saw mill . . . the rigging

loft . . . the paint shops . . . the timber shed. Along with the rest went the new frigate *Columbia*, almost ready for launching, and the sloop of war *Argus*, completely finished.

Grimly satisfied that his duty was done, Captain Tingey stepped into his gig and rowed for Alexandria. Behind him the fire roared on, as new explosions erupted at the fort on Greenleaf's Point, where another demolition team was at work.

The brilliant glare made the job easier for General Ross's men on Capitol Hill. As one group burned Sewall's house, others turned their attention to the rest of the nearby buildings. A grim-looking officer rode up to Andrew Hunter's door and began interrogating Mrs. Hunter. Where was her husband? Not at home. When did he leave? In the morning. Why? To keep the children from seeing "such a horrid scene." When would he be back? She didn't know. Desperately she invited him to go to the sideboard and help himself, then gingerly asked a question of her own: did the British plan to burn the city generally, or only the public buildings? The officer said that all depended: where no resistance was made, private property would be safe, especially if everyone remained at home. But wherever there was resistance, or arms found, that place would be burned.

Outside, the policy was once again being demonstrated. Searching Tomlinson's Hotel, across from the Senate wing of the Capitol, Ross's men found guns and ammunition. It was instantly set on fire.

Now for the Capitol itself. With the eruption of trouble, most of the 3rd Brigade had come up. Moving into Capitol Square, they deployed into line, facing the building. A sharp command, and they fired a volley into the windows of the eastern façade. The practical purpose was, of course, to discourage any further sharpshooting, but it all seemed symbolic as well. It served as a formal announcement that this citadel of republicanism was being officially possessed in the name of His Majesty the King.

Stepping forward, Lieutenant de Lacy Evans led a party that quickly broke down the doors, and for the next hour the troops turned sightseers, roaming through the empty halls and chambers. Admiral Cockburn took a small bound copy of a Treasury report, which he kept as a souvenir. Someone with more extravagant tastes cut out the portaits of Louis XVI and Marie Antoinette, hanging in the room adjoining the Senate Chamber.

Lieutenant Scott took nothing, but he too was among the sightseers, staring with awe at Benjamin Labrobe's handsome Corinthian columns in the Hall of Representatives. It all seemed so much more grandiose than the cramped quarters of the House of Commons back home. He rather suspected that this nation which boasted so loudly of its republican simplicity was actually "somewhat infected with an unseemly bias for monarchial splendour."

Enough musing. The time had come to destroy this ambitious building. The prospect raised no qualms—the British leaders in America were committed to the destruction or ransom of public property—but it did raise a question of method. The Capitol was so well built it seemed to defy burning. At first Ross and Cockburn were inclined to blow the place up, but word spread to the few remaining citizens in the neighborhood. They bitterly protested that the explosion would wreck their homes too, and they had done nothing to oppose the British. The General relented; he would try using fire.

Naval Lieutenant George Pratt was put in charge. He was considered an expert at this sort of business, but at first things went rather slowly. In the House wing, three-man teams tackled each room on the lower floor. The first chopped the woodwork into kindling; the second sprinkled a bucket of rocket powder about; and the third applied the torch. This started a number of local fires, but nothing spectacular.

Upstairs, Pratt was having little better luck with the Hall of Representatives. At first his men fired rockets into the roof, but nothing happened. It turned out to be covered with sheet iron. Finally they piled the mahogany chairs, desks and tables high in the center of the room, added some of the rocket powder, and fired more rockets directly into the pile. Similar measures were taken with the Senate wing, and Lieutenant Pratt's efforts were at last rewarded.

Within minutes both wings were ablaze. The limestone outer walls might only crumble and crack, but there was more than enough to burn inside—the red morocco chairs of the Senate . . . the secret journals of the House, so carefully locked in a special drawer . . . the law library of Elias Bardinot Caldwell, clerk of the Supreme Court . . . the baize curtains of the House . . . the 740 books purchased in Europe in 1802 as a nucleus for the Library of Congress . . . the handsome gilt eagle surmounting the clock above the Speaker's chair . . . and the clock itself, whose hands pointed to 10:00 as the fire began.

Flames surged through the doors and windows, up through the roof, and fanned out into the night. The Navy Yard might make a better pyrotechnical display, but this was far more disastrous. The southwesterly breeze caught the sparks and carried them toward the streets to the north and east.

Four more buildings were soon blazing . . . among them the two houses built by George Washington on North Capitol Street. Up in smoke went the Congressional papers so laboriously moved there for safety by the assistant House clerk Mr. Frost.

Lieutenant Gleig had rarely seen anything so grand. The 1st and 2nd Brigades were reorganized now, and as they marched down the turnpike toward the city, the glare was so bright the men could easily recognize each other's faces. "Except for the burning of San Sebastián," Gleig later decided, "I do not recollect to have witnessed, at any period of my life, a scene more striking or more sublime."

It was anything but sublime to the terrified inhabitants remaining in Washington. Mrs. Andrew Hunter watched in horror from the top floor of her house as the flames leaped through the rigging of the ships at the Navy Yard—"You never saw a drawing room as brilliantly lighted as the whole city was that night." Dr. James Ewell, still with his family at Mrs. Orr's house, heard a noise like thunder as the fire burst through the roof of the Capitol . . . then was even more startled by a tremendous pounding on the Orr front door. Five or six British soldiers tramped in, but to Mrs. Ewell's relief it was not rape they were after—only a little food. Their hosts instantly produced a cold ham, bread and butter, wine —anything that might keep them satisfied.

Then a new cause for alarm. Glancing outside, Ewell saw every room of his own house lit up with flames. He dashed to the scene, hoping to save his medical library . . . and happily discovered that it was just the glass in his windows reflecting the fire at the Capitol.

But the house had been plundered, and as Ewell contemplated the shambles, the Reverend Alexander McCormack, rector of nearby Christ Church, came up and offered to take him to General Ross and Admiral Cockburn. Perhaps they could help, the minister suggested; he had met them and they were "perfect gentlemen."

Walking down the street a few steps, they approached an officer heavy with braid and lace. Putting on his best church manners, McCormack performed the honors, introducing Ewell to "General Ross."

"My name is Cockburn, sir," came the answer in the quick, high-pitched voice of the Admiral.

That straightened out, Ewell explained his troubles, saying he thought private property was safe; yet his was stolen, even though left in the care of servants.

"Well, sir," said the Admiral, "let me tell you it was very ill confidence to repose your property in the care of servants."

With this brief lecture on the dangers of the servant class, the Admiral seemed inclined to let the matter drop, but at this point Ross came up and was far more sympathetic. If Ewell would point out the house, he'd post a sentry there.

To the General's amiable embarrassment, it turned out to be the very house he had picked for his headquarters. Ross gallantly declared he "could never think of trespassing on the repose of a private family." He would order his things out at once.

Ewell was no fool. Realizing that his best bet was to keep the General there, he begged him to stay. Ross finally consented—any small room would do—but the doctor gave him his own bedroom, the one with the good mattress.

But the General wasn't ready for bed just yet. Parting with Dr. Ewell, he and Cockburn gathered together a small force of perhaps 150 picked men, and with each commanding a separate detachment, they started up Pennsylvania Avenue about 10:30 P.M. A single officer on foot led the way. Behind, the men marched two abreast, swiftly but silently. When somebody started talking, the officer broke in sharply: "Silence! If any man speaks in the ranks, I'll put him to death!"

Here and there along the avenue the bolder citizens peeked from open windows. As William P. Gardner watched them pass his place, four officers on horseback rode up and politely said good evening.

"I presume you are officers of the British Army," responded Gardner, making perhaps the most self-evident comment of the night. Assured that they were, he said he hoped individuals and private property would be respected.

The officers pledged this on their honor, but urged everyone to stay at home. Then one of them, who turned out to be Admiral Cockburn, asked pleasantly, "Where is your President, Mr. Madison?"

Gardner said he didn't know, but supposed he was by now far away. After a few minutes more of casual conversation, the officers excused themselves, explaining they were on their way to "pay a visit" to the President's House, which they understood was a little ways ahead.

Soon they were at the 15th Street "bend," where the Avenue was interrupted by the grounds of the executive mansion. Here the force halted while arrangements were made at the low brick boardinghouse kept by Mrs. Barbara Suter for a late supper for General Ross and his staff. Then on again, up 15th Street, while the dismayed Mrs. Suter set about killing chickens and warming bread.

Now another stop, this time near the Treasury pump. While the troops crowded around, ignoring their officers' warnings of poisoned water, Admiral Cockburn sent a thoughtful message ahead. Not knowing Dolley Madison's movements, he offered her an escort to any place of safety she might choose. But she was gone, of course, and there was no need for further amenities. The forced moved on to the President's House.

Nothing startled them like the dining room. There the table was perfectly set for 40 people. The servant boy Paul Jennings had done his work well—the wine stood in the coolers packed in ice. Sampling cold cuts and what Captain Harry Smith termed "super-excellent Madeira," the unexpected guests hugely enjoyed themselves. The crystal goblets were raised in a joyous toast to "the health of the Prince Regent and success to His Majesty's arms by sea and land."

Cockburn had a special joke. Somewhere along the way he had corralled the Washington book dealer Roger Chew Weightman—probably impressed as a guide. Now the Admiral plopped the miserable Mr. Weightman down in a chair and told him to drink to "Jemmy," as Cockburn almost invariably called the President.

That over, the Admiral expansively told his victim to help himself to a souvenir. Weightman suggested something valuable, but Cockburn said no, the expensive things must feed the flames, and handed him instead a few odds and ends off a mantelpiece. The Admiral himself chose an old hat of the President's and a cushion off Mrs. Madison's chair—joking that the latter would remind him of her seat, or so a letter written three days later delicately implied.

By now others too had joined the souvenir hunt. Ranging from Madison's medicine chest to a pair of rhinestone shoe buckles, the variety was endless. Lieutenant Beau Colclough Urquhart of the 85th Foot fancied a ceremonial sword. Captain Harry Smith was more practical: he went upstairs and taking off his grimy, sweat-stained shirt, helped himself to the Presidential best. Downstairs, with both the meal and the joke well digested, a soldier swept the plates and silver into a tablecloth and made off with the evening's best haul. Outside, the guards—unable to join the fun—amused themselves by hacking up an abandoned carriage.

A block away at Octagon House, French Minister Serurier watched and worried. The blacks were saying that the British planned to burn not only the President's House but all the homes of government officials. He wondered just how far his diplomatic immunity would carry him, camped as he was in the residence of one of the city's leading figures. He hastily sent a messenger to the President's House with a letter asking General Ross to send a guard to protect him "against an accident or a mistake, which could easily happen despite the intentions of His Britannic Majesty's officers."

The messenger found Ross in the Oval Room, piling together all the furniture he could find. The General took time out to send back a reassuring reply: "The French King's house would be as respected as if His Majesty were there in person."

Now the preparations were finished, and the job of starting the fire was turned over to the efficient Lieutenant Pratt. His sailors quickly got torches from Nordin's beer house opposite the Treasury, and once again the familiar scene unfolded. The huge dining room sideboard . . . the red velvet cushions of the Oval Room . . . the pianoforte from Andrew Hazlehurst . . . the President's half-filled portmanteau . . . the $28 guitar—all of it went up in one roaring bonfire.

As the flames soared skyward, the force turned its attention to the long, brick Treasury Building just to the east. The men had high hopes here, taking the name literally, and felt almost cheated when they found no money at all. But there were plenty of old records to burn—some going back to the Revolution—and the building was soon blazing nicely.

As the flames got going, someone discovered a fireproof vault on the ground floor, and the men managed to break it open. To their immense disgust, it too had nothing but old files.

Now at last the night's work was done. General Ross and his staff retired to Mrs. Suter's and were soon joined by Admiral Cockburn. The meal made little impression one way or the other, but Mrs. Suter was so undone she was sure that General Ross was the suspicious man she had seen lurking around several days earlier.

Heading back down Pennsylvania Avenue, Admiral Cock-

burn had an afterthought. Hailing a man standing outside
McKeowin's Hotel, the Admiral asked where he could find
the offices of the *National Intelligencer*. The editor, Joseph
Gales, Jr., whom he liked to call "Dear Josey," had told some
"tough stories" about him, and now there was a score to settle.

The man hailed was Chester Bailey, the contractor who
ran the New York–Philadelphia mail stage. Pleading that
he was a stranger in town, he said he had no idea where the
paper's offices were. Actually, he knew perfectly well that
they were right across the street.

Cockburn turned to two other bystanders, who also equiv-
ocated. Whatever else he might have been, the Admiral was
no fool, and he made it clearly understood that he wanted no
more of this nonsense.

The bystanders got the point, and showed him the building
themselves. A soldier then broke into the office and emerged
with the last issue of the paper, assuring its readers that the
city was safe. General Ross attempted to keep it as a souvenir, but couldn't fit it into his pocket. "Damn it," he said, al-
lowing himself a rare vulgarity, "My pocket is full of old
Madison's love letters; I have no room for this trash."

Cockburn now ordered the building burned, but was immediately confronted by Mrs. Pontius D. Stelle and a Mrs.
Brush, two ladies who lived in the block. They begged him
to hold off, or their houses would go too. The Admiral listened carefully and finally agreed not to burn the place
down. Instead, he would wreck it in the morning. "Be tran-
quil, ladies," he added cheerfully, "you shall be as safely protected under my administration as under that of Mr. Madison." He then bade everyone a polite good night and,
together with Ross, headed back to Capitol Hill.

A single sentry was left on guard at the *National Intelligencer* office. This lone soldier was the total British occupa-

tion force in central Washington that night. The rest of the men of the 3rd Brigade bivouacked on Capitol Hill, while the 2,300 of the 1st and 2nd Brigades remained at the edge of the city, watching the flames from the heights just inside the toll-gate. Lieutenant Gleig sensed a feeling of awe in the air. When the men talked at all, it was in whispers.

For the capital's scattered population, it was more a night of sheer terror. Some of those still in the city huddled in St. Patrick's Church, where the Catholic priest, William Matthews, led them in prayer. Urged to flee, Father Matthews remarked, "Why should I? I have more business here now than ever before." Beyond the District Line, thousands of refugees converged on the houses of friends and strangers—the Fries family alone took in 18 frightened children. Many people had no place to go and simply roamed through the woods and fields. One poor woman found at daylight that she had wandered ten miles.

Others, sure at least of safety, could afford the luxury of more effusive emotions. On the road to Falls Church, Virginia, Mordecai Booth glanced back at the glare and found it "a sight so repugnant to my feelings, so dishonorable, so degrading to the American character, and at the same time so awful, [it] almost palsied my faculties."

The fire dominated everything. It glowed brightly at Baltimore 40 miles away, where the citizens gazed in alarm from the rooftops. It caught the eye of the watch officer of the British bomb vessel *Meteor*, far down the Potomac, who dutifully noted in his log, "Saw a large fire NNW." It lit the farmhouse just above Georgetown where Jacob Barker and Robert de Peyster left the portrait of George Washington for safekeeping. It hovered over General Winder at Tenleytown, two miles farther on, as he tried in vain to regroup his shattered army. It rose and fell across the horizon, spurring on Secretaries Armstrong and Campbell as they hurried to-

ward Frederick, Maryland, where the government was to reconvene.

Typical of this chaotic night, none of the other administration leaders was going there. At the moment, they were
hopelessy scattered about the Virginia countryside. James
Madison, Attorney General Rush and the rest of the Presidential party rode to Salona, where the President expected to
meet his wife. Secretary of State Monroe went to Wiley's
Tavern, near Great Falls. Secretary of the Navy Jones was
with his family and Dolley Madison's entourage, struggling
through the clogged roads toward the Salona rendezvous.
They finally decided they would never make it and spent the
night at Rokeby, the home of Mrs. Madison's friend Mathilda
Lee Love. Here, the First Lady sat silently by an open window, where she too watched the great, angry scar in the sky.

Relief finally came from the heavens. Toward dawn one of
Washington's patented thunderstorms rumbled in, wetting
down the fires and ending the danger that the flames might
spread to the whole city. But the storm brought no relief
from the heat and only dampened the spirits of the capital's
bedraggled residents. On Benjamin Homans's barge above
Georgetown, Miss Brown mourned over the soggy remains
of her pink and white bonnet.

Dawn, August 25, the fresh British troops from the 1st Brigade took over the work of destruction. The rest of the army
now camped on Mrs. Gerard Gibson's estate, still on the edge
of the city but blessed with a cool, inviting spring. Here the
weary, soot-smeared men of the 3rd Brigade filled their canteens and rested in the first light of another stifling day.

No rest for George Cockburn. By 5:30 the Admiral was on
the move again. Somewhere he had found an old white mare
with a long mane and tail that appealed to his sense of
whimsy. Now, with its foal trailing behind, he rode it up

Pennsylvania Avenue to inspect the results of his night's work.

Across town Captain Wainwright of the *Tonnant* was on the move too. Taking a party of sailors and marines, he went to the Navy Yard around 8:00 A.M. to see if the Americans had missed anything in their effort to wreck the place themselves. Surprisingly, the cooper's shop, two timber sheds, another shed full of pitch and rosin, and a good deal of hardware had escaped completely. Wainwright's trained hands fixed that.

Before leaving, they also stopped by the Yard's most conspicuous embellishment, the Tripoli Monument. Dedicated to the naval heroes who fell in the Barbary Coast Wars, this was a gaudy affair, dripping with sculptured symbolism, but nevertheless a source of great pride to a young country with very little past. The British visitors gleefully stole a bronze pen from the hand of History; and reaching high to a figure representing Fame covering the deeds of her sons with a palm and crown of glory, some agile tar took the palm right out of Fame's hand.

Wainwright's men weren't gone 30 minutes before another visitor arrived: the commandant of the Yard, Captain Tingey himself. He had been rowed back in his gig from Alexandria, and now at 8:45 he stepped ashore, risking capture any minute, to see how things were. To his amazement, the brand-new schooner *Lynx* had somehow survived both his own and Wainwright's efforts. She floated serenely perfect alongside a smoldering pier, and his men quickly hauled her to greater safety.

Everything else was gone, except for his and Lieutenant Haradan's houses. Wainwright had respected these as private property, but not so Tingey's neighbors. They were mostly poor, unskilled hands who picked up a meager living working around the Yard. They had little to lose, and few had bothered to flee with the vast majority of Washington's citizens. Now all authority was gone, and they were ranging through the Yard, salvaging hardware and looting the commandant's house. Tingey saved a little, but friends soon persuaded him to go. The British were bound to learn he was there, and it was just too dangerous. After all, he had been born in England; they would certainly charge him with treason. The Captain rowed gloomily off, as the looters went back to work.

About the same time Captain Wainwright's men raided the Navy Yard, Major Timothy Jones led another British column up Pennsylvania Avenue. During the long night of burning no one had gotten around to the rather pedestrian brick building that housed the State, War and Navy Departments just west of the executive mansion. Now the men of the 1st Brigade, followed by some 30 blacks carrying powder and rockets, were on their way to remedy the omission.

As they reached the scene, a lone horseman darted out from nowhere. It was John Lewis, erratic grandnephew of the sainted Washington. Long ago Lewis had run away to sea . . . suffered impressment by the Royal Navy . . . escaped and ever since had been burning with vengeance. At last the moment had come. Possibly fortified by a dram or two, he charged the head of the column in a wild, one-man confrontation. He fired his pistol, hit no one, caught a blast of return fire, and fell from his horse mortally wounded.

Now the work could proceed. The Americans had moved most of the current records, but there was still plenty of fuel. Fed by such varied kindling as Secretary Jones's furniture and undistributed copies of the army's *System of Drum-Beating*, the fire quickly mushroomed through the building.

That finished, the detachment headed back east along F

Street. Next on their schedule was a visit to the Patent Office and Post Office, which shared Samuel Blodgett's empty hotel building at 8th Street. Here they had an unexpected encounter with Dr. William Thornton, the Superintendent of Patents.

Dr. Thornton was one of those universal men, essentially eighteenth-century, who aspired to be an expert on everything. Born in the Virgin Islands, he took his medical degree at Aberdeen University, drifted to America, and within a couple of years had submitted the winning design for the U.S. Capitol. Characteristically, he had no architectural training whatsoever. He was obviously Jefferson's kind of man, and in 1802 was put in charge of Patents. He never took his administrative duties seriously; rather, he used his time to pursue his interests. He wrote poetry, sketched beautifully and kept notebooks showing an incredible range of interests: better treatment for the insane . . . a steam gun . . . a phonetic alphabet . . . shorthand . . . a talking machine . . . education of the deaf . . . black colonization . . . asbestos . . . taxidermy . . . artificial ice.

At the moment he was working on a new kind of violin, which he kept in his room at the Patent Office. He had left it there in his flight the previous evening, but it was still very much on his mind. Returning at daylight for some breakfast in Georgetown, he heard that the British hadn't touched the Patent Office yet. Perhaps he might still be in time to save the violin, and maybe some of the other inventions and prototypes stored in the building.

Rushing to the city, he found Major Jones in the act of burning the War Department offices. The Major seemed to be in charge of the morning's operations, and he quickly agreed to the rescue of the violin. Thornton then checked home, recruited an assistant and hastened to his office.

He was just in time. The British troops had arrived and

were preparing to burn the building. There was no sign of Jones, but a Major Waters told him to go ahead—save the violin and any other private property.

This gave the doctor an inspiration. Turning to Waters, he announced that practically everything in the building was private property. Clearly the course to follow was to take out the few items of public property, burn them in the street, and leave the building alone. Otherwise he could never get out the hundreds of inventors' models that filled the place. Hitting his stride, Thornton dramatically warned that "to burn what would be useful to all mankind would be as barbarous as to burn the Alexandria Library, for which the Turks have been condemned by all enlightened nations."

Thoroughly shaken, Waters said they'd better see Major Jones. The Major, it turned out, was now at the offices of the *National Intelligencer*, carrying out Admiral Cockburn's instructions to wreck the place. When reached, he cheerfully accepted Dr. Thornton's arguments, and the Patent Office was saved.

The *National Intelligencer* was another matter. Cockburn himself was on hand to make sure the place was destroyed. He even helped carry out Gales's reference library, which was burned in back of the building. Then he watched with approval as Jones's men smashed the presses and hurled the type out the windows. "Be sure that all the c's are destroyed," the Admiral joked, "so the rascals can't abuse my name any more."

Gales's home might have gone next, but for a quick-witted housekeeper. She closed the shutters and chalked on the front door "For Rent."

Cockburn would have appreciated that. Along with his toughness, he had a sort of zestful joy for combat that allowed plenty of room for tricks, recklessness, improvisation —almost anything except stodginess. It was his hard luck to be teamed with the quiet Ross and the stuffy Cochrane, but today his judgment was vindicated—he had pulled it off —and he was understandably full of high spirits and pleased with himself.

"Now did you expect to see me such a clever fellow?" he asked a wide-eyed young lady standing at her door. "Were you not prepared to see a savage, a ferocious creature, such as Josey represented me? But you see I am quite harmless; don't be afraid, I will take better care of you than Jemmy did!"

Introduced to Mrs. Hunter, he bubbled over with praise for American ladies—they made excellent wives and good mothers—but they were so prejudiced against him. "Dear Josey" had told so many lies about him, he was afraid he'd never be a favorite. The Admiral added that he had now paid Josey back by scattering his type, but had left a special line to be printed in the next edition of the paper. The line, unfortunately, remains a mystery; it was apparently missed by the editors when they later cleaned up.

In contrast to Cockburn, General Ross seemed very subdued. He never returned to the center of town, spent most of his time either at the camp or at the Ewell house on Capitol Hill, commiserating with the doctor on the hardships of war. Yes, he was sorry he had burned the Library of Congress; no, he would never have burned the President's House had Mrs. Madison been there. He mourned the wounding of Commodore Barney; he upbraided a rude enlisted man; he listened sympathetically to the appeals of frightened citizens.

He countermanded his own orders to burn the Marine Barracks when he learned that the fire would endanger the whole neighborhood. He agreed that the Bank of Washington was private property and should be respected. He apparently overruled Cockburn's decision to burn Captain Elias Caldwell's house. Ammunition had been found there, and by the Admiral's standards that was enough. But Dr. Ewell rushed to the rescue, playing the keys he knew would move the General: Caldwell was a brave man . . . he was just doing his duty . . . another case of private property. The house was saved.

But all Ewell's eloquence didn't help when it came to saving the three ropewalks owned by Renner & Heath, Tench Ringgold, and the Reverend Dr. John Chalmers. The British had had enough of the upstart American Navy, and anything useful to it—private property or not—must be destroyed.

Lieutenant James Scott led a party of seamen to one of the ropewalks—he never knew which—spread the hemp along the center of the building, poured some barrels of tar on top, and lit the mixture. The other walks were treated the same way. In less than half an hour all were a mass of flames. Great clouds of heavy black smoke rolled up, hiding the sun completely—the most spectacular display of the day.

The war seemed to be getting uncomfortably close to the Virginia militiamen guarding the far end of the long bridge across the Potomac. All that smoke and fire, and here they were, the nearest soldiers to the enemy in the whole American Army. Squinting hard across the river, the corporal in charge felt sure he could see redcoats getting ready to cross the bridge.

There was only one thing to do. The predawn storm had broken the draw, so he quickly set fire to his end of the bridge. Seeing the smoke and commotion—and deciding that it must mean an American attack—the guard at the British end did the same.

On the Washington side, a woman with several children stood watching in dismay. She couldn't see the flames across the river; only that the British had set fire to her end . . . apparently wrecking her last chance to escape the whole dreadful nightmare. In a sudden panic, she grabbed her children, ran through the mounting flames, and out onto the bridge.

Another minute and she would be trapped between the two
fires. Risking their own lives, three British soldiers dashed
after her and carried the family to safety.

The encounters were of all kinds as victor and vanquished
rubbed elbows most of the day. Mary Ingle, a precocious 13-
year-old, challenged a British officer who boasted he was
using a silver goblet of "old Jemmy Madison's" as he drank
from the pump outside her front door. "No Sir," called
Mary. "That isn't Mr. Madison's goblet. My father and a
whole lot of gentlemen have got all his silver and papers and
things and gone." Before she could say any more, a parental
hand was clapped over her mouth and a strong arm dragged
her inside.

Some confrontations had more serious overtones. James
McLeod, proprietor of the Washington Hotel near the Trea-
sury, was robbed by a British soldier at the point of a musket.
Valette's barber shop was then plundered by the same man.
He was finally caught ransacking the Norval family's house
by a couple of officers sent to the scene.

Neither Ross nor Cockburn tolerated looting. Both knew
how easy it was for an army to get out of hand in an occu-
pied town. At least seven men were flogged—some for
trivial offenses. They took their punishment with the stoicism
of Napoleonic veterans, although one man was heard to complain that it was "damn hard, after being in the service 18
years, that I should be flogged for taking a damn Yankee
goose."

The most serious moment came as the two commanders
were sitting down for their midday meal at Dr. Ewell's. Suddenly a dirty, blood-streaked prostitute came running up
screaming, "Oh, I am killed, I am killed! A British sailor has
killed me!"

Headquarters exploded in an uproar. While Dr. Ewell
dabbed at her wounds, Cockburn ordered all his sailors to be

mustered on parade: the man she picked out would be shot at once. But the woman was incoherent, couldn't possibly identify her assailant or even the circumstances of this particular encounter. In the end Ewell persuaded the Admiral that her wounds were superficial and perhaps it was best to let the matter slide. Still mortified, Cockburn gave him six gold doubloons to take care of the case. Suddenly some of the fun had gone out of his day.

There were other encounters too, but the one that both sides thought about the most never came off. This was, of course, the union between the black man and the English liberator. The white citizens of Washington had long dreaded the possibility of a slave uprising. Sir Alexander Cochrane, for his part, had long relished the idea of "thousands" of blacks flocking to his colors. Now here the British were, right in the American capital, and nobody came.

Once again, the answer went deeper than anyone cared to penetrate: the blacks trusted neither side. There were exceptions, of course—Charles Ball and his friends fighting with Barney; the "colonial marines" serving Ross as skirmishers —but the vast majority wanted no part of it. Now that the British were here, the inclination was to hide rather than rejoice. A man like Michael Shiner stayed and watched not because he saw the hope of a better life, but because a white lady stopped him with the reassuring rhetorical questions: "Where are you running to? What do you reckon the British would want with such a nigger as you?"

And so the hours of tension passed, while all the time the shimmering August heat grew worse. Great thunderheads were piling up in the northwest, but there was still not a breath of breeze when one more British detachment left Capitol Hill around 2:00 P.M. Consisting of four officers and 200 men, it marched down Delaware Avenue to Greenleaf's Point, where the Eastern Branch flowed into the Potomac.

The Americans had destroyed the fort there, but the magazine remained, and the detachment had orders to get rid of its 150 barrels of powder.

A deep well on the point seemed ideal for the purpose, and the troops began rolling the barrels to the edge and dropping them in. Unknown to everyone, there was not enough water to cover the powder, and the contents of the barrels (plus some of the barrels themselves) soon rose high above the surface.

No one ever knew just how it happened. Some said a soldier accidentally tossed a lighted brand down the well; some said he did it on purpose, as the safest way to extinguish it; some said he threw a cigar; some said nobody threw anything: it was the barrels tumbling down the shaft that struck sparks off the stone siding. Whatever the cause, the result was the same—an ear-splitting explosion that blew well, powder, dirt, buildings and human beings into a huge, jumbled, mangled mass.

It was worse than any single moment at Bladensburg. Some of the men were blown to pieces, and no one knew exactly how many were killed. Estimates ran from 12 to 30. The 44 badly injured were carried back to the Capitol, where Ross established a makeshift hospital in the big empty hotel on Carroll Row.

Calm slowly returned to the city, but not the hot, still calm of before. The black clouds to the northwest were rolling closer, muttering with thunder, and flashes of lightning blinked across the sky. It grew steadily darker. A sudden breeze kicked up the dust on Pennsylvania Avenue, and large drops of rain began to fall. Old Washingtonians knew they were in for a really big storm.

But not like this. Nobody could remember anything else that came near it—the crashing thunder, the blinding rain, that howling, lashing wind. It plucked Lieutenant Gleig right off his horse. It picked up the two British 3-pounders as though they were toys. It carried away the foremast of the schooner *Lynx*, just saved by Captain Tingey. It ripped the roof off the Patent Building, just saved by Dr. Thornton.

It caught General Ross at the Gerard Gibson estate, checking on his reserves camped there. He and his staff took shelter in the house, but Mrs. Gibson wanted no part of the place, as it trembled and shook in the wind. Terrified, she fled to the garden and clung to a fence. The General gallantly rushed into the storm and hauled her back, assuring her that there was no danger, that all would be well in the end.

Cockburn sat the storm out in the Ewells' dining room, amiably chatting with the doctor. Suddenly the front door flew open and in stamped four men with a dripping white flag. Led by the Reverend James Muir, it was a "peace" delegation of three clergymen from Alexandria, Virginia. They had battled their way through the storm to explain that their city was completely defenseless—what surrender terms could they expect? It all seemed so anticipatory, Cockburn asked whether Captain Gordon's squadron was in sight yet, coming up the Potomac. No, it turned out, no one was near; they just wanted to know the terms when their time came.

For once in his life the Admiral was virtually nonplused. He wasn't used to these people who surrendered without even an enemy in sight. Improvising as best he could, he said that if there was absolutely no resistance, their persons and property would be safe . . . that the British would take but pay for whatever they needed. With that, he ran out of ideas, and the delegation politely bowed themselves out of the room and back into the storm.

Nor was Alexandria the only place attempting to surrender. The people of Georgetown had been trying for two days. During the evening of the 24th, Mayor John Peter led a delegation of leading citizens in the first attempt to negotiate terms. They apparently never made contact—they were on the wrong road—but the same group was at it again bright and early on the 25th. This time they reached Ross and offered to give up the town if only the British would spare their houses.

The General turned out to be a surprisingly good bluffer. He let them believe he was interested, but actually he had no intention of going farther west. There were rumors that the American Army had rallied on the heights above Georgetown, and he certainly didn't want to get trapped.

By late afternoon Ross was determined to head back to the fleet right away. The explosion at Greenleaf's Point had wiped out some of his best men; the storm had torn his organization to shreds. Now there were reports of American reinforcements coming on . . . of 12,000 men massed for a great counterattack. His pickets said they could even see weapons glittering on the heights above the Potomac. As for himself, he had already accomplished more than he ever hoped. More than he dreamed. Why stretch his luck?

As evening approached, staff officers quietly alerted the various unit commanders to be ready to fall back after dark. Secrecy was all-important. Not a word to the men or the people of the city. Where the sudden bustle of activity required some explanation, the inhabitants were fed vague, misleading rumors: There were hints of a move on Annapolis; and Dr. Ewell got the distinct impression from General Ross that the army would be heading for Georgetown next, to destroy Foxhall's Foundry. A curfew was set for 8:00 P.M.— everybody to be in their houses by then.

Assistant Commissary General Lawrence scurried about in a spurt of last-minute activity. Ranging into the country, his men rounded up some 60 head of cattle for a supply of beef on the hoof. Others assembled a motley collection of vehicles to carry the wounded: 10 or 12 carts and wagons, 1 oxcart, 1 coachee, several gigs, and 49 horses to draw them.

Even so, the army would not be able to take all its casualties. The 44 badly injured at Greenleaf's Point couldn't be moved, and nothing was more upsetting to General Ross. "I am much distressed at leaving these poor fellows behind," he confessed to Dr. Ewell. "I do not know who is to mitigate their sufferings."

The doctor took the hint. He assured Ross that Americans were a humane people—"of the same origin as yourself" —and that he personally would look after the men left behind. That settled, the General gave a last, long look at the battered forms lying in Carroll Row and continued his preparations.

At dusk the campfires blazed brightly on Capitol Hill and at the larger encampment on the edge of the city. Occasional figures, silhouetted or caught in the flickering light, hovered about doing ordinary chores. It was, of course, the oldest of *ruses de guerre*. While a handful of men played out a charade, the great mass of the army stole away in the night. Falling in at 8:00 P.M., the 3rd Brigade led the way . . . then the 2nd . . . then the 1st, silently marching out Maryland Avenue, the exact way they had entered 24 hours ago.

By midnight they were at Bladensburg again, passing the scene of yesterday's struggle. A pale moon shone over the field, faintly lighting the white forms of the dead, still unburied but now stripped of their clothing. Crossing the bridge, they stopped an hour while the men collected knapsacks and loaded some of the battle casualties into the carts and wagons. Here again Ross was forced to leave many behind—83 altogether. This time he entrusted them to Commodore Barney, still at Bladensburg resting from his own wound. The two leaders made an informal arrangement, calling for mutual exchange of all prisoners later.

Shortly after 1:00 A.M. on the 26th the British were on their way again, this time marching for Upper Marlboro by the most direct route. The 60 head of cattle were in front . . . then the hodgepodge of creaking vehicles . . . and finally the three brigades, with the 85th Foot acting as rear guard. Beyond that, there was no order. The men were so tired they barely knew where they were going. Many had filled their haversacks with flour at Bladensburg, but now it seemed much too heavy and most of them threw it away. Captain Harry Smith always said that if it hadn't been for that flour marking the route, his column would never have found its way home.

At 7:00 A.M. they halted for five hours, then on again until they reached Upper Marlboro at dusk. And so it went— town by town, retracing their steps to the fleet. Not a shot was fired at them all the way; not a bridge destroyed nor a tree chopped down to check their progress. They had seen few enemy troops on the way in; they saw none on the way out.

Yet there were casualties—not killed, or wounded, or prisoners, but a remarkable number of stragglers and deserters. A total of 111 men simply vanished. Some were like Sergeant Michael McNamara of the 85th Foot, or Private Edward Kelly of the 44th, who apparently wanted only a new start in a new land. But others were little more than armed marauders, taking time out to pillage the countryside. They stayed away from the big estates of the Federalist country squires—these often had British guards. They concentrated instead on the small holdings of the poor dirt farmers, robbing their homes, their crops, their hen houses.

Robert Bowie, the former Democratic-Republican Gover-

nor of Maryland who had property near Nottingham, decided to do something about it. Coming over to Upper
Marlboro on August 27 shortly after the British left, he con-
sulted the town's patriarch, Dr. Beanes. The doctor, of
course, had played host to Ross and Cockburn on their way
to Washington, but the latest British visitors were a different
sort. He agreed with Bowie, recruited several local people,
and working together, they soon had six or seven of the
stragglers in jail. All was going well until one escaped and
got back to Ross's force.

In the early hours of August 28, a party of British horsemen rode up to Beanes's front door, crashed into the house,
and pulled the doctor out of bed. Two house guests, ex-Gov-
ernor Bowie and two other local figures were seized too, and
all were carried back to the fleet as hostages for the immediate release of the stragglers. This was soon done, and the
Americans were freed—except Dr. Beanes.

Ross was furious at the old man. Whether the General felt
misled by the doctor's earlier hospitality, or whether Beanes
had in fact given some sort of pledge during Ross's visit, was
never made clear. Whatever the facts, the General certainly
felt an enormous breach of faith had occurred, for he normally was most gracious to individual Americans—especially to those, like Beanes, whom he regarded as "gentlemen." This time the "gentleman" was bundled aboard the
flagship *Tonnant* and thrown in the brig.

"To our no small surprise, we saw our friend Dr. Bean
brought in as a prisoner," Lieutenant Gleig noted in his diary
on the 28th, showing that the case had stirred a certain
amount of interest even at the subaltern level. But the young
Lieutenant was really more concerned with basic things—
his weariness on the 29th during that last 20-mile march to
Benedict . . . the glow he felt as the sailors cheered his brigade, boarding ship on the 30th. In 12 incredible days they

had marched 50 miles into the enemy's country, captured his capital, burned the public buildings, and got back safely again. Now at last Gleig could relax, take a bath, wear fresh clothes. "The luxury I enjoyed in turning into clean sheets is beyond description."

CHAPTER EIGHT

Shock Waves

Twenty miles west of Washington, the Reverend John A. Dagg—rushing with his militia company on August 25 to relieve the captured capital—began meeting frightened soldiers hurrying the other way. They assured him the British were right behind them.

Twenty miles north of Washington that same afternoon a man named Milligan burst into Brookeville, Maryland, with the news that the British had just burned nearby Montgomery Court House and were on their way to Frederick. At Montgomery Court House General Winder could see no sign of them, but he too felt he knew just where they were. "There remains no doubt but that the enemy are on the advance to Baltimore," he wrote General Stricker of that city, "and will be tonight full half-way. . . ."

For his intelligence, Winder was still depending largely on Colonel McLane, the Collector of the Port of Wilmington, who during the past two days had consistently managed to place the enemy between himself and the American Army. McLane's latest contribution was a flash that the British had brought their ships up to Washington and were landing 2,000 reinforcements at Greenleaf's Point. Together with the "6 to 7,000" Winder felt they had at Bladensburg, the force bound for Baltimore was "overwhelming." The General apparently missed or never got a copy of the new, concise report sent by Captain Henry Thompson, stationed on the road to Baltimore: "There is not an Englishman this side of Bladensburg."

It was not surprising. The situation at headquarters verged on chaos. After reaching Tenleytown on the night of the 24th, Winder had paused, hoping to collect his shattered army. But the men melted away as fast as they came in, and by midnight the three miles separating himself from Georgetown, and maybe the British, began to seem very thin. By the light of the fires raging in the capital, he retired five miles farther west . . . then at dawn moved still farther back to Montgomery Court House, some 12 miles from the city. Here maybe he could make a respectable showing.

No such luck. Colonel Beall could muster only 100 of his 800 men from Annapolis . . . Sailing Master John A. Webster, only 50 of the 400 flotillamen. General Stansbury's 1,400 militia from Baltimore County had all but vanished: there were only 15 or 20 left under the faithful Captain Edward Aisquith. Colonel McLane scoured the countryside in a fruitless search for others: "I find the road full of straggling militia looking toward Baltimore. I have prayed, I have begged, I have threatened, all to no purpose. Those drones on the public persist in running away. . . . From a disorganized militia, Good Lord deliver us."

The Colonel might also have prayed for a quartermaster. The army's baggage train had strayed off to Virginia; there was no bread, no meat, no tents, no supplies of any kind.

Turning up at Montgomery Court House during the afternoon, Jacob Barker and Robert de Peyster were appalled by
the situation. Worse, nobody seemed to be doing anything
about it. Hurrying to Baltimore, they sent back five or six
wagons loaded with all the hard bread they could find—
paid for completely out of their own pockets. Meanwhile
Winder dashed off a frantic plea to Secretary Armstrong in
Frederick to send flour and salt beef . . . making sure, he
added, to pick a route safe from the ubiquitous British.

Armstrong did his best, but he was "somewhat indisposed"
and thoroughly disgusted. Through his aide Major Daniel
Parker, he sent a caustic message to Major General Samuel
Smith of the Maryland Militia, hoping a better defense would
be made at Baltimore than at Bladensburg—"that story will
not tell well." More bitter than ever at the course of events,
the Secretary now had a new cause for complaint. He and
Secretary of the Treasury Campbell had gone to Frederick,
specifically designated by Madison as the place where the
government would reconvene, and now nobody else was
coming.

Certainly it was the last thing on the President's mind. He
and Dolley Madison spent most of the 25th still floundering
around the Virginia countryside looking for each other. During the morning Madison had ridden from Salona back to
Falls Church, hoping to find his wife at Wren's Tavern. She
meanwhile had left Rokeby and visited Salona in hopes of
catching him. Neither, of course, had any luck. Mrs. Madison
then continued west to Wiley's Tavern on Difficult Run,
while the President returned to Salona to learn she had just
left. He immediately set out after her but was held up along
the way by the great storm that swept the area that afternoon. Madison finally reached Wiley's toward the end of the
day, and here at last he found the First Lady.

Both were still traveling with their respective parties, but there was little time for reunion. Midnight, Madison set out again—now with Rush, Jones, Mason and the State Department chief clerk John Graham—planning to cross the Potomac at Conn's Ferry and rejoin Winder in Maryland. When it proved impossible to cross at night, Jones went back to look after the ladies, while Madison and the others waited till dawn of the 26th. It was 6:00 P.M. by the time they wearily rode into Montgomery Court House, only to find that Winder was no longer there. Taking such men as he could, the General had started for Baltimore around noon.

The Presidential party, now escorted by a troop of dragoons, picked up the trail. But it proved impossible to catch up with Winder that night. Around 9:00 P.M. they finally halted at Brookeville, eight miles farther on. This was a small Quaker community—normally a quiet, idyllic retreat—but for the past week it had swarmed with refugees and troops. Yet somehow the town never lost its composure. As Mrs. Caleb Bentley told one of her unexpected guests while spreading the table for a fourth or fifth time in a single evening, "It is against our principles to have anything to do with war, but we receive and relieve all who come to us."

Nor was it any different when the nation's Commander-in-Chief asked to spend the night. All hands went to work in the Bentley kitchen; beds were spread in the parlor; campfires were kindled in the yard outside. The villagers filed in to pay their respects, and the President received them gravely.

At 10:00 P.M. he found a moment to dash off a quick letter to James Monroe, who was now with Winder's force, camped at Snell's Bridge several miles closer to Baltimore. Madison always felt safer in matters of war when Monroe was around, and this time was no exception: "I will either wait here for you to join me, or follow and join you, as you may think best. . . . If you decide on coming hither, the sooner the better."

Although frail and 63, President James Madison personally took the field as the British invasion force approached Washington in August, 1814. This portrait, painted three years later, is a good likeness of him at the time.

Dolley Madison, the President's indomitable wife, watched with a spy-glass from an upper window of the President's House as the fighting developed. When all was lost, she joined the flight from the city — after seeing to the safety of George Washington's portrait.

Vice Admiral Sir Alexander Cochrane, commander-in-chief of the British expedition. He brought to the job organizing ability, good connections, and a strong distaste for Americans.

Rear Admiral George Cockburn, second-ranking naval officer of the expedition. Daring and resourceful, he successfully overrode the top command's qualms and engineered the capture of Washington. Here he stands, magnificently oblivious of his handiwork.

Right, Brigadier General William H. Winder, the lackluster defender of Washington, whose army was routed at Bladensburg. *Below*, Commodore Joshua Barney, whose flotillamen contributed one of the few American bright moments. *Below, right*, James Monroe, the restless Secretary of State, who personally scouted the advancing British and later, with less success, rearranged the American lines.

Lossing's Pictorial Field Book of the War of 1812

Library of Congress

The Peale Museum

Two contemporary British conceptions of Washington's ordeal.

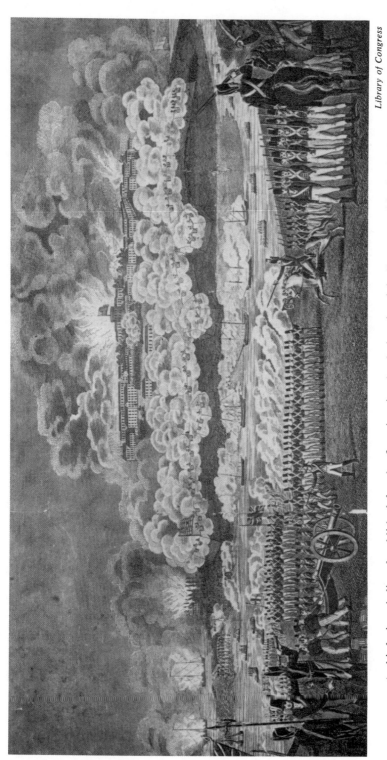

A third view, believed published for the first time in a book since it originally appeared in the *Stationer's Almanack*, London, 1815.

The President's House before the fire.

Somewhat the same view afterward.

"The Fall of Washington, or Maddy in Full Flight." In this derisive English print the onlookers speculate that the President is off to join "his bosom friend" Napoleon in exile.

With slaves plodding by in chains and Liberty watching from the sky, this curiously ambiguous print shows the ruins of the Capitol after the fire.

slender were the remains of the Columns that carried the heavy entablature. — The sketch below is an exact copy of two Columns, excepting that my paper does not admit of their being of proportionate heighth: but the Blocks stand upon one other in the manner represented, and at the lowest pin which I had placed in the center of each block, to keep them getting into place is bare. Of the fallen the Vaulting of the rooms have been beaten down; but is not a single arch in the which requires to be taken. In the North wing the beautiful columns which surrounded Court room have shared the than Columns of the Hall and in the Senate Chamber lished Columns of 14 feet block are burnt to live down. All but the Vaults they stand a most magnificent ruin.

steady while the colonnade had below might fortunately there whole building down but Doric Co the Supreme fate of the Cori Representatives the Marble po shafts in one have fallen is ruined.

Called to Washington to rebuild the Capitol, architect Benjamin H. Latrobe made this sketch for Thomas Jefferson, showing two of the damaged columns in the House chamber.

Major General Samuel Smith, the American commander at Baltimore, next target of the British force. Through his enormous drive he ultimately assembled some 16,000 troops and over 130 guns for the city's defense.

Major George Armistead commanded all-important Fort McHenry, guarding the entrance to Baltimore harbor. He and apparently he alone knew that the fort's magazine was not bombproof.

Francis Scott Key, a poetically inclined Georgetown lawyer, was on a flag-of-truce boat with the British fleet as the attack began. He had come to negotiate the release of an American civilian held prisoner — only to be detained himself until the battle was over

Landing at North Point near Baltimore, Major General Robert Ross was leading his redcoats toward the city, when cut down by American sharpshooters. In this rare 1816 print he slumps from his horse as a British rocket streaks by.

In the ensuing Battle of North Point (or Patapsco Neck, as it is called in this primitive view) the Americans were defeated, but the British thrust was blunted. After a day of cautious probing, the invaders returned to their ships.

Meanwhile Fort McHenry was attacked by the British fleet, while Francis Scott Key watched from his flag-of-truce boat, trying to see if "our flag was still there."

Fort McHenry's huge American flag measured 42 by 30 feet. Major Armistead hoped it would be "so large that the British will have no difficulty in seeing it at a distance." Made by Mary Pickersgill, it cost exactly $405.90 — as meticulously noted in the receipt below.

Disappointed at Baltimore, the British force — now heavily reinforced — headed for New Orleans. Here on January 8, 1815, it was crushed by Andrew Jackson. If he looms larger than life in this detail, taken from an old handkerchief, that was just the way he seemed to the American defenders.

Monroe was thinking along the same lines. He too felt military matters were handled better when he himself was around. And on top of that, nothing seemed more dangerous than this fragmented government—the President and the Secretaries of State, War and Navy in four different places. His love of action had carried him along during the day. Winder had been so sure the British were marching on Baltimore . . . had even gone ahead to get everything ready for the troops. But new reports were coming in suggesting that the General was off on another false scent.

The latest dispatches said that the enemy were definitely heading back to their ships . . . that serious disorders were breaking out in the abandoned capital. Worst of all, there were rumors of that perennial nightmare in times of crisis—a slave rebellion. General Robert Young, bringing reinforcements from Fairfax County, was already holding up his men on the south side of the Potomac. General Walter Smith's District Militia and Major Peter's Georgetown artillery were clamoring to get back to protect their homes in Washington.

Everything seemed to call for strong central authority. Early on the morning of August 27—even before Madison's letter reached him—Monroe wrote the President, urging they return to Washington at once. Then he turned up himself at Brookeville to drive home the point, but Madison needed no prodding. On receiving Monroe's letter, he had immediately written Jones, Armstrong and Campbell to hurry back. Then a special note to Dolley—"my dearest" —assuring the group at Wiley's Tavern that Washington was safe again. "We shall accordingly set out thither immediately; you will all of course take the same resolution."

At noon they started out: the President; the faithful Richard Rush; the self-assured Monroe; and the guard of 20 dragoons, jangling in martial splendor—an almost ludicrous touch in the light of the past week's shambles. Behind lay the smiling Bentleys and the tranquillity of Quaker Brookeville. Ahead lay the chaos and uncertainty of the ravaged capital. Nobody knew what to expect. "I know not where we are in the first instance to hide our heads," Madison confessed in his note to Dolley, "but shall look for a place on my arrival."

An almost eerie quiet hung over Washington; it had been that way ever since the British left. Pennsylvania Avenue stood broad and empty, with Joe Gales's type still scattered over the 7th Street intersection. General Ross's horse still lay, legs stiff in death, outside the ruins of Robert Sewall's house. The rubble of the Capitol still smoldered quietly in the sun. Contrary to all the wild rumors, there was no slave rebellion—the blacks still wanted no part of either side—but here and there occasional figures did dart in and out of the deserted buildings.

Looters. The capital's poor had always been a problem. Largely drifters and unskilled hands brought in to work on the public buildings, they had been left high and dry when the projects were finished or the money ran out. Even in good times they seemed to "live like fishes, by eating each other," to quote one shrewd observer, and these were anything but good times. The empty buildings . . . the disappearance of all authority . . . a sense of the waste of war in the air . . . all brought out the worst in them regardless of race. Once it was clear the British were gone and the American government not yet returned, they quickly went to work.

Alexander McCormack's groceries . . . a case of domestic striped shawls left at Long's Hotel . . . the contents of Congressman Abijah Bigelow's desk at his boardinghouse— anything was fair game. The files in the War Department's fireproof vault survived the British Army, but not the town's own looters. They continued to run wild at the Navy Yard, where they not only broke open Captain Tingey's locked door but took the lock itself.

This wholesale plundering was in full swing on the morning of August 26, when Dr. William Thornton returned to the city. The colorful Superintendent of Patents had saved his building the day before; now he was back to make sure it was still standing. It was; but a quick look around convinced the doctor that there were plenty of other problems to tackle.

Thornton was not a shy man. Realizing he was the only functionary in town, he quickly appointed himself a sort of unofficial mayor. (For his authority he later recalled that he had once been named a justice of the peace.) Plunging into his new role, he appointed guards at the ruins of the various government buildings. He shut the gates of the Navy Yard. He visited the British wounded at Carroll Row. He established useful relations with Sergeant Robert Sinclair of the 21st Foot, who had been left in charge of them. He waited on Dr. James Ewell, "to thank him in the name of the city for his goodness toward the distressed, who, being in our power, and especially in misery, were no longer enemies." He appointed a commissary to look after the injured's needs. He appointed citizen guards to patrol the streets at night. He made an odd arrangement with Sergeant Sinclair to include British soldiers in these patrols.

About 3:00 P.M. Dr. James Blake, Washington's official Mayor, returned to the city. Embarrassed at getting back so late, he failed to appreciate the ceremonial flourish with which Dr. Thornton handed over his borrowed authority. Nor did he like Thornton's idea of using captured enemy soldiers to help guard the capital. Backed by a citizens' meeting, Blake rejected the plan and set up his own system of patrols.

The individualistic Thornton retired in a huff and thereafter contented himself with taunting letters to the editor about mayors who disappeared in times of crisis.

But once again Thornton had risen to the occasion. Now the job was done. The looting stopped. Order restored. Around dusk Captain Caldwell's cavalry turned up, adding the reassuring sight of American uniforms; and Mayor Blake himself walked the streets all night, his musket at the ready. By 5:00 P.M. on August 27, when the Presidential party re-entered Washington, all was quiet in the city.

Not so down the Potomac. The rumble of distant gunfire came drifting up the river. It was clearly that British naval squadron, so often reported, yet all but forgotten in the recent excitement. Was the city now in for a new set of horrors? The rumble ominously continued for about two hours. Then, around 8:30, came a deep, teeth-rattling explosion. It shook the ruins of the Navy Yard, where Captain Tingey was toting up a list of losses. It rattled the windows at the Thorntons, where they were excitedly exchanging experiences with the Cuttses and other neighbors. It broke in on the quiet, serious conversation at Secretary Rush's house, where he, Madison and Monroe were assessing the military and political situation. The whole city seemed to pause . . . and listen for what would come next. But there was nothing —just silence.

On the quarterdeck of the frigate *Euryalus* Captain Charles Napier studied Fort Washington and tried to figure what the explosion meant. The British diversionary squadron under Captain James Gordon had been inching up the Potomac for ten days now, fighting shoals, current and contrary winds. Far behind schedule, the men watched the glow in the sky on the 24th and guessed correctly that Washington had already

fallen. They kept on anyhow. They might come in handy if
the army ran into trouble on the way back. But it was hard
work, and now this big fort, looming high on the Maryland
side, looked like the biggest obstacle of all.

They had been bombarding it for two hours when Captain Napier saw to his surprise that the garrison was retiring
—and then this appalling, earth-shaking explosion. The British guns fell silent as the crews watched a great mushroom of
smoke rise over the equally silent fort. It was too late in the
evening to investigate, but it looked as though the defenders
had blown the place up.

To Napier, it seemed incredible. The position was good;
its capture would have cost at least 50 men. Moreover, the
winds were so much against the British that a serious check
could have upset the whole expedition.

Yet the incredible had happened. Captain Sam Dyson,
commanding the 60-man garrison, had orders from Winder
to blow up his fort and retire, if attacked by land. Of course
he *wasn't* being attacked by land, but he heard rumors of
troop reinforcements coming ashore on the Patuxent, and he
feared he might be caught between them and this squadron
on the river. It wasn't a very convincing story—and didn't
sit at all well with the court-martial that later convened—
but that was the way he told it. In any event, Dyson spiked
his guns without firing a shot, led out his men, and set off the
3,346 pounds of powder in the fort's magazine.

Coming ashore early the following morning, the British
toted up their good fortune: 27 guns, 564 cannon balls,
countless small arms and ammunition. Best of all, the way was
now completely open to the rich port of Alexandria, only six
miles farther upstream.

Others realized this too. As the squadron got under way
again, down the river from Alexandria came a small boat
flying a flag of truce. Around 10:00 A.M. it eased alongside

the frigate *Seahorse*, flagship of the expedition, and three of the town's leading citizens climbed aboard the warship. They were led to Captain Gordon's cabin, where the Captain asked politely what he could do for them.

Jonathan Swift, spokesman for the group, began by saying that when the British reached Alexandria, he hoped that Gordon would show as much respect for private property as Admiral Cockburn and General Ross had displayed in Washington. They had "immortalized their names" and here was a fine opportunity to emulate their splendid example.

Captain Gordon said dryly that he didn't need any prompting to do what was right. Pressed for details, he said he would respect shops and houses but planned to seize all ships and cargoes waiting for export. Most unfair to Alexandria, Swift pleaded. The citizens were "all Federalists," yet they were being made to suffer far more than those people in Washington.

Gordon remained unmoved. Nor would he say exactly what his surrender terms were. Everyone would find out once he arrived.

The disappointed delegation went back to Alexandria, where the Committee of Vigilance was already doing its best to soften the town's fate. The biggest danger seemed to be that someone might try to rescue them. This could easily lead to shooting and incur the wrath of the British commander. The man to watch was clearly Brigadier General John P. Hungerford, whose 1,400 Virginia Militia were hurrying toward them, only 24 miles away.

The committee whipped up a resolution, urging Hungerford to lay off. It explained that Alexandria had no military force to protect it, that the committee intended to surrender at discretion, "and therefore think it injurious to the interests of the town for any troops to enter at this time."

The upside-down logic of urging the relief force to stay

away for fear of spoiling the surrender seemed lost on the committee, but it overwhelmed Lieutenant Colonel R. E. Parker, the officer in Hungerford's command who first got the message. Passing it on to the General, Parker added his own postscript: "I send you a copy of an instrument just received and make no comment on it—my heart is broke."

Meanwhile Captain Gordon's squadron crept closer. At 7:00 P.M. most of the ships anchored about two miles south of Alexandria, but the bomb vessel *Aetna* continued up, standing ominously off the town at dusk.

At 8:30 P.M. the Committee of Vigilance decided to try their luck with Captain Gordon again. This time they chose a local businessman named William Wilson as their spokesman. His firm had close commercial ties with England and perhaps that might do some good. Wilson went aboard the *Seahorse* at 9:30, pleaded the town's cause for three hours, but Gordon remained unimpressed.

Monday morning, August 29, the British squadron drew opposite the waterfront, turned its guns on the town, and this time Captain Gordon delivered his terms in the most specific manner possible: all naval stores, public or private, to be delivered up; all scuttled vessels to be raised and handed over; all goods intended for export to be surrendered; all goods sent out of town since August 19 to be retrieved and given up; all necessary provisions to be supplied the fleet, but at current prices. The crisp English officer who brought the terms told Mayor Charles Simms that he had exactly one hour to accept them.

The Committee of Vigilance briefly wrangled over a couple of points. They couldn't make the citizens raise their own scuttled ships; they couldn't retrieve the goods already sent out of town. Very well, the officer said, he would make those concessions—but nothing else.

The committee quickly capitulated. Gordon's ships eased

alongside the wharves, and for the next three days the sailors scurried back and forth, salvaging the scuttled boats and loading the rest with the flour, beef and tobacco that filled Alexandria's warehouses. There was no friction: the town's merchants watched sadly from a distance, while the English tars conducted themselves perfectly. "It is impossible that men could behave better than the British behaved while the town was in their hands," Mayor Simms wrote his wife a few days later with just a little too much enthusiasm.

Alexandria wanted only to keep things pleasant, and for that reason it was all the more disturbing when the city fathers learned on the 29th that General Hungerford was hurrying to save them in spite of their resolution. His force was now only ten miles away. Once more the Committee of Vigilance sent out a messenger to him—this time not with a mere resolution, but with an order not to come any closer and interrupt their arrangements with the enemy. Hungerford answered coldly that he acted only under the authority of the federal government . . . and kept marching. No one knows what might have happened had he reached the town, but when only three miles away, he received new orders from Washington to halt where he was and detach some of his men for other duties.

So that hurdle was past, but a new crisis arose on September 1—due, strangely enough, to a joke. That afternoon two of the U.S. Navy's real fire-eaters—Commodore David Porter and Captain John O. Creighton—were lurking not far from Alexandria when they heard that some British officers were dining there at Tripplett's Hotel. Hoping to seize them by surprise, Porter and Creighton came galloping into town on horseback, but some Tory warned the officers and they escaped in time.

Still hoping to stir a little mischief, the two American captains now rode to the waterfront. Here they spied a young

British midshipman, John West Fraser, who was supervising a
work detail loading one of the captured ships. Roaring up
from nowhere, Creighton seized Fraser by his cravat and
tried to carry him off. It was an unequal struggle—the
Captain was a remarkably burly man and Fraser perhaps 14
years old—but as luck would have it, the midshipman's
cravat broke, and he scrambled to safety aboard the ship.

Instantly the alarm gun sounded . . . the *Seahorse* hoisted a
signal to prepare for battle . . . the sailors hurried to their action stations . . . and the squadron's guns were once again
trained on Alexandria. Women and children fled through the
streets, and Mayor Simms frantically scribbled out an apol-
ogy while a British officer stood at his elbow with the buf-
feted midshipman in tow.

A delegation soon made its way to the *Seahorse* conveying
official regrets: the town had no control over the perpetrators
of the outrage . . . it shouldn't be held responsible . . . it
would take steps to see such a thing didn't happen again . . .
guards would be posted at the head of each street leading to
the waterfront. Finally mollified, Captain Gordon annulled
his signal for battle stations, and Alexandria heaved a huge,
collective sigh of relief.

"Alexandria has surrendered its town and all their flour and
merchandize," Margaret Bayard Smith wrote her sister from
Washington on August 30. "What will be our fate I know
not. The citizens who remained are now moving out, and all
seem more alarmed than before."

The capital trembled at the thought of another enemy visit,
and indeed there seemed no reason why the British couldn't
bring their boats and barges six more miles and complete the
job Ross and Cockburn had begun. To French Minister Serurier the threat posed a delicate diplomatic problem. "Your

Highness will understand," he wrote Talleyrand in Paris, "that I do not wish them to find me a second time in this residence, and find myself having to give dinners to their generals or squadron leaders. To avoid this possibility, I am thus determined, my Lord, to leave tomorrow for Philadelphia. . . ."

And how would he explain this runaway to the Americans? It would be easy: "Upon leaving, I shall say to the people of Washington that I stayed with them as long as they were in danger, but now that danger is past, I am going to travel for a while. . . ."

Such deviousness wasn't necessary. Most of Washington not only expected the British again but wanted to surrender in advance. "The people are violently irritated at the thought of our attempting to make any more futile resistance," Mrs. William Thornton noted in her diary on the 28th.

That same morning the irrepressible Dr. Thornton buttonholed Mayor Blake. The time had come, he urged, to send a deputation to the British fleet at Alexandria and ask for terms. There was nothing wrong with Thornton's courage—he had proved that—but as a practical man, he wanted to save the rest of the city, and as a good Federalist, he saw no salvation in Madison's hands.

The Mayor brushed him aside, and Thornton next went to the President himself, who was returning from an inspection of the Navy Yard with James Monroe and Richard Rush. The people, Thornton began, wanted to capitulate. Madison rejected the idea, but Thornton pressed on. The citizens had a right to surrender, he said, notwithstanding the presence of the government.

That was enough for Monroe. With Armstrong and Winder both miles away, the President had put him in charge of the whole defense effort. Turning to Thornton, he declared he had the military command, and if he saw any delegations proceeding to the enemy, he would bayonet them.

This put an end to it. Since the government was determined to resist, Thornton would do his best. The next time his wife saw him, she was distressed to find him buckling on his sword to go out and fight.

Monroe was the catalyst. Full of energy, he seemed to be everywhere at once. He had a battery planted on Greenleaf's Point, another near the half-burned Potomac Bridge, a third at Windmill Point—all aimed down the river. He soon had the demoralized Georgetown volunteers posted on the heights above the town, and backed them with 300 to 400 Alexandria militia, who never had the opportunity to defend their own homes.

He sent orders to a colonel across the river to shift his guns to some better positions for engaging the enemy. When the colonel questioned his authority, Monroe rode over and gave the order in person. The colonel remained adamant, and Monroe told him to obey or leave the field. The colonel left, but the guns were moved.

A new spirit filled the capital. Monroe was firm, confident, respected, well known, and above all trusted. In this last respect, ironically enough, he was guilty of one significant lapse. He carefully concealed his role in forming the disastrous battle lines at Bladensburg. Writing his friend George Hay at this time, he confided that this was something "which I mention in particular confidence, for I wish nothing to be said about me in the affair."

But good men too occasionally stumble, and at the moment it was perhaps just as well that James Monroe's deception went undetected. What the capital needed more than anything else was faith, and this he supplied in generous measure.

Washington got another lift with the return of Navy Secretary William Jones on the afternoon of the 28th. He had left Mrs. Madison and his own family in Virginia, crossed into Maryland in a vain effort to catch up with the President, and finally arrived alone from Montgomery Court House. Now he was full of optimistic ideas on using the navy. Seeing an opportunity to trap the British up the Potomac—or even capture their ships if they tried for Washington—he ordered Commodore John Rodgers, marking time in Baltimore, to hurry down with "650 picked men."

But for Madison personally, the best lift of all came with the unexpected return of "my dearest" Dolley on the afternoon of the 28th. She had started right out on receiving his message from Brookeville, attended by Navy Department clerk Edward Duvall. She never got a second note, warning her to hold off, and now came riding into town in a carriage belonging to Richard Parrott, the Georgetown ropewalk owner. Rolling past the ruins of the President's House, she went straight to the Cutts home on F Street. It must have been a strange feeling—this was where she and Madison lived when they first came to Washington in 1801.

The President met her there, and they decided to stay with the Cuttses until more permanent arrangements could be made. The news quickly spread that the First Lady was back, and the Thorntons and Smiths dropped by to pay their respects. It was a different Dolley Madison they found. For once her sunny warmth was missing. She was depressed— could hardly speak without tears—and almost violent on the subject of the English. A few troopers passed by, and she exclaimed how she wished for 10,000 such men "to sink our enemy to the bottomless pit."

August 29, and two more familiar figures appeared— Secretaries Campbell and Armstrong, back from their futile trip to Frederick. Campbell was seriously sick and soon resigned his post. Armstrong, active and ready for business, dis-

covered that the whole capital was against him. Always detested by the Federalists, for months he had barely been
suffered by the Virginia-oriented Democrats. Now both factions declared him the architect of the disaster.

He was blamed for everything. Forgetting the President's
uninspired leadership, Winder's appalling generalship and all
the other contributing causes, most people saw only John
Armstrong's misassessments—and in these they even saw
treason. A torrent of false charges poured on him. He was
said to have lost Washington deliberately in a plot to move
the capital north. He was said to have ordered Captain Dyson
to blow up Fort Washington without firing a shot. He was
said to have been in touch with a relative in the advancing
British Army. He was said to have drawn a million dollars
from the Treasury the day before Bladensburg, planning to
join the army on the Canadian front and seize the reins of
government. "The movements of this fiend should be nar-
rowly watched," warned the Georgetown *Federal Republican*.

In his proud way, Armstrong tried to ignore it. On the afternoon of his return, he rode down to Windmill Point,
intending to inspect the District Militia. His appearance set
off an uproar. Apart from politics, the officers were mostly
men of property with heavy investments in Washington.
They shuddered at the thought of Armstrong trying to move
the capital. Charles Carroll of Bellevue, one of the largest
landholders, refused to shake hands; various officers laid
down their swords rather than serve under him; and as their
version of this chivalric gesture, the enlisted men working on
the ditches threw down their shovels.

Either at this time—or even earlier—General Walter
Smith's 1st Brigade held a meeting at which the men passed a
formal and unanimous resolution: they would no longer serve
under Armstrong, that "willing cause" of the city's capture.

Smith hastily sent his aide Thomas McKenney and his brigade inspector Major John S. Williams to alert Madison, adding his assurance that "under the orders of any other member
of the cabinet, what can be done, will be done."

The President sent back word that he would give the matter his "immediate, deliberate, and earnest consideration."

That evening Madison dropped by the Seven Buildings for
a quiet talk with his Secretary of War. Feeling was running
high against them both, the President began, but especially
against Armstrong. It would be best if he didn't go near the
local troops. In fact, a message from General Smith indicated
that "every officer would tear off his epaulets" if he had anything more to do with them. Monroe got along with them
nicely, Madison added tactlessly; the Secretary of State had
been doubling as Secretary of War, but with Armstrong's return, that expedient was out. They must think of something
else.

Armstrong took all this to mean that the President was
proposing some other person—undoubtedly Monroe—to
handle the situation in the District, while he continued as
Secretary of War for everywhere else. Remarking that the
feeling against him was all based on lies, he went on to say he
obviously couldn't remain in the capital with part of his functions exercised by someone else. He must exercise his whole
authority or none at all. If he couldn't do the job effectively,
he'd resign . . . or perhaps retire from the scene and visit his
family in New York.

The President felt resignation was going too far—it
might have a bad effect—but he rather took to a "temporary retirement." Then, after a long but dignified argument
over Armstrong's share in the recent disasters, Madison
closed the conversation by going back to the Secretary's offer
to visit his family for a while. Tomorrow morning, nudged
the Chief Executive.

Next morning, as anticipated, John Armstrong was off
. . . but it would still be some time before he got to New
York. For most of four days he smoldered in Baltimore, spill-
ing out his anger to friends. The more he thought about it,
the more outrageous the charade seemed. Finally on September 3 he announced his resignation in a long, stinging letter to
the Baltimore *Patriot and Evening Advertiser*. Perhaps as a
deliberate slight, he confirmed it on the 4th in a curt, two-
sentence note to Madison.

With Armstrong gone, the President immediately named
James Monroe as Acting Secretary of War, and the change
was noticeable at once. Monroe's first move was to try and
trap the British at Alexandria. To accomplish this, he had
some Virginia Militia, several District units anxious to redeem
themselves, and Commodore Rodgers's "650 picked men,"
just summoned from Baltimore. More important than the men
themselves, he had three highly enterprising naval officers to
manage the effort: Rodgers, Commodore Oliver Hazard
Perry and Commodore David Porter. All were established
national heroes and proven gunnery experts.

The plan was simple: place batteries along the Potomac
below Alexandria and pound the British as they returned
down the river. But it took time to haul the guns to the selected
positions—and even more time to plant them. Long before
the Americans were ready, the British at Alexandria smelled
danger. At 5:00 A.M., September 2, Captain Gordon's flagship
Seahorse slipped her moorings and began working downstream. The rest of the squadron followed, and with them
went no less than 21 prize vessels. Their decks bulged with
13,786 barrels of flour, 757 hogsheads of tobacco, and countless tons of cotton, tar, beef and sugar.

The following morning, the 3rd, Commodore Rodgers left
Washington in hot pursuit. Boiling down the Potomac with a
small flotilla of cutters, he hoped to send three fire vessels

against the tail end of the British squadron. There was a brief pause opposite Alexandria when he noticed that the town fathers of that docile community hadn't yet put back the American flag. This fixed, he hurried on and caught up with the enemy around noon. He seemed to be in luck: the bomb ship *Devastation* had run aground and looked like an easy mark.

But then luck failed. The wind died, and Captain Thomas Alexander of the *Devastation* turned out to be a most resourceful opponent. He pushed off his own cutters and barges, breaking up Rodgers's attack and scattering the American boats. John Moore, a young midshipman from the *Seahorse*, towed the nearest fire vessel ashore, and the others were easily turned aside. Rodgers later tried again with two more fire vessels, but had no greater success. Such a weapon was child's play for men who had spent 20 years battling Napoleon.

The British ships up front had more serious trouble. They soon came up against Commodore Porter's batteries posted at the White House, a bluff on the Virginia shore. By September 3 he had ten guns in place, a furnace for heating shot, entrenchments for his supporting infantry, and a huge white banner proclaiming in bold letters, "FREE TRADE AND SAILORS' RIGHTS."

Taking no chances, Gordon sent several of his ships ahead to soften Porter up, while the rest hung back, collecting under the guns of his two frigates for an all-out dash. All the 4th and the morning of the 5th the two sides traded hundreds of cannon balls with remarkably little effect. The log of the *Erebus* recorded one of the few dark moments: "Found one cask of rum shot through . . . lost 50 gallons."

Noon, September 5, and Gordon was at last ready. Noting that the British trajectory was usually too low to reach the Americans high on their bluff, he added an almost Nelsonian touch: he weighted his ships to port so his starboard guns would fire higher. Then the *Seahorse* and *Euryalus* advanced, with the prizes and smaller vessels trailing behind. Soon all the British warships were pounding the bluff, and now their shots began to tell. Porter's men hung on for an hour and a quarter, but it was a hopeless mismatch—13 effective guns against a combined naval broadside of 63 pieces. Knowing he couldn't stop the enemy and seeing his own men starting to fall, Porter withdrew as Gordon sailed triumphantly by.

But the British commander's troubles weren't over. A little farther down the river on the Maryland side, Commodore Perry was waiting for him with some more guns planted at Indian Head. Gordon expected another long duel, but it turned out to be short and easy. The Americans had only one gun heavy enough to do any damage, and it soon ran out of ammunition. Early on the morning of the 6th Gordon sailed by unmolested and continued on his way.

For a badly shaken Washington there was only one consolation. The second British diversion—Sir Peter Parker's foray up the Chesapeake in the frigate *Menelaus*—suffered an unexpected setback. The dashing Captain had an easy time of it the first two weeks, but then overreached himself. On the night of August 30 he landed near the village of Moorfields on Maryland's Eastern Shore and led a party of marines and seamen against a strong force of local militia. Parker hoped to take them by surprise, but they were more than ready for him. The British attack collapsed under a withering fire.

Next morning a young American soldier exploring the battlefield came across an exquisitely made leather shoe neatly marked by a London booter: "No. 20169, Parker, Capt., Sir Peter, Bt." Returning it during a truce that day, a militia officer remarked, "We guess that your captain was not a man to run away without his shoes."

The hunch was right. Sir Peter Parker—reckless sailor, ruthless disciplinarian, spoiled child of patronage, but no less a hero to his men—had been mortally wounded during the attack.

Victory-starved Americans treated this single death as a major military stroke. The British cooperated with wildly exaggerated lamentations. In these golden days of aristocracy, the nobleman who fell in battle could generate an almost ritualistic outpouring of national grief. An authorized biographer depicted Parker, smiling as he fell, urging his men onward; actually, he only managed to gasp a rare piece of wise advice: "Pearce, you had better retreat, for the boats are a long way off." Parker's first cousin, Lord Byron, wrote a touching eulogy grieving for his departed comrade—while privately confessing that he hardly knew the man and "should not have wept melodiously except at the request of friends."

Yet in the last analysis, Sir Peter Parker's misfortune was a small affair for both British and Americans. The overwhelming fact was the capture of Washington . . . and now, the surrender of Alexandria. For Madison and his advisers this latest disaster was especially humiliating—in some respects even worse than Bladensburg. This time they knew what the enemy was doing; they had a Secretary of War they trusted; they had three of their most exciting commanders in the field; they far outnumbered the foe—and still they couldn't win.

But at least the British were no longer breathing down their necks. Washington could start picking up the pieces. Captain Tingey set about recovering the hardware looted from the Navy Yard. The *National Intelligencer* advised its readers that Admiral Cockburn had not succeeded in destroying the paper's account books, and subscribers were expected to pay up. The city's hard-working doctors turned to the task of healing the wounded—both friend and foe. Some of the British casualties, in fact, became pampered favorites. Col-

onel Thornton received a bedpan from his namesake Dr.
Thornton, and when the English surgeon Dr. Monteath died,
Dr. Ewell asked for the Marine band to play at the funeral.

Some 120 British prisoners posed a more difficult problem.
Many claimed to be deserters, and it was hard to say for sure.
To be on the safe side, General Mason sent them all to Frederick, where those who made a convincing case were par-
celed out in pairs to interior towns like Leesburg, Winchester
and York.

Meanwhile the hunt began for spies and traitors who might
have helped the British achieve their lightning coup. To the
stunned administration leaders, there had to be some better
explanation than their own ineptitude. The Washington jail
soon housed suspects like Richard H. Lee, charged with
supplying the enemy with melons and useful intelligence . . .
Peter Ramsay, said to have guided the invaders around the
city . . . William Wilson of Alexandria, who showed too
much interest in Commodore Porter's fortifications down the
Potomac . . . L. A. Clark, an enterprising purveyor of re-
freshments to thirsty American soldiers. "It is a most horrid
thing," Clark wrote General Winder on August 28, "that I
should be kept under guard, supposing I piloted the enemy
into Marlboro on Monday last, when it is known by Capt.
Buck, Capt. Carberry, Lt. Rodgers, and a number of the officers of the 36th Regt. that I was at the Wood Yard on that
day selling liquors."

Presumably Mr. Clark's loyal customers rallied to his side,
for all the suspects were soon released. In the excitement of
the chase, the hunters missed some genuine if rather small
game—Ross's informants Calder and a shadowy figure named
Brown . . . Thomas Barclay's clerk George Barton, whom
chance placed so fortuitously at Bladensburg.

Along with the mopping up, Washington turned to the
challenge of resuming normal government functions. Ob-

viously, those cracked and blackened walls that studded the city would no longer do, yet it seemed all-important to get going again. To Madison and the administration leaders, it was a matter of re-establishing confidence, of getting on with the war. To the local inhabitants, it was all that and their pocketbooks too. Already the old cry was going up again to move the capital. Heavy investors like John P. Van Ness shuddered at the thought, and even the clerks and grocers knew that government was the town's only industry. Things had to happen fast.

The President and Mrs. Madison moved into the Cutts house for a month . . . then to John Tayloe's far more imposing Octagon House, now vacated by French Minister Serurier. The government departments were established in various private homes, and Congress in Blodgett's Hotel, displacing the Post Office and Patent Office. But any hope that a truly useful role had finally been found for this white elephant of a building quickly vanished. The Representatives and Senators couldn't stand the hot, cramped quarters and again began talking about moving the capital. Daniel Carroll, Thomas Law and other leading landowners hastily put up a large brick hall near the ruined Capitol, and here in the so-called "Brick Capitol" the legislators were happy again. An important crisis was past.

Gradually, the various departmental valuables and papers were brought back from their hiding places in the country. The "Gilbert Stuart" was retrieved by Jacob Barker. The navy's trophies were unloaded from Benjamin Homans's canal boat. The Library of Congress books were gone forever, but Thomas Jefferson sold his personal library to the government to form the nucleus of a new collection.

Buried among the salvaged War Department files was a single letter that might have changed everything. Dated July 27, 1814, it was addressed to "the Honourable James Madison" and came from an anonymous seaman, apparently impressed on one of Admiral Cockburn's ships. Obviously sent at the risk of the writer's life, it warned the President that

> Your enemy have in agitation an attack on the capital of the United States. The manner in which they intend doing it is to take the advantage of a fair wind in ascending the Patuxent; and after having ascended it a certain distance, to land their men at once, and to make all possible dispatch to the capital; batter it down, and then return to their vessels immediately. In doing this there is calculated to be employed upwards of seven thousand men. The time of this designed attack I do not know. . . .
>
> (Signed) Friend

Somehow it was smuggled ashore and sent on its way. Postmarked "New York, August 1," it must have reached the President's House two or three days later. Here, the harried Madison (or some equally harried aide) bucked it to Winder . . . who filed it. Once again, as so often happens, a vital piece of intelligence was lost. Once again the truth was passed over—perhaps because the circumstances seemed so preposterous—while a dozen false leads were eagerly snapped up, because they seemed so plausible. And once again, what might have been anticipated came as a total surprise.

And surprise it was—not just in Washington but throughout the country. Even after word spread of the British landings, the capital seemed perfectly safe. "We have full confidence in the officer to whom, for six weeks past, the protection of the District has been entrusted," declared the New York *Gazette and General Advertiser* on August 23, the day before the roof fell in. "All look with confidence to the capacity and vigilance of the Commanding General," echoed the Baltimore *Federal Gazette and Daily Advertiser,* "and we feel not a doubt that his foresight and activity will leave nothing undone that our security requires."

The paper was no less confident the following morning. Unlike Winder, it correctly predicted that the British would head for the "pass" at Bladensburg, but there was nothing to fear. "Thermopylae" would be held, declared the editors, borrowing a not entirely happy analogy. "We of this town know our Leonidas well, and his fearless band."

Even the experts agreed. Commodore Rodgers, hurrying down from Philadelphia with his seamen, paused at the Susquehanna to drop an encouraging line to his wife Minerva. Dated 4 P.M. on the 24th—the very moment of disaster— his letter reassured her: "Everybody in high spirits and no fears are entertained regarding the safety of Baltimore or Washington."

Then the shattering truth, spreading slowly from town to town, carried along by the cumbersome mail stages that linked the country together. Philadelphia got its first inkling when the Baltimore Pilot Stage rumbled up to the City Hotel during the evening of the 25th. The first details were sketchy—just the army mauled at Bladensburg, Winder falling back. But at 11:00 P.M. an express rider pounded up with the dreadful news that Washington was lost.

By 1:00 A.M. on August 26 the Pilot Stage was rolling on north, now carrying proof sheets of the first Philadelphia extras. They were printed too soon to mention the capital's fall, but the dispatcher managed to scribble on the wrapping, "The enemy has entered Washington after a severe battle." Around 5:00 P.M., after the standard 16-hour journey, the stage arrived in New York, and by seven o'clock the whole city knew.

"DISASTROUS INTELLIGENCE," proclaimed the *Commercial Advertiser*'s Extra, first on the street. "PAINFULLY IMPOR-

TANT," declared the more conservative *Gazette and General Advertiser* the following morning.

As sometimes happens, the national mood went from one extreme to the other. Complacency gave way to panic; confidence to despair. The wildest rumors swept the land: Barney dead . . . Georgetown wrapped in flames . . . Armstrong lynched at Frederick . . . Baltimore's fashionable 5th Regiment wiped out . . . 15,000 British troops led by Lord Hill in person . . . the dreadful Admiral Cockburn driven in triumph through the capital "with a *miss* at his side."

"I have just heard that Washington is in ashes," Minerva Rodgers frantically wrote the Commodore on August 25, "I am bewildered and know not what to believe but am afraid to ask for news." She was sure of only one thing: that the enemy was at hand and that Rodgers was in deadly peril: "Oh my husband! Dearest of men! All other evils seem light when compared to the danger which threatens your precious safety. When I think of the perils to which your courage will expose you, I am half-distracted, yet I would not have you different from what you are. . . ."

Along with alarm went a sudden surge of anger, indignation and shame. "In what words shall we break the tidings to the ear?" asked the Richmond *Enquirer* on August 27. "The blush of shame, and of rage, tinges the cheek while we say that Washington has been in the hands of the enemy." The Winchester, Virginia, *Gazette* didn't bother with rhetorical questions as it tore into the administration leaders: "Poor, contemptible, pitiful, dastardly wretches! Their heads would be but a poor price for the degradation into which they have plunged our bleeding country." Philadelphia's *United States Gazette* demanded these men resign, and failing that, "they must be constitutionally impeached and driven with scorn and execration from the seats which they have dishonored and polluted."

The scorched walls of the Capitol itself blossomed with accusing graffiti: "John Armstrong is a traitor" . . . "Fruits of war without preparation" . . . "This is the city of Madison" . . . "George Washington founded this city after a seven years' war with England—James Madison lost it after a two years' war."

It was hard to stand up against this sort of battering. The small, frail President seemed more shriveled than ever. Visiting him during these dark days, the lawyer-essayist William Wirt wrote his wife: "He looks shaken and woe-begone. In short, he looked as if his heart was broken."

One night four other visitors turned up. Led by Alexander C. Hanson, editor of the Georgetown *Federal Republican* and archfoe of the administration, they had come not to add to Madison's miseries but to warn him of a plot on his life. Nothing definite was ever smoked out, but a corporal and six privates were hastily assigned to guard the President.

They were never needed. The first wave of anger soon gave way to new sympathy for the man. Steaming down the Hudson from Albany, Washington Irving felt it deeply when news reached the boat at Poughkeepsie that the capital had been taken. A fellow passenger snorted in derision and said he wondered what "Jimmie Madison" would say now.

"Sir, do you seize on such a disaster only for a sneer?" Irving stormed at the man. "Let me tell you, sir, it is not now a question about Jimmy Madison or Johnny Armstrong. The pride and honor of the nation are wounded. The country is insulted and disgraced by this barbarous success, and every loyal citizen would feel the ignominy and be earnest to avenge it."

The press quickly caught the change in mood. "The spirit of the nation is roused," proclaimed the influential *Niles' Weekly Register*. "War is a new business to us, but we must 'teach our fingers to fight.'—and Wellington's *invincibles* shall be beaten by the sons of those who fought at *Saratoga* and *Yorktown*."

Opposing factions drew together in the crisis. The very depths of the disgrace seemed to call for a new unity that would demonstrate to Britain in particular, and the world in general, that the American experiment could work. "Believe us, fellow citizens," pleaded the anti-administration Albany *Register*, "This is no moment for crimination and recrimination, which necessarily follows. . . . Let one voice and one spirit animate us all—the voice of our bleeding country and the spirit of our immortal ancestors."

Even Alexander C. Hanson's venomous *Federal Republican* joined in the call for solidarity, showing that it was not just a passing impulse that prompted his concern for the President's safety. "The fight will now be for our country, not for a party," declared Hanson, who nevertheless couldn't resist adding that old scores would be settled later: "When the enemy is expelled, we will then call to account, in the mode prescribed by the paramount law of the land, the traitors who may appear to be guilty. . . ."

One after another the disaffected rallied to the cause. Former Governor Thomas McKean of Pennsylvania urged a huge rally in Philadelphia to stop looking at the past; look only to the present and the future. In Cincinnati General William Henry Harrison forgot his differences with the administration and appealed to the governors of Ohio and Kentucky to send help at once. New York's Rufus King, darling of the Federalists, called for all-out defense. When the question of money arose, King had a ready answer: "Let a loan be immediately opened. I will subscribe to the amount of my whole fortune."

Even New England, hotbed of the antiwar movement, rose to the occasion. Governor Martin Chittenden of Vermont, who in 1813 had tried to keep his militia from serving outside the state, declared that the war had assumed a whole new character: "The time has now arrived when all degrading party distinctions and animosities, however we may have differed respecting the policy of declaring, or the mode of prosecuting the war, ought to be laid aside; that every heart may be stimulated and every arm nerved for the protection of our common country, our liberty, our altars, and our firesides."

The people needed no prompting. They were already on the way. "Our county is all alive and will be down soon to the relief of our friends," Colonel Sam Ringgold of Boonsborough, Maryland, wrote General Winder on August 26. "Sir, believe me, this country is all on fire and raising [troops] of their own free will and at their own expense," Captain John Sterrett, the U.S. Army barrack master at Carlisle, Pennsylvania, wrote the War Department on the 30th. He added that he had turned the barracks over to the quartermaster and was coming himself.

"To stand with folded arms and look on the scene as a mere spectator is not to be borne," Colonel J. A. Coles wrote James Monroe. Coles was awaiting court-martial as a result of the defeat at Chrysler's Farm on the Canadian front, but now he begged Monroe to suspend his arrest and let him serve at least as a private.

Corporal Robert Thompson was only a disabled veteran with an honorable discharge, but the loss of the nation's capital was too much for him too. "It makes me again resort to arms," he wrote the government on September 3, "though I feel rather unable, owing to my wound, which plagues me in damp weather, but in spite of it, I'll go."

They came from near and far. At Frederick, Maryland, Captain John Brengle's company of 84 men was raised August 25 on the impulse of the moment; in four hours they were on their way to Washington. In the remote Richland District of South Carolina the citizens raised 100 men and

$3,000 to buy their supplies. "Conflagration and rapine will
never bow the spirit of the American people," the Richland
Citizens' Committee wrote the War Department. "Our
enemy, we hope, will find that they have miscalculated our
resources and our spirit." They added that they did need a
bugle.

In the big coastal cities the outpouring was enormous. On
August 30 alone the Philadelphia *General Advertiser* ran 23
notices calling on various groups to report for duty, or announcing the formation of new volunteer units. The paper's
advertisements reflected a new concern for military affairs:
the Washington Rifle Co. needed a bugler . . . "Gentlemen
wishing uniforms embroidered in a prompt and neat manner
will please apply to No. 2 Carter's Alley" . . . John Gathen
offered the latest in pom-poms, noting that "pom-poms have
been adopted by the United States in place of feathers." A
strong editorial argued the value of the pike as a military
weapon; it was, the writer assured any skeptics, known as
"the queen of arms."

While Philadelphia's raw recruits explored the art of war,
thousands of their fellow citizens began digging entrenchments. They came from every walk of life—62 carpenters
. . . 200 printers . . . 30 teachers . . . 140 crewmen from the
frigate *Wasp* . . . 400 watchmakers, silversmiths and jewelers
. . . some 15,000 men altogether.

Early every morning the groups working that day got
their assignments and began to dig. At 10:00 A.M. the drum
beat for grog. At noon it beat for dinner and more grog. At
3:00 P.M., and again at 5:00, there were breaks for still more
grog. At 6:00 the drum finally beat retreat, at which point
the General Orders suggested tactfully: "For the honor of the
cause in which we are engaged in, freemen to live or die, it is
hoped that every man will retire sober."

The women did their bit too. Meeting on August 30, 100

of Philadelphia's fairest turned out 120 riflemen's uniforms in two days. At nearby Frankford the young ladies sewed a standard of "elegant colors" for the local artillery company. Miss Mary Dover made the presentation, promising a blushing Captain Thomas Duffield that the girls would "fly to meet you on your return."

The scene was repeated up and down the seaboard. In these hectic days it almost seemed as if John Jacob Astor were the only person still carrying on a normal life. The rich New Yorker hoped to operate the next flag-of-truce vessel for Europe—highly desirable since the ship would enjoy free passage through the British blockade. On August 22 he wrote Monroe asking the government's approval, but if the letter reached Washington at all, it went up in the flames that engulfed the State Department. Naturally there was no reply. August 27, Astor fired off another letter. Although by now he well knew of the capital's fate, he was so absorbed in his project that he ignored recent events completely. Not a word of worry or regret; just a touch of petulance:

> Perhaps my letter of the 22nd has not been received or you had not time to write. I hope no other arrangement has been made and that the ship which I have prepared will receive the Flag, as otherwise it will expose me to unpleasant circumstances, if not some discredit, as I have long since advertised her.

He urged Monroe to write; sent along his own man to wait for an answer; and threw in a paragraph that couldn't help but catch the eye of a hard-pressed administration leader: "Myself with a number of other wealthy citizens are much engaged to form a system for a national bank to relieve the country from its present pressure as respects finance."

Perhaps that was what did it. The economy was in chaos

. . . recent events would make it harder than ever to raise
money . . . Astor's help could be a lifesaver. Monroe hastily
scribbled a note to the State Department clerk: "Mr. Graham
to inform Mr. Astor that his vessel will be employed, but
owing to present state of affairs, must be delay."

There was so much to do. Washington was deluged these
days not only with offers of assistance but with demands of
every sort. New York's Robert Fulton was in town lobbying
for funds to finish his "floating steam battery"—said to be
the answer to that city's defenses. Major General Barker of
the Virginia Militia was demanding reinforcements, additional artillery, better equipage and more provisions for his
state's northern counties. Governor Joseph Alston of South
Carolina was demanding better protection for Charleston.
The Philadelphia Committee of Safety seemed to want the
moon—even the transfer of General George Izard's army
from the Great Lakes to the Schuylkill.

Monroe and William Jones desperately fenced them off.
Fulton got $40,000, but most of the demands were out of the
question. The government, the harassed Secretaries explained,
couldn't be everywhere at once. The limited forces available
had to be used where the danger was greatest.

That was just the trouble. Every local official thought *his*
danger was the greatest. By September 6 Cochrane was in the
Bay again, and Gordon had passed the last obstacle down the
Potomac. Soon they would be reunited—ready to strike
somewhere—yet the available intelligence was hopelessly
contradictory.

Baltimore or Norfolk would be next, declared some people
at Benedict who had overheard the British talking. "Nothing
was said about going to Baltimore, but a great deal about taking New London or Long Island and making winter quarters
there," reported Major William Barney after interrogating
three British deserters at Annapolis. "There cannot be a

doubt that Richmond will be their next object," announced the *Virginia Patriot*, citing sources "which may be depended on."

"As soon as the army is all reembarked, I mean to proceed to the northward and try to surprise Rhode Island," Admiral Cochrane privately wrote Lord Melville, First Lord of the Admiralty, on September 3, as the British fleet worked its way back down the Patuxent. Once there, he went on to explain, he would land and rest the troops till the end of October. Then, bolstered by reinforcements from England, he would move southward again, take Baltimore, and head on down the coast. "As the season advances, I propose going to the Carolinas, Georgia, etc., and ending at New Orleans, which I have not a doubt of being able to subdue and thereby hold the key to the Mississippi."

The plan had much to recommend it. A shift to Rhode Island would divert the Americans. Their newspapers were already filled with rumors of Lord Hill coming over with a huge army to attack New York. This would look like the opening move. It would draw thousands of troops from the Baltimore area and, just as important, keep Madison from reinforcing his army in Canada.

Above all, it would get Cochrane's men out of the Chesapeake during what was known as "the sickly season." Nothing weighed more on British minds. In August 1813 Admiral Warren's force had been swept by a mysterious fever that struck down 500 of his 2,000 men. Vaguely attributed to noxious vapors rising from the swamps, it was thought to be a seasonal phenomenon that the Americans could perhaps survive but certainly not a civilized people. "The sickly season here is about at its height," the Fleet Captain Edward Codrington wrote his wife, "and from the uncommonly cadaverous appearance of the natives who are in health, the country with all its beauty of scenery is not fit for the habitation of social man."

So they would head north for a while, but they would be back, and then it would be Baltimore's turn. This lively, brawling seaport up the Bay sat at the top of the list of British hates. It had supplied 126 of the privateers that ravaged British commerce. It was generally considered a "nest of pirates." It was, in Admiral Cochrane's mind, "the most democratic town and I believe the richest in the union."

A special fate awaited this most special target. There might be some excuse for respecting private property in Washington, but not here. "Baltimore may be destroyed or laid under a severe contribution," Cochrane wrote Earl Bathurst on August 28. Writing Melville six days later, he no longer talked of ransom; instead, he was worried about a delicate problem that might spoil his plans for total destruction:

> As this town ought to be laid in ashes, if the same opinion holds with H. Maj.'s Ministers, some hint ought to be given to Gen'l Ross, as he does not seem inclined to visit the sins committed upon H. Maj's Canadian subjects upon the inhabitants of this state.

It was not that Ross lacked zeal, Cochrane hastened to add. It was just that he was soft. "When he is better acquainted with the American character," the Admiral observed, trotting out his favorite simile, "he will possibly see as I do that like Spaniels they must be treated with great severity before you even make them tractable."

Admiral Cockburn thought Ross was soft too, but with that went pliability, and this could be turned to advantage. Time and again on the road to Washington he had won the General over to his own schemes; now he went to work again. Like everybody else, Cockburn wanted to get at Baltimore; but unlike Cochrane, he wanted to do it right away —while the British were still in the Chesapeake . . . while the Americans were still demoralized . . . before they had time to organize the city's defenses, build fortifications, bring in new troops, arouse the nation. As for the "sickly season," the dangers were vastly exaggerated. He had been here last year, and he knew.

Ross leaned the other way. For Cockburn it wasn't as easy as those days when they were in the field together. Now he was back on the *Albion;* while the General was on the *Tonnant,* where Cochrane could see him all the time.

But Cockburn did have a powerful ally on the *Tonnant.* This was Lieutenant George de Lacy Evans, Ross's Deputy Quartermaster General. Although nominally a junior staff officer, Evans had the General's ear. He had always sided with Cockburn in those discussions on the road to Washington. It was no different this time.

Ross still leaned the other way. But he was doubtful enough to ask his Deputy Adjutant, Captain Harry Smith, for his opinion. Smith was all against an attack just now: rumors planted by the British themselves had already drawn too many American troops to Baltimore; a brilliant stroke like the capture of Washington could rarely be repeated; the approach up the Patapsco River could be easily blocked; too many of the men had dysentery; and most important of all, there was so little to gain and so much to lose. Washington was a tour de force; Baltimore would be at best an anticlimax and could be a disaster.

"I agree with you," Ross nodded. "Such is my decided opinion."

Smith had been appointed to carry Ross's dispatches back to England, and with this in mind, he now asked if he could tell Lord Bathurst that there would be no immediate attack on Baltimore. Yes, said the General, he certainly could.

On September 3 Smith left. As he headed for the gangway to catch the launch to the frigate *Iphigenia*, the General walked beside him. Reaching the rail, they shook hands, and on an impulse Smith asked once again, "May I assure Lord Bathurst you will not attempt Baltimore?"

"You may," said Ross, not a doubt in his voice.

Certainly it looked that way. On September 4–5 a flurry of orders went out to the various commanders, dispersing the fleet on new assignments: Admiral Malcolm to take most of the warships and all the transports to a point south of Block Island . . . Captain Sir Thomas Hardy to take 13 of the ships and relieve Admiral Cockburn in the Chesapeake . . . Cockburn to take the *Albion*, now loaded with prize tobacco, dispose of it in Bermuda, and rejoin Cochrane at a secret rendezvous apparently south of Block Island.

As the ships started on their separate ways, Admiral Cochrane sent a hearty "well done" to all hands:

> The Commander-in-Chief cannot permit the fleet to separate without congratulating the Flag Officers, Captains, Commanders, officers, seamen, and marines, upon the brilliant success which has attended the combined exertions of the Army and Navy employed within the Chesapeake. . . .

And so, with the felicitations of their grateful chief, the captors of Washington moved down the Bay convinced that their mission, for the present anyhow, was completed in these waters.

CHAPTER NINE

Focus on Baltimore

"All is now confusion and consternation here—everybody moving that can get off, under the full expectation that the enemy will be here tomorrow night," reported the Baltimore correspondent of the New York *Commercial Advertiser* on August 25, the day after the debacle at Washington.

Other cities might fear they were next on the British list, but the Baltimoreans *knew* it. The place was only 40 miles from Washington . . . several of the British deserters said the fleet was heading there . . . General Ross himself confirmed it, according to one of those obliging southern Maryland squires who enjoyed such easy access to the enemy.

Besides these immediate clues, there were other more underlying reasons to expect an early visit. Boasting a population over 45,000, Baltimore was the third biggest city in the Union—a target of obvious importance. Its bulging warehouses and crowded waterfront invited the closest attention of the prize-conscious British leaders. Its record of harassing the enemy was unparalleled—over 500 British ships captured or sent to the bottom by Baltimore privateers.

And it had a reputation to go with its record. No city had done more to fan the war fever. In one anti-Federalist riot a crowd even killed a distinguished Revolutionary leader and maimed the venerated Richard Henry Lee, seemingly just because they wanted peace. "Mobtown" was the gentlest epithet applied by the British press.

Yet at the moment brawling, bellicose Baltimore was anything but warlike. As the shattered remnants of Stansbury's and Sterett's militia tumbled in from Bladensburg, a wave of defeatism swept the city. "You may be sure this is the most awful moment of my life," one of the stunned inhabitants, David Winchester, wrote a relative in Tennessee. "Not because, if the place is defended, I shall put my life at hazard in common with my fellow citizens, but because I am positively sure we shall not succeed."

Few even contemplated a defense. "I think the only way to save the town and state will be to capitulate," wrote Private Henry Fulford, back home from his harrowing day at Bladensburg. "We shall have to receive the British without opposition and make the best terms we can," echoed a local shipowner in a letter to New York. He added that he had to close now; he was off to scuttle his own vessel in the harbor.

Postmaster Burrall hastily made plans to shift the mails out of town. The banks began moving their specie to York, Pennsylvania. Many members of the Committee of Vigilance and Safety—just formed to organize the city's defense—seemed more interested in arranging capitulation than resistance. One of the committee's most prominent members, John Eager Howard, desperately tried to stem the tide. Pointing out that he had four sons in the field and as much property as anyone, he said he would rather see his sons killed and his property in ashes than surrender and disgrace the country.

The city's military leaders rose to the occasion too. As the disastrous details of Bladensburg and Washington rolled in on August 25, Brigadier General John Stricker, commanding Baltimore's own militia brigade, stalked into the Council Chamber where the Committee of Vigilance and Safety was meeting. With him came Commodore Perry, in town to take over the new frigate *Java;* Captain Robert T. Spence, another senior naval officer; and Major George Armistead, commanding the regulars at Fort McHenry, which guarded the entrance to Baltimore's harbor.

Together they called for all-out resistance. Burying the usual service rivalries, they also urged that a single over-all commander be appointed for the city's defenses. The man they wanted was Major General Samuel Smith, commanding the 3rd Division of Maryland Militia, the main body of troops in the area. The committee agreed and appointed a delegation led by John Eager Howard to wait on Smith. They returned so quickly it seemed the General just might have been waiting in the wings. He accepted, subject to one condition: he wanted Governor Levin Winder's sanction, including whatever extended powers might be necessary to do the job.

That condition told a lot about Sam Smith, as he was universally known. After twenty years in Congress—first as Representative, now as Senator—he knew all the pressure points of the body politic. Military authority from some citizens' committee didn't mean much, but from the Governor himself—that was different. Especially if, as here, the Governor also happened to be the uncle of Brigadier General Winder, the regular army officer commanding the District. A clash of authority seemed likely, and Smith wanted to cover himself.

This kind of shrewdness, coupled with hard-driving ambition, sound judgment and a freewheeling style, had carried Sam Smith a long way. Born in Pennsylvania, he grew up in Baltimore, the strong-willed son of a wealthy merchant. In the Revolution he organized a company, joined George Washington, and shared the trials of Long Island . . . White Plains . . . the Brandywine . . . Monmouth. For the defense of Fort Mifflin he got a sword and a vote of thanks from Congress. Yet even in those dark days he still had a streak of personal ambition that set him aside from the rest of that band of heroes. Somehow he got back to Baltimore every winter for recruiting and business, and long before the war was over he resigned his commission and went home to make money.

He prospered mightily—iron, shipping, banking, land, everything he touched—and was soon in politics too. Elected to Congress in 1792, and later to the Senate, he was not so much a legislator as a manipulator. Often he lost: he fought Jefferson on foreign policy; Madison on militia matters; and Gallatin on anything. But always he survived—another tribute to his agile mind. Like many successful politicians of the day, he was a power in the state militia, and during the invasion scare of 1813 he proved his worth by organizing Baltimore's defenses with a furious flurry of energy.

Now at 62 he was as shrewd, tough and ambitious as ever. Maybe not the ideal man for the long winter at Valley Forge, but for the short haul no one had more drive or commanded more respect. Significantly, three of the leaders who proposed him were regulars, who traditionally hated to serve under a militia officer. This time they had no qualms, for here was a man who could get things done.

So an express galloped off to Annapolis, and by the 26th he was back with the Governor's blessing. It proved a masterpiece of evasion, for apart from avuncular considerations,

Levin Winder was faced with a most delicate problem. Normally General Winder, a regular, outranked Smith, a militia officer. But if called into federal service, Smith, a major general, outranked Winder, a brigadier. The hitch was that nobody had called Smith into federal service. Under the Presidential order of last July, General Winder had the authority but never exercised it. On the other hand, Governor Winder had no authority in such matters at all. The Governor solved the problem by simply *implying* that Smith had been called into federal service:

> By the requisition of the President of the United States of the 4th of July last, one Major General is required of this state. In conformity to which, you have been selected.

That was good enough for Sam Smith. "The endorsed copy of a letter from His Excellency Governor Winder was received by me this day, and I have in consequence assumed the command agreeably to my rank," he quickly wrote General Winder, who was hurrying toward Baltimore to organize the city's defense himself. And if that didn't get across the point, the rest of Smith's message showed the tone of command already creeping into his pen: "Do me the favor to send me information by the dragoon of your situation, the number of troops with you. We want the tents and equipage of Stansbury's Brigade. . . ."

Winder was thunderstruck. Arriving in Baltimore at 3:00 A.M. on the 27th, he rested a few sleepless hours, then went to see Smith. It was a stormy session: Winder protesting that he still had command, that the Governor had no power to name anybody; Smith insisting he was now in charge and expected to give the orders. In the end Winder got nowhere, but whatever his merits as a general, he was too decent a man—

too good a patriot—to sulk or walk out. Swallowing his pride, he said he'd do whatever Smith asked, until the issue could be settled by Washington.

"General Winder has in a manner much to his honor I conceive, consented to waive his pretentions to rank for the present," Commodore Rodgers wrote approvingly to Secretary of the Navy Jones later that day. Rodgers had been present during the whole confrontation, and as a regular himself he agreed with Winder's legal position. But he had been in Baltimore since the night of the 25th, had seen the panic firsthand, and knew how desperately a strong leader was needed. Somehow he managed to give his sympathy to Winder and his support to Smith without alienating either of those sensitive warriors.

He himself was a tower of strength these trying days. As senior officer of the U.S. Navy, his presence alone gave new heart to Baltimore, while his 300 seamen from Philadelphia were the first tangible evidence that help was on the way. By combining them with the 500 flotillamen in town—plus Commodore David Porter's force, soon down from New York—Rodgers put together a makeshift "brigade," which he made as conspicuous as possible.

Meanwhile he worked on the civilian leaders, supplying a touch of moral rectitude that balanced nicely the bludgeon of Sam Smith. He even extracted a personal pledge from the Committee of Vigilance and Safety that they would defend the city "to the last extremity." Calm returned, and on the 27th Porter was able to write Secretary Jones that, thanks in no small measure to Rodgers's efforts, "The citizens of Baltimore have recovered from their panic, and I hope, Sir, the Navy may yet be enabled to render some service to their country."

But there was so much to be done. The best of the Maryland Militia had been at Bladensburg, and on the 27th they were still hopelessly scattered. When Sam Smith issued a call to Stansbury's men to report, only 600 showed up. His somewhat imperious order telling Winder to bring on Stansbury's tents and equipage was ludicrous—everything was still lost in Virginia. Even Sterett's elite 5th Regiment seemed to have vanished. Want ads blossomed in the *Patriot and Evening Advertiser* pleading with Pinkney's Riflemen and the American Artillerists to reassemble, ready to fight again. An even more revealing ad summoned to the Court House "Elderly men, who are able to carry a firelock, and willing to render a last service to their Country."

It was a situation made for Sam Smith, and every Baltimorean soon knew it. On the 27th the citizens were told to collect all the wheelbarrows, pickaxes and shovels they could find. On the 28th they started digging. A line of fortifications gradually took shape along the eastern edge of the city—the side most exposed to a British landing.

The new commanding general seemed everywhere at once. Impatient and highhanded, he hurled himself at every obstacle. August 29, the Pennsylvania and Virginia Militia began coming in; Smith wanted no more "Bladensburg Races" and drilled them mercilessly from reveille to 7:00 P.M. August 30, Commodore Rodgers and the naval contingent left briefly on their futile attempt to stop the British squadron on the Potomac; Smith fumed and stormed . . . urged Rodgers to come back immediately. August 31, Quartermaster Paul Bentalou announced he had no money and could get none from the War Department. Smith charged over to the Committee of Vigilance and Safety and engineered an immediate loan of $100,000 from the Baltimore banks.

That same day he scored an especially characteristic stroke when the War Department ordered five 18-pounders at Fort McHenry to be transferred to Washington. "The guns belong to the U.S.," he wrote the Committee of Vigilance and

Safety, "but the carriages are the property of the City. I have therefore not conceived myself at liberty to deliver them without the consent of your Committee. I consider these guns as indispensable. . . ." The committee took the cue and told the War Department that it could have the guns but not the carriages. That way, they were of very little use to anybody, and Washington quietly capitulated.

September 1, the units crowding into town began battling over the few available wagons—Smith intervened and divided them up: one wagon for every 100 men. Arbitrary, but it worked. September 2, the troops were running out of bread because all the bakers were drilling. Again Smith stepped in, released the bakers from service, told the contractors to hire them and start making biscuits. September 3, military traffic ground to a halt; the streets were clogged with caissons, carts, wagons of every sort. Once again Smith exploded into action, ordering a bridge of scows across the inner harbor. It looked a little visionary, but in two days 30 scows were in place and the bridge operating.

Sam Smith was not a man to delegate authority, and his headaches came in all sizes. One minute he was straightening out the different countersigns used by the sentries . . . the next he was trying to dispose of 40 head of surplus cattle brought along by a Virginia brigade . . . the next he was rounding up kettles for a Pennsylvania outfit . . . the next he was shelling out $20 for John Bouldin's map of North Point. Bouldin had tried in vain to collect through the regular channels, finally had gone to the General himself. Smith didn't hesitate: North Point was a place that interested him greatly. Lying 12 miles east of Baltimore at the tip of the peninsula where the Patapsco emptied into the Chesapeake, it looked like a good place for the British to land.

In the hubbub around headquarters it sometimes seemed as if nothing got done, but actually a great transformation was taking place. A week ago Hampstead Hill was a placid green rise to the east of town; now the dirt was flying. "They are throwing up entrenchments all around the city," an unidentified young lady wrote her brother in New York, who passed her letter on to the *Evening Post*. "White and black are all at work together. You'll see a master and his slave digging side by side. There is no distinction whatsoever."

The citizens worked in relays, depending on the ward where they lived. They reported at 6:00 A.M. and toiled till dark. Everybody joined in. When 12-year-old Sam W. Smith, the General's nephew, disappeared from home, the family knew just where to find him—out on Hampstead Hill, digging away with the rest.

A less visible but equally important change was the sudden flow of money for defense. A week ago the talk was of paying ransom; now it was of buying guns, tents, provisions, forage. Washington had said it had no cash; very well, the Baltimoreans declared, they would finance their own needs. With just a little prodding from Sam Smith, the local banks ultimately advanced $663,000 for the cause. Less spectacular, but more poignant, were the hundreds of donations showered on the town by its loyal citizens—Samuel Chase, $100; Thomas McCormick, $3; William J. Alcock, $24, to mention only a smattering.

And where cash was impractical, the people came through with goods and services. The variety was a nightmare to the city comptroller: Luke and William Enson, 3,000 bricks . . . Dr. Henry Karl, 2 bundles of lint . . . C. White & Sons, 5 barrels of whiskey . . . David Wilson, 2 barrels of shad . . . "A Citizen," 3 tons of hay.

But the biggest change of all was the mass of volunteers pouring in from every direction. A week ago Baltimore lay wide open; now troops seemed to fill every inch of space: the 56th Virginia jammed into Piper's Ropewalk . . . the 38th

U.S. Infantry had tents on Hampstead Hill . . . five companies from Pennsylvania were in Oliver's Ropewalk . . . Colonel Hood's Annapolis militia camped by the hospital.

It grew so crowded even the generals were squeezed. Thomas Forman, commanding Maryland's 1st Brigade, thought he had staked out fairly comfortable quarters in a vacant house. Next thing he knew, a pack of artillerymen moved in and left him boxed into a single small room.

Few of these reinforcements brought much equipment—adding to the bedlam at headquarters. Quartermaster Bentalou was bombarded with demands for horses, and somehow managed to come through: 99 for the Maryland artillery . . . 24 for the Marines . . . 16 for Rodgers's seamen. The navy contingent, understandably, was unprepared for this kind of shore excursion, but Deputy Commissary Officer James Calhoun performed heroics in filling their needs. Somewhere he got them tents, canteens, camp kettles, knapsacks, all the things no one else could find. Still there was so much to do —hundreds of militia were without shoes; some 2,000 men had no cartridge boxes; most of the Pennsylvania companies didn't even have ammunition.

With such a conclave of amateurs, personnel problems were bound to arise. Several Quakers had been scooped up in the general draft; now they wanted their release as conscientious objectors. Some troops from Elkton began worrying about their own town's safety and asked to go home. Captain Jacob Squires's Pennsylvania volunteers wanted to be transferred from a Maryland regiment to some outfit from their own state. Sam Smith did his best to cope with them all, but his thin veneer of patience must have been tested when Lieutenant Colonel Henry Trimble of Stansbury's brigade asked that his battalion be allowed to remain camped apart from the rest of the brigade. "Should we be removed," Trimble explained, "the harmony of our camp may be destroyed by our men intermingling with others with whom they are unacquainted."

Somehow Trimble was dealt with, and the preparations went on. By September 4 Quartermaster Bentalou estimated there were 15,000 troops on hand. That day General Forman enthusiastically wrote his wife, "We have assembled seven generals: Smith, Winder, Stricker, and Stansbury of Baltimore, Douglass and Singleton of Virginia; and your humble servant. This morning all the general officers with their aides and brigade majors assembled at 6 o'clock to view the grounds and country surrounding Baltimore. The parade was splendid and interesting. . . ."

All seemed in perfect harmony as this array of braid and cocked hats swung by the serried ranks, but beneath the surface General Winder still seethed at the thought of being just one of seven. He had been appointed by the President of the United States in person to command the 10th Military District—which certainly included Baltimore—yet this fractious militia officer had brazenly seized control, and apparently nothing could be done about it. Logic . . . precedent . . . a quick trip to Washington . . . an ingenious suggestion that he be given an on-the-spot promotion to outrank Smith—Winder had tried everything, and the War Department paid no attention. It was bad enough coping with Armstrong's evasions, but it especially hurt when James Monroe—Winder's good friend—took over and even confirmed Smith's command.

Worse was to follow. When Winder got his formal assignment from Smith on September 5, he found his job was to defend the Ferry Branch of the Patapsco. This backwater was the western anchor of the city's defense line, yet it was to the east that Baltimore's fate would most likely be decided. Clearly he was on the shelf.

"After the candour which I have uniformly evinced to-

ward you," the General wrote Smith on the 6th, "I cannot
for a moment suppose that in the assignment of my command
and station any other motive than that of a just regard to my
rank and other circumstances influenced you, and yet I cannot but believe that in a review of the arrangement you have
made you will be satisfied that it is unjust as relates to my
rank and situation and in derogation from the ordinary principles of military service."

Smith never even answered. Tact was not one of his high
points. By now, in fact, he had thoroughly ruffled the feelings
of three of his generals; and Judge Joseph Nicholson, a leading citizen, pronounced him an outright demagogue. The
commanding general let none of it bother him. On this 6th of
September, in fact, while Winder was pouring out his heart,
Smith was absorbed in his fortifications. Monroe had just sent
him Captain Sam Babcock of the U.S. Army Engineers to
take charge of that specialized area, and the man was full of
ideas: build a new earthwork on Hampstead Hill, big enough
to hold a thousand reserves . . . collect bricks and stones at
various points for barricading the avenues on short notice
. . . occupy the city's new stone cathedral—ideal for a last,
desperate stand.

But where was the enemy against whom these desperate
measures were contemplated? Along with his other precautions, Sam Smith had stationed lookouts along the Chesapeake, but they had little to report. From the Goodwin house
near the tip of North Point, day after day Major Josiah
Green sent back a laconic "There is nothing of the enemy
below." From the dome of the State House at Annapolis,
Major William Barney (the Commodore's son) could only
say, "There is nothing in sight." Occasionally Governor
Winder himself would clamber up the creaking ladder and
take a turn with the glass. But the eyes of the statesman were

no sharper than any others in catching a sign of the next British move.

All thoughts were on Rhode Island as the advance units of the British fleet lay at anchor about ten miles southeast of the Potomac on the morning of September 6. They were waiting here for Captain Gordon's squadron to emerge from the river, but no one anticipated any change in plans. Admiral Cochrane in the *Tonnant* remained convinced that the "sickly season" ruled out for the moment any further operations in the Chesapeake; General Ross had been persuaded; Lieutenant Evans, having tried in vain for Baltimore, was holding his tongue; and Admiral Cockburn was glumly preparing to hand over his Bay command to Captain Hardy in the *Ramilles*. To Cockburn it must have been some consolation that he himself was taking the prize tobacco to Bermuda, where he could personally deal with the prize agent.

Thirty-five miles north, Admiral Poultney Malcolm was just leaving the Patuxent with the troop convoy. It had taken an extra day to water and provision the crowded transports; but now all was ready, and at 8:30 A.M. the *Royal Oak* got under way. With the rest of the convoy wallowing astern, she made the difficult turn by Solomon's Island, crept into the Bay, and swung south after the rest of the fleet.

But it was slow going. After several hours Malcolm was still only three miles off Cedar Point when the lookouts sighted a sail bearing down from the north. It proved to be a small American sloop flying a flag of truce, and at 1:20 P.M. the *Royal Oak* headed into the wind to receive the stranger. She eased alongside, and two men in civilian clothes scrambled aboard the warship.

One of them was well known to the British, although Malcolm had personally never met him. This was John S. Skinner, the American prisoner-of-war exchange agent, who often visited the fleet. He was an enterprising young politician from Baltimore with a bluff, casual manner that appealed to Admiral Cockburn. More fastidious acquaintances like John Quincy Adams found him a little hard to take. "Ruffian, patriot and philanthropist are so blended in him," Adams observed, "that I cannot appreaciate him without a mingled sentiment of detestation and esteem."

The other visitor was Francis Scott Key, the charming Georgetown lawyer whose tactical suggestions had added to the chaos of Bladensburg. Both he and Skinner were on an official mission to win the release of Dr. William Beanes, the elderly physician from Upper Marlboro who had been seized by the British for his part in jailing Ross's stragglers.

Dr. Beanes was well connected, and his friends had gone right to work. On August 30 James Monroe and General Mason, the Commissary General of Prisoners, were approached through Dr. Thornton. The interview was encouraging, but nothing happened. On the 31st Maryland's Governor Winder wrote Ross a strong letter on the doctor's behalf. Beanes's neighbor and patient, Richard West, rushed it to British headquarters, but Ross remained unmoved. September 1, West headed for Washington to try a new tack. Deciding a knowledgeable government lawyer might be the answer, he called on his wife's brother-in-law—Francis Scott Key.

Key went to the President, requesting permission to visit the British fleet under a flag of truce and negotiate for the doctor's release. Madison approved the project and passed him on to General Mason. The General dashed off a note to Skinner in Baltimore, alerting him to get a flag-of-truce boat ready for the trip down the Bay. On the 2nd Mason formally appointed Key and Skinner to undertake the mission jointly —Key knew the case and Skinner knew the British.

Mason next armed his two emissaries with a strong letter to Ross setting forth the American government's grounds for demanding Beanes's release. The doctor was a 65-year-old noncombatant, "taken from his bed, in the midst of his family and hurried off almost without clothes." Seizing him this way was a "departure from the known usages of civilized warfare."

Key and Skinner were also given a letter of instructions covering certain contingencies. It was expected that the British would argue that Beanes had given Ross at least a tacit pledge to refrain from any hostile act; that he had broken this pledge when he jailed the stragglers; that he thereby forfeited any claim to noncombatant status. The American answer: Once Ross had withdrawn from the area, Beanes was relieved of any pledge he might have given. Finally, if the British still refused to release the doctor as a noncombatant, Key and Skinner were authorized as a last resort to give a receipt for him—as in the case of an exchanged prisoner of war— together with a complete statement of the American position.

The administration's deep concern with Dr. Beanes's fate was more than altruistic . . . more than a matter of legal principle. At this time prisoners of war were customarily exchanged, with regular books kept on each side's "debit" and "credit" balance. If Washington conceded that the doctor was just another prisoner, Mason feared "it would at once induce the enemy to seize and carry off every unarmed citizen of whatever age they have in their power."

With everything set, Key hurried back to Georgetown; packed a few things; sent a reassuring note to his mother; and arranged for his wife and children to stay with his family in Frederick while he was gone. Meanwhile Mason notified Colonel Thornton, senior officer of the British wounded still in Washington, that a flag of truce would be going down the

Bay, and he offered to forward "any open letters that you or any of the prisoners may choose to send to the British army." The men gratefully scribbled away and soon had a bulging packet ready.

Early September 3, Francis Scott Key was on his way. First, a stop at Mason's office to pick up the pouch . . . then to Carroll Row for the British letters . . . then on north to Baltimore. He arrived on the morning of September 4, somehow located Skinner, and handed him Mason's instructions along with the packet of letters.

Monday, September 5, and they were off. Boarding Benjamin and John Ferguson's packet—name unknown—they glided out of the Basin . . . past the star-shaped Fort McHenry on the right . . . down the broad, shallow Patapsco . . . and into the Chesapeake. To Skinner, the whole business shouldn't take very long. He was pessimistic about rescuing Beanes, but whatever happened, they should find Cochrane and Ross off the Patuxent . . . make their pitch . . . and be back in Baltimore in a couple of days.

As expected, they sighted the first British sails shortly after noon on the 6th, but from that point on nothing went according to calculations. Boarding the *Royal Oak*, Skinner and Key quickly learned from Admiral Malcolm that this was only the troop convoy. The main part of the fleet— including Cochrane, Ross, and of course Dr. Beanes—was much farther south off Tangier Island. Malcolm, however, sent their letters ahead by dispatch boat and assigned the frigate *Hebrus* to escort the sloop for the rest of the trip down the Bay.

Continuing south on the morning of September 7, the two vessels finally sighted Cochrane around noon—not loafing off Tangier, as everyone supposed, but beating hard up the Chesapeake. The ships quickly closed, and at 2:10 P.M. the

Tonnant's anchor chains clattered down. Soon a small boat rowed over from the flagship and brought back the two Americans—just in time to dine with the Commander-in-Chief.

The meal began with elaborate courtesy. Skinner found himself seated on Cochrane's right; Key on the right of Captain of the Fleet Codrington, who had just been promoted to rear admiral. There were, however, few introductions, and it was some time before Skinner realized that the quiet, plainly dressed officer on his right was none other than General Ross, the man they had come to see.

But all was small talk at the table. Then as the wine flowed freely, Codrington began ranting about David Porter—clearly the American he detested the most. Skinner took it for a while, then answered with a few hot words of his own. Ross, always the perfect gentleman, saved the day by inviting Skinner to Admiral Cochrane's cabin, where they could discuss their mutual concerns. They retired, leaving the far more diplomatic Key still at the table.

Ross opened the discussion, and it was immediately clear that he had already digested not only Mason's appeal on behalf of Dr. Beanes but also the mail from the wounded British prisoners. They had weighed heavily on his conscience—should he really have left them?—now it was an enormous relief to know they were getting the best care and attention. "All that has been said on that point by the Commissary General of Prisoners in his letter to me has been confirmed by their own letters; and I wish you therefore to say to him and to the friends of Dr. Beanes that on that account, and not from any opinion of his own merit, he shall be released to return with you."

It was as simple as that. The job was done before the legal arguments could be trotted out . . . before the play on sym-

pathy could be made . . . before Key's tact and persuasive-
ness could even be tested. And it was clear that none of these
weapons would have worked had it not been for those grateful British prisoners. Ross, normally the most humane of warriors, had nothing but contempt for the old doctor; Cockburn wanted to send him in chains to Halifax. Beanes himself
received exceptionally harsh treatment for an era when
prominent prisoners of war—especially wealthy ones—
were handled with courtly consideration. He was kept shut
up in the forecastle, scorned and ignored by the whole crew.

Ross officially conveyed his own strong feelings in a letter
he now wrote to Mason. Again, he had nothing good to say
about Beanes; he just wanted to return a kindness: "I shall accordingly give directions for his release. . . ."

But not yet. In a sudden change of strategy, Admiral
Cochrane had dropped his plan of going to Rhode Island and
decided to hit Baltimore instead. To protect the secrecy of
the operation, he certainly couldn't release Beanes, or let Key
and Skinner go, until the attack was over.

Perfectly understandable. But what prompted the change
remains a mystery. Most probably it was intelligence gathered by the *Menelaus*, just back the previous evening from
her foray up the Chesapeake. Despite Sir Peter Parker's
death, a great deal had been accomplished. Off Baltimore,
Parker had even taken the tender *Jane* all the way up the Patapsco, sounding the channel and examining the forts that
guarded the harbor. "I captured a boat laden with fruit close
to the forts," he proudly wrote Cochrane the day he died,
"and a boat which came to us from the harbor with an officer
in her, mistaking us for a friend, only escaped by a momen-
tary calm between the lands."

Good ammunition for a forceful officer like Lieutenant de
Lacy Evans, who wanted to go to Baltimore anyhow. Armed

with new arguments that the attack would be easy, it's likely he went to work on Ross . . . and certain that Ross went to work on Cochrane. The Admiral remained dubious but finally agreed.

The decision was reached early on September 7. Until then the *Tonnant* still lay off Tangier, and all orders reflected the original plan. But at 10:30 A.M. the squadron suddenly weighed anchor and began heading north. Orders went out to the *Asia*, guarding the Capes, to hurry and join up. Other orders went to Cockburn, just starting his passage to Bermuda: forget that and rejoin the fleet. Fortunately he had only gone eight or ten miles, and by 12:10 P.M. was back in signaling distance. An urgent message from the *Tonnant* greeted him: "Signify how many marines you can land; examine all seamen, then report how many are used to small arms."

This was more than a matter of planning for Baltimore. Word arrived from the shore about this time that Captain Gordon's squadron was in trouble coming down the Potomac. The Americans were building batteries along the bluffs, trying to trap him there. It might be necessary to go up the river and blast him loose.

For a while Cochrane hovered off Smith Point, apparently hoping for better news, but by midafternoon he decided he could wait no longer. All thoughts of Baltimore were shoved aside, and at 4:00 P.M. the fleet weighed anchor and headed directly for the Potomac.

It must have been some time during this hectic afternoon that Cochrane took a moment to apologize to Key and Skinner for his lack of hospitality. He regretted, the Admiral said, that he couldn't put them up on the *Tonnant* during their stay, but she was so crowded with staff officers that there just wasn't any room. He invited them instead to move to the frigate *Surprize*. She was commanded by his son Sir Thomas Cochrane, and he was sure they'd be perfectly comfortable. The unexpected guests gratefully accepted.

September 8, the British fleet streamed into the Potomac, with the *Surprize* now towing the flag-of-truce sloop. General Ross came aboard the *Albion* to coordinate with Cockburn any landing they might have to make. Long after dark they kept going—to the amazement of the Americans peeking from the shore. The local traders found it hard enough to navigate these tricky waters even in broad daylight.

By dawn on the 9th Cochrane's ships were 20 miles upstream, still inching ahead. Then at 6:30 A.M. they finally saw what they came for. There, standing down the river toward them, was a cluster of sails. It was, of course, Captain Gordon and his squadron. They had safely run the gauntlet and were now home free with their 21 prizes.

So it was back down the Potomac and on to Baltimore. At 5:40 P.M. the last of the fleet cleared the river and started up the Bay, and by 10:00 they were all off the Patuxent again. It seemed a good omen when Admiral Cochrane picked the mouth of this friendly river, which had served them so well in the past, as an appropriate place to stop for the night.

Dawn, September 10, and they were on their way again —stud sails set and under a full press of canvas. Yet it was one of those lazy days that sometimes mark a busy campaign, and nobody did very much. On the *Brune* the men cut up 20 hammocks to make into haversacks for the sailors assigned to the army. On the *Golden Fleece* Lieutenant Gleig amused himself watching the excitement that erupted along the shore at the sight of His Majesty's ships.

The whole countryside was in an uproar. Everywhere lookouts were lighting signal fires . . . home guard units were firing off alarm guns . . . horsemen were frantically galloping back and forth. When the fleet passed Annapolis around 7:00 P.M., the scene was especially chaotic. People flew from their houses; wagons top-heavy with furniture jammed every road that led out of town.

Annapolis was sure its turn had come. The city had no decent defenses and wanted only to save itself. Resistance was "useless," declared Judge Jeremiah T. Chase, chairman of the Committee of Safety . . . "an act of extreme folly and temerity," said Jonathan Gossaway, the state Adjutant General. Governor Winder himself more or less wrote the place off. For most, the main concern was to keep Lieutenant H. A. Fay, commanding the local detachment of 42 regulars, from doing something foolish . . . like firing back at the British. Now, as those enemy sails came pouring over the horizon, the citizens naturally fled.

But the British didn't even pause at Annapolis. Instead, they skimmed right by and continued on up the Bay. All afternoon Major Barney counted them from his perch atop the State House dome, oblivious to the panic in the streets below. From time to time he sent expresses to Baltimore, filling in Sam Smith on his latest calculations: 12:00 noon, 6 or 7 sail below Plum Point . . . 1:30 P.M., 12 ships in sight . . . 4:00, he could now see 31—"they get along rapidly, studding sails out on both sides." By 9:00 it was too dark to count, but he sent along a final message from his man at Chew's Farm 15 miles below: as of 8 o'clock there were 50 ships altogether, all heading north under a full press of canvas.

Baltimore was ready. By September 10 Sam Smith had 16,391 men packed into a network of land and water defenses covering the eastern and southern approaches to the city. From the Bel Air Road northeast of town a line of earthworks curved south past the hospital . . . along the brow of Hampstead Hill . . . and down to the Sugar House at the edge of the harbor. Over-all, the line boasted 62 guns supported by over 10,000 troops. Most of them were militia—but not all. Several hundred tough navy gunners manned the crucial segment that faced the road coming in from North Point. In honor of the Commodore, this section was appropriately named "Rodgers' Bastion."

At the harbor Sam Smith's problem was complicated by the nature of local geography. Lying 12 miles up the Patapsco River from the Chesapeake Bay, Baltimore could be reached by the lighter British warships. Approaching the city, moreover, the river split at Whetstone Point into two branches, and both had to be considered in planning defense. The right-hand fork, coming in from the Bay, was called the Northwest Branch, and it led straight to the main waterfront. The other fork—the Ferry Branch—curved off to the west, but at Ridgely's Cove it still came within a mile of town.

Sam Smith began by sealing off the Northwest Branch at its mouth. There was already a boom here, running from a projection called the Lazaretto to Whetstone Point, but it looked flimsy, so Smith backed it up with a line of barges, bristling with cannon. At the Lazaretto itself he had a three-gun battery manned by some of Barney's flotillamen.

At Whetstone Point, the other anchor of the barrier, Smith could count on the only permanent fixture in the whole defense system: picturesque, star-shaped Fort McHenry. Largely built between 1798 and 1800, the fort—along with its system of outworks—was there to defend both the Northwest Branch to the east and the Ferry Branch to the west. Its red-brick masonry had a sturdy, spunky look that endeared itself to Baltimoreans, but how good it really was, nobody knew.

Sam Smith was taking no chances. Fortunately, he had a

good head start, for during the scare of 1813 he had greatly strengthened the place. Among other things, he had improved the "water batteries" close to the river, built a furnace for heating shot, and installed 15 36-pounders from the *L'Eole*, a French warship stranded in the port. Now he extended the harbor boom around the tip of Whetstone Point and beefed up Major Armistead's 250-man garrison with hundreds of regulars, flotillamen, Sea Fencibles, militiamen and Judge Nicholson's Artillery Fencibles. These last were a company of gentlemen volunteers who had their own hot coffee specially brought out from the city every morning. By September 10 at least 57 guns and about 1,000 men were crammed into the little fort.

Even so, it was just possible that the British might break into the Ferry Branch west of Fort McHenry and enter the city from Ridgely's Cove. To forestall this, Sam Smith counted on two small works that backed up the main fort and lay a mile or so to the west. At the first, an earthwork ambitiously christened Fort Babcock, he put six guns with Sailing Master Webster and 52 flotillamen. The second, a somewhat stronger position called Fort Covington, was entrusted to a company of Sea Fencibles. If there was time, a boom would be laid across the Ferry Branch too, but this was a matter of low priority, for in truth, Sam Smith saw comparatively little danger to the west.

General Winder knew it all too well. Vaguely charged with "the defense on the Ferry Branch," the architect of Bladensburg took his assignment as a slap, and every day confirmed his hunch. It turned out that Forts McHenry, Babcock and Covington were all under his command, but not the garrisons that defended them. He commanded the 905 regulars, but 600 of them were out of his reach at Fort McHenry. His Virginia Militia were mostly military leftovers that no one else could use. He had only enough cartridges for twenty rounds per man. He had no artillery, no engineers, no work force. Nothing was more inspiring than the sight of thousands of Baltimoreans trooping out each morning to dig the earthworks to save their town—but none of them came General Winder's way.

His complaints to Smith went unanswered; a letter to Monroe protesting the whole command setup got sympathy but no action. There was much to be said for Winder's position, the Secretary conceded, but the fact remained that Smith had taken command at a time when the defense of Baltimore hung in the balance, and any change during the present emergency "might cause some derangement there injurious to the public interest."

When Winder again protested, Monroe lost patience. "There can be but one commander," he answered, and that of course was Smith. "I thought this idea was conveyed in my last. Finding that you do not so understand it, I hasten to correct the mistake and to express my full confidence that you will do everything in your power to promote the success of our arms in defense of our Country."

Slowly, painfully, relentlessly, General Winder finally learned that in war a routed commander rarely gets a second chance.

Sam Smith never gave the matter a thought. His labors went on—so effectively that Baltimore's problem swung from a lack of preparation to a surfeit of confidence. As reports drifted in that the British were down the Bay again, a feeling of lassitude swept the city. The 3rd Brigade dispensed with its morning drills. Captain Brengle's company of Frederick Volunteers, so prompt to the rescue, now asked to go home. General Forman expected his brigade would be discharged by September 13 or 14—"then home with all speed to see my darling wife."

Even stern, conscientious Commodore Rodgers was not

immune. Writing a friend in Philadelphia on the 9th, he observed that Baltimore "now has nothing to fear even should the enemy make his appearance tomorrow. It is understood, however, that he has descended the Bay, and whatever might have been his intentions, that he will not now attempt an attack on this place. . . . I hope to leave here in two or three days for Philadelphia, as I begin to feel tired of playing the soldier."

Perhaps too many others felt the same way—explaining the lack of excitement Saturday night, September 10, when Major Barney's ship-sightings began arriving from Annapolis. General Winder sent a hurry call for cartridge boxes . . . Judge Nicholson's Fencibles, in town for the weekend, hastily reassembled to march back to Fort McHenry . . . but on the whole, Baltimore spent a quiet, uneventful Saturday night.

Sunday the 11th began quietly too. The city rustled with rumors, but nothing really new since last night's dispatches from Annapolis. While Sam Smith and Commodore Rodgers huddled over a scheme to sink block ships in the Northwest Branch, most of Baltimore went to church as usual. At the Wilkes Street Methodist Church, some soldiers stacked their arms outside the door and joined the congregation.

Suddenly, toward 1:30 P.M., the quiet of the Sabbath was shattered by the sound of three shots fired from cannon on the courthouse green. As the Wilkes Street Methodists buzzed with excitement and the troops scrambled for the door, the minister quickly closed his Bible. "My brethren and friends," he announced, "the alarm guns have just fired. The British are approaching and commending you to God and the word of His Grace, I pronounce the benediction, and may the God of battles accompany you."

At the Light Street Methodist Church, the Reverend John Gruber was even more to the point: "May the Lord bless

King George, convert him, and take him to heaven, as we want no more of him."

Outside, it was bedlam. Troops were racing to their positions; wagons bulging with women, children and furniture rattled north on Charles Street, heading out of town. Families of the "poorer sort" (to borrow the phrase of still another Methodist minister, the Reverend James Stevens) fled on foot—some even carrying little children on their backs.

Breasting the stream of refugees, Private Mendes I. Cohen, an 18-year-old recruit in Judge Nicholson's Fencibles, hurried to get back to his post at Fort McHenry. Like the rest of his company, Cohen had come into town the previous evening, but somehow missed the midnight summons to report for duty at once. Now he was trying to make up for lost time, but late as he was, he couldn't help pausing at the observation station on Federal Hill. In the shimmering haze 12 miles down the Patapsco, he could make out the whole British fleet standing into North Point.

This was just the way Sam Smith thought it would be. He was always sure the biggest danger lay to the east . . . in a British landing on the jagged peninsula that jutted into the Bay between the Patapsco and Back rivers, ending at North Point. That was why he had put nobody to the north and only Winder to the west. Now he was clearly right, and he lost no time making his next move. Determined to avoid anything like the four-day game of peekaboo that preceded Bladensburg, he ordered Brigadier General John Stricker to take his 3rd Brigade, totaling some 3,200 men, and head for North Point at once.

Stricker was the natural choice for this assignment. A Revolutionary War veteran slightly younger than Smith, he had occasionally served under the commanding general in militia operations and seemed to be one of the few officers who could get along with the old man. His 3rd Brigade was also well chosen. These troops came from Baltimore, were highly motivated, and included most of the 5th Regiment and Pinkney's riflemen, who were all veterans of Bladensburg. While this was not entirely a recommendation, nevertheless there was something to be said for experience, and the 5th had at least made a brief stand.

Mixed in with the Baltimoreans were three companies of volunteers recently arrived from Pennsylvania and Captain Thomas Quantrill's ardent young blades from Hagerstown, Maryland. Six shiny 4-pounders under Captain John Montgomery perhaps looked more fearsome than they really were.

At 3:00 P.M. the men fell in and headed east on Baltimore Street. Led by fife and drum, they presented the usual mixture of dashing uniforms and civilian dress. They ranged from military dandies like Captain Aaron Levering's Independent Blues, with their stylish red cuffs and white cross-belts, to rank amateurs like Private John Smith of the Union Volunteers. He soon lost his knapsack containing "a swan's-down vest, a pair of nankeen pantaloons, a linen shirt, and striped cravat." Tramping down Baltimore Street, they presented less a picture of martial splendor than one of earnest endeavor. Yet there was something poignant about them too, and as they passed the house of the Reverend John Glendy, he blessed them and prayed for their safety and success.

Moving on to the Philadelphia Road, they continued east . . . past the earthworks on Hampstead Hill . . . past the seamen already manning the guns at "Rodgers' Bastion" . . . and finally turned right into Long Log Lane, a somewhat rambling road that led ultimately to North Point. Three more miles, and at 8:00 P.M. they reached a one-room Methodist meeting house lying at the edge of the road. To their left was a branch of the Back River picturesquely called Bread and Cheese Creek; to their right, a major inlet of the Patapsco called Bear Creek. At this point, the peninsula was less than a mile wide, making it ideal for defense. In fact, with that end in view, Sam Smith had already stocked it with rations for 3,000 men and enough hay for 200 horses.

Here Stricker halted for the night, taking the precaution of posting his riflemen at a blacksmith's shop two miles farther down the road and his cavalry still another mile ahead at Robert Gorsuch's farmhouse. The men lay down to sleep, but it was a restless night for the clerks and young blades who made up most of the brigade. North Point and the British fleet lay only seven miles away; a man couldn't help wondering what the morning would bring.

It was a restless night at Baltimore too. By sunset the lookouts on Federal Hill had counted 47 to 50 British sail, including ten transports "all within the bar." On Calvert Street, Postmaster Burrall once again made ready to move the mails—this time to Ellicott Mills, ten miles west of town. At his new museum on Holiday Street, Rembrandt Peale bedded down his wife and eight children. Others could flee, but he had staked his fortune on this place, and he hoped his family might give it residential status in case the British sacked the city.

On Hampstead Hill 10,000 men fretted behind the earthworks, now at last completed. At Fort Covington Lieutenant Newcomb and 80 sailors took over from the Sea Fencibles, now worn out by fever. In the Northwest Branch Lieutenant Charles Ridgely, acting skipper of the sloop of war *Erie*, lined her up with the gun barges blocking the channel, cleared her decks, and loaded her guns on the side facing downstream. At the Lazaretto, Lieutenant Solomon Rutter went over the night signals he had just worked out with Major Armistead at Fort McHenry: "Enemy in sight or approaching—one gun, one false fire, one blue light, repeated until answered."

Armistead himself was worn to the bone. Professionally, there was the loneliness of command—he and apparently he alone knew that Fort McHenry's magazine was not bomb-proof. Personally, there was an aching concern for his wife Louisa. He had sent her off to safety at Gettysburg, but she was expecting a baby and he continued to worry. Friday night he dreamed she had presented him with a son; tonight there was no time to dream, or even to sleep.

Eight miles down the river from Fort McHenry Lieu-tenant Gleig of His Majesty's 85th Foot was spending an equally sleepless night aboard the transport *Golden Fleece*. It was often that way the night before battle, and Gleig listened enviously to the heavy breathing of his more hardened com-rades lying asleep beside him. He tried every trick he knew —he must have counted to 10,000—nothing did any good. In the end he gave up and paced the deck, from time to time studying the dim outline of the Maryland shore. He lis-tened to the tide washing against the side of the ship, and at midnight to the clang of a dozen ships' bells echoing across the water.

Nearby on the sloop *Fairy* General Ross and Admiral Cockburn were putting the final touches on their landing plan. They had transferred from the *Albion*, so as to get far-ther up the Patapsco and closer to the shore. Now everything was set, although not quite the way Cockburn had hoped. He wanted to lead the barges and cutters up the Patapsco and storm Fort McHenry—rather like the assault on Barney in the Patuxent—but he had been overruled in favor of a two-pronged attack instead. Now the troops would go ashore at North Point and advance up the peninsula to assail Balti-more by land, while the bomb vessels and frigates would ad-vance up the river to strike the city by water.

Once taken, there would be no mercy. A new letter had arrived from Governor Prevost in Canada, telling of fresh atrocities by the Americans, and Admiral Cochrane was determined to retaliate on Baltimore. As he always said, you had to treat these people like spaniels. The troops were appropriately equipped for serious business. The ammunition allotment was increased from 60 to 80 rounds per man, and all frills were to be left behind. Lieutenant Gleig—always the officer and gentleman—resigned himself to sharing a hairbrush with another man.

Quite aware of these harsh plans, John Skinner and Francis Scott Key waited out the night, back on their own flag-of-truce boat. They had been transferred to her during the day —either because, as Key later recalled, Cochrane needed the *Surprize* himself as a shallow-draft flagship; or because, as Skinner told it, he had demanded that they suffer through the attack at least on a vessel flying their own colors. In any event, they weren't yet free to leave. When Skinner had broached this possibility during the afternoon, Cochrane had simply smiled and said, "Ah, Mr. Skinner, after discussing so freely our preparation and plans, you could hardly expect us to let you go on shore in advance of us."

They had, nevertheless, achieved one thing. They persuaded General Ross to release Dr. Beanes from confinement. The old gentleman immediately joined them, and now the three Americans wondered and waited together—still the unwilling guests of this hostile armada lying quietly under the stars.

At 2:00 A.M. on the 12th the silent ships came suddenly to life. A gun brig moved close inshore, prepared to rake the beach if any Americans appeared. Barges and cutters swarmed around the transports, taking off the troops and then rendezvousing near the *Fairy*, where the commanders were still in conference. At 3:00 A.M. the whole collection of small craft began moving toward the shore, and in little more than half an hour a thousand men were landed. At 6:30 the columns formed, ready for marching. The general order was much the same as on the march to Washington, with a few variations. For one thing, they now had eight guns drawn by teams of horses. For another, this time there was an extra brigade of seamen and marines, drawn from the whole fleet. It boasted some 600 men and more than made up for the casualties and desertions suffered during the Washington campaign. There were other minor changes, but the command remained the same. Leading them all was General Ross, and by his side was the gusty, rambunctious figure of Admiral Cockburn. At 7:00 A.M. the bugles sounded, and the British force—now 4,700 strong—started for Baltimore.

CHAPTER TEN

North Point

General Stricker wondered where the British could be. At first an early action seemed so certain—at 7:00 A.M. his cavalry had reported the enemy landing in force . . . at 7:30, that they were already approaching Robert Gorsuch's farm only three miles away. As his scouts retired, Stricker quickly sent back his baggage and ordered his troops up to a line he had carefully picked out.

Here he protected the junction of the only two roads leading out from Baltimore. On his right was Bear Creek, on his left a marsh bordering on Bread and Cheese Creek. Behind him was a wood offering good cover in case of emergency; ahead a strong timber fence and an open field of fire. Deploying his force, Stricker posted the 5th Regiment on the right, the 27th on the left, his six guns in the middle, across the single road that continued on to North Point. Then he established two lines of reserves to the rear—and began waiting.

One hour . . . two hours ticked by, and still no British came. The soldiers marked time as best they could, but there was a good deal of grumbling. Although Sam Smith had provided rations, in a rare oversight he forgot the cooking equipment. Stricker scribbled an urgent note to headquarters—send pots and camp kettles as soon as possible.

Then another irritation. Along with the cavalry, Stricker had sent his riflemen forward to harass the British whenever they appeared. But it was a nervous morning for them too, and at some point the rumor spread that they had been flanked. They came tumbling back to the main line, and now it seemed too late to reorganize and send them out again. Resigned to the ways of militia, the General put them on his right wing and continued waiting.

Around 11:00 a new report threw a little more light on the delay. A scout said the British advance had stopped at the Gorsuch farm and were "feasting and frying." Unable to fathom any military reason for such behavior, Stricker chalked it up to an Englishman's arrogance. But when Captain Aaron Levering offered to lead his Independent Blues to punish the enemy, the General swallowed his pride and decided to continue waiting.

Noon, and he changed his mind. The thought now occurred that maybe the British were purposely holding off, planning a bayonet charge after dark. The militia were notoriously unreliable at night, and squeamish any time about bayonets. Rather than risk this sort of engagement, Stricker decided to provoke a fight now.

Everyone volunteered to go. In the end Stricker built his force around Captain Levering's Blues and Captain Benjamin Howard's Mechanical Volunteers, two of the 5th Regiment's best companies. To this nucleus he added 80 riflemen under Captain Edward Aisquith, a handful of cavalry and a single gun. With Major Richard Heath in over-all command, this grab-bag of soldiers—totaling 250 men altogether—moved out at 1:00 P.M. and headed down the road toward North Point.

For half a mile nothing happened . . . then suddenly a shot from somewhere ahead. All caution now, Captain Levering and his Blues edged on a few yards, then came to a rise that looked out over a stretch of open ground. Across the way they could see three men—one with a spyglass— watching them. The American muskets and rifles exploded in a volley of fire, and when the smoke cleared away, the men were gone.

To Admiral Cockburn, this sudden blast of American gun- fire proved the point he had been trying to make to General Ross: their advance guard of 50 to 60 men was too far ahead of the main force. Now there was nothing left to do but put on a brave front and stand the enemy off until more troops arrived.

Up to this point the morning had been a picnic. Pushing ahead from North Point, the British advance burned the Todd house . . . carved a Union Jack over the mantel of the Lodge family's living room . . . and enjoyed a leisurely breakfast at the Gorsuch farm. For this they had plenty of time, because already the men were getting strung out and it seemed a good idea to consolidate.

While Ross and Cockburn were still enjoying Mr. Gor- such's eggs and country butter, three captured dragoons were brought in and briefly questioned. How many troops were defending Baltimore? About 20,000, the prisoners answered with loyal exaggeration. "But," asked Ross, "they are mainly militia, I presume?" Yes, the dragoons conceded, that was so. Relieved, the General observed that he didn't care "if it rains militia."

As the British officers stood up to go, Mr. Gorsuch somewhat deferentially asked if he should prepare supper for their return. "No," smiled Ross, "I'll eat in Baltimore tonight—or in hell."

Starting down the road again, the advance guard once more drew ahead of the light companies, and it was at this point that Admiral Cockburn warned Ross that they were really much too far ahead of the rest of the force. This wasn't the way it was done in Virginia, where the troops were always kept well collected. Ross knew all that—this wasn't the way it was done going to Washington either—but Major Brown, who led the advance guard there, had been wounded at Bladensburg; the officers who now led the advance guard were inexperienced. But Cockburn had a point, and the General was just about to call a halt when those American guns opened up.

Happily, the British return fire quickly discouraged the militia. They faded back into the woods, and the action simmered down to occasional, ragged shooting. Seizing the first lull, Ross told Cockburn that he himself would go and hurry on the light companies. Starting back along the road he had just come, the General was riding all alone when a final American volley rang out. A bullet pierced his right arm and buried itself in his chest. Staggered by the blow, he toppled off his horse.

No one knows how many minutes passed before the light companies appeared, hurried along by the sound of firing ahead, to find their leader lying alone in the dust. But when the first man reached him, Ross was still quite conscious and managed to gasp, "Send immediately for Colonel Brooke."

Colonel Arthur Brooke, commanding the 44th Foot and second-ranking officer in the entire army, was soon at Ross's side—as were Cockburn, Captain Duncan MacDougall and other staff officers. A mile or so to the rear Lieutenant Gleig was marching along with the 85th Foot, when MacDougall came galloping back shouting for a doctor. Gleig sensed something dreadful had happened, and his worst fears were confirmed when his company reached the spot a few minutes later. The troops marched silently by, pretending not to notice.

Ross sensed the effect on his men, and asked to be covered with a blanket. He was gently dissuaded—by now it was far too late to hide the truth. The surgeon began binding his wounds, but the General felt it was useless. Pulling a locket from his tunic, he handed it to Cockburn: "Give this to my dear wife, and tell her I commend her to my King and country."

Someone commandeered a passing rocket wagon to carry him back to the fleet, but Ross declined to use it. Faintly he said he wouldn't deprive his men of a weapon so important to their success. Then a cart from George Stansbury's farm was found, and he was carefully placed in that.

At last the cart started off with Ross's aide, Lieutenant Haymes, in attendance. As it bumped and jolted along the road, the General suffered terribly and finally lapsed into a coma. Seeing the end was near, Haymes stopped, and they rested beside a tree. Once Ross came to long enough to murmur, "My dear wife." When they finally reached the beach, he was quite dead and had been wrapped in the Union Jack.

The shooting of General Ross produced no cry of triumph from Major Heath's hard-pressed men—they didn't know they had done it. Later Captain Aisquith's riflemen, the Independent Blues and the Mechanical Volunteers would each claim the credit. They would tell how Captain Levering of the Blues pointed out the target to his men . . . how the Mechanical Volunteers saw and fired first . . . how Aisquith's sharpshooters reminded one another, "Remember, boys, General Ross rides a white horse today." (Actually, the General's horse was black.) The arguments would rage for years, but at the time, Major Heath and his men knew only that they had accomplished their mission. They had been sent to pick a fight, and they got one.

But they had casualties too in this brief encounter. Privates Daniel Wells and Harry McComas had been apprentices together in the saddlery business; they enlisted together in Aisquith's Rifles; now they fell together near the same peach tree. Lieutenant Gregorius Andre tried to take a last shot from the top of a fence; next instant he too was dead. Sergeant Alexander Mackenzie also went down, but he was luckier. Dr. Sam Martin scooped him up across his saddle and galloped to safety.

The troops on the main line rested their muskets along the fence, knowing their turn was next. They didn't have long to wait: around 2:30 P.M. the first rockets began whizzing by. The militia crouched low, but this time they didn't run. By now they had heard all about these weird contrivances, and everyone said they were really quite harmless. Still, even the officers looked a little uncertain when faced with the real thing, and the men got their greatest reassurance when their own 4-pounders answered with a roar of defiance.

The British opened up with their guns too, and for a while the infantrymen on both sides relaxed and watched the artillerymen show off their wares. They accomplished very little beyond digging up dirt and sending a shower of branches cascading down upon the troops. Finally, a British rocket fell short, set fire to a haystack, and the blaze soon spread to the nearby Boulden family farm. Then another fire broke out in a small log house lying directly in front of the American position. Between the smoke from the fires and from the can-

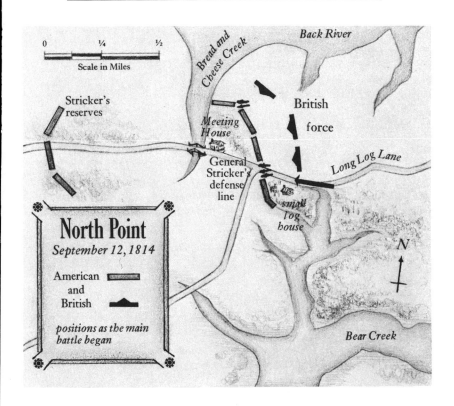

North Point
September 12, 1814

American
and
British

positions as the main
battle began

Scale in Miles

0   ¼   ½

Stricker's reserves

Bread and Cheese Creek

Meeting House

General Stricker's defense line

small log house

Back River

British force

Long Log Lane

Bear Creek

N

non, it was hard to see what was going on.

But Stricker did notice that most of the British firing was concentrated on his left. Anticipating an attack there, he began strengthening that side of his position. Calling up his second line, he put the 39th Regiment to the left of the 27th . . . then two of his guns still farther to the left . . . then the 51st all the way on the flank, but at right angles to the rest of the line. Presumably this was to cover a turning movement, but there were those who felt it was a waste of firepower to put these men at right angles to the enemy. Worse at the mo-

ment, the maneuver caused a great deal of countermarching
and confusion among the green troops of the 51st.

A somewhat puzzled Lieutenant Gleig watched the Americans marching back and forth perhaps 600 yards away. It
struck him as an enormous waste of effort, and it amused him
to see the militiamen dodge past any spot where a British cannon ball had hit. They seemed to feel if one had landed there,
another was sure to be on the way.

In contrast, the British professionals were smoothly moving
into position with no fuss or commotion. The 85th Foot and
the other light infantry spread out along the entire front,
backed by the 44th Foot and the brigade of seamen. The 21st
stood in column on the main road. The 4th tramped through
a hollow toward the extreme right. The army's new commander, Colonel Brooke, planned a surprise blow on the
American left—just as Stricker expected. As the 4th picked
its way slowly to the flank, the rest of the troops marked
time—the 21st dodging occasional cannon balls on the road
. . . the 85th lying in the grass . . . the seamen munching
biscuits from their haversacks.

By 2:45 all was nearly ready; Colonel Brooke and Admiral
Cockburn rode the full length of the line on a last-minute
inspection. The Admiral proved a conspicuous target in his
gold-laced hat, and the American guns seemed to follow him
the whole way. "Look out, lads," muttered a sailor. "Here's
the Admiral coming—you'll have it directly."

About 3:00 Brooke gave the signal . . . the orderly bugler
sounded the charge . . . the other bugles took it up all along
the line. The troops moved silently forward, and for a moment all was quiet with the Americans too. Then a crash of
artillery, and the Yankee version of grape came screaming
across the meadow: old locks, horseshoes, nails, bits of bro-

ken muskets, anything that could be crammed into a gun.

The British troops began falling, but still they came on, crouching low, sometimes crawling on their hands and knees. To the Americans—raised on tales of redcoats impervious to any kind of fire—this seemed a good omen, but they held their musket fire, and not a voice was raised on either side.

Now the British were less than a hundred yards away. Suddenly a single militiaman impulsively jumped over the fence . . . ran forward a few yards . . . knelt and fired his musket. It seemed to break the trance. With a great yell, the troops behind him began firing too, and in seconds the whole line blazed with musket fire.

The British answered with one of their organized huzzahs and began shooting as they charged—totally contrary to the best European practice. Cochrane later wrote Lord Melville somewhat apologetically that this breach of decorum was necessary because the Americans just wouldn't stand up to an honest bayonet charge.

Oddly enough, the 4th Foot—whose flanking movement was the key to the whole attack—played little part in these dramatics. As so often happens in war, they took much longer than anyone expected to complete their assignment. Now they were just emerging from some thickets on the American left when the rest of the line charged.

It made no difference to Captain Lewis Weaver's frightened militiamen that as yet they had no real opposition. Stationed with the rest of the 51st Regiment on the far left, they felt very much alone. Then came all that firing (the way they were facing, it was behind them), and now that ominous crackling in the bushes on their flank. . . .

They broke and ran. Then the rest of the 51st collapsed

too, and as the men ran across the rear of the American position, they carried part of the 39th Regiment along with them. Long before that clever British flanking movement could even develop, the American left was gone.

The British charge did the rest. For twenty minutes there was a frantic firefight along Stricker's center and right, with the militia grimly hanging on. Above the din, Captain Lowrie Donaldson could be heard shouting to his men to shoot low; then some redcoat aimed low at him, and he too was down. Private Uriah Prosser, an old shoemaker and Revolutionary War veteran, was killed fighting alongside his son. A hundred others fell too, as the whole American line finally gave way.

The British troops swarmed over the timber fence and into the woods, where a dangerous game of hide and seek began. One shrewd Yankee, finally cornered, started arguing for his right to keep a silver dagger, which he claimed as "private property." Another American hiding behind a tree, took a shot at Lieutenant Scott, which only grazed him but brought down William Edmonston, clerk of the frigate *Melpomene*. Then, to everyone's horror, Edmonston was finished off by a saber blow from another British officer, who mistook him for a skulker.

As the Americans streamed back through the woods, General Stricker fought to keep some semblance of order. The last thing he wanted was another Bladensburg, with the troops dispersing and heading for home. Somehow he managed to herd them together behind the 6th Regiment, which lay in reserve nearly a mile to the rear. Here he rallied and re-formed them—just the way the military textbook said to do.

But they were still dead tired; so he finally pulled the whole force all the way back to Worthington's Mill, near the northeast end of Sam Smith's earthworks. Now at last they could be really rested and reorganized.

That was all right with the men. They had been badly mauled—some 163 killed and wounded, another 50 taken prisoner. But they also felt a touch of satisfaction. They had met "Wellington's Invincibles"—fought them at long-range for nearly two hours, face-to-face for 20 minutes. In the end they were beaten, but certainly not disgraced. They brought off all but two of their guns, and here they were, still intact, willing to try again tomorrow.

Admiral Cockburn's aide Lieutenant James Scott was satisfied too—"a second edition of the Bladensburg Races," he called it. But there was one big difference between this and Bladensburg: Colonel Brooke now commanded the army. He was anything but sure of himself . . . his casualties already totaled 300 . . . the day was nearly over. It was all enough to give a man pause—and pause he did. Late afternoon the bugles sounded halt, and the army prepared to camp for the night by the Methodist meeting house, less than half a mile farther along the road to Baltimore.

On the Patapsco Admiral Cochrane was making greater progress in carrying out his part of the two-pronged advance. After landing the last of the troops and supplies at North Point, he shifted his flag to the *Surprize* and at 1:30 P.M. ordered the frigates and bomb vessels to head upstream for Baltimore. As they got under way, Cochrane knew nothing of Ross's death or the change in command, but he could plainly hear the gunfire ashore, and he struggled to get his ships in position to support the advancing army.

It was a back-breaking job. The Patapsco was not only shallow, but full of unexpected shoals, and the squadron had only two or three pilots who knew the water. The *Seahorse* went ahead to feel the way, but she ran aground almost immediately. For nearly four hours she was either stuck or warping slowly through the mud. On the *Severn* Captain Nourse sent his small boats ahead to take soundings. In the ship's launch Midshipman Robert Barrett worked with the stream and kedge anchor until he was literally covered with slime.

At 3:30 the *Surprize* finally anchored at a point about five miles below Fort McHenry. Here she was joined by the *Severn* flying Cockburn's flag, and the other frigates and brigs. The five bomb vessels and the rocket ship *Erebus* continued creeping closer until they anchored only two and a half miles from the fort.

No one knew how the Americans might react, but Cochrane was taking no chances. He ordered every ship to have grapnels ready in case the enemy tried fire vessels, as they had on the Potomac. Torpedoes were always a menace, although the Admiral considered them outlawed by the rules of war. He issued careful instructions on towing them clear of endangered craft. Sets of passwords and countersigns were distributed for use in the night.

Sweeping his glass along the shoreline, Cochrane discovered one defense measure he didn't know how to counter. The Americans were busy sinking block ships across the mouth of the Northwest Branch. These would effectively keep him from storming the inner harbor, either to bombard the town or to carry off the prize goods he thought about so much. There was no alternative but to capture Fort McHenry first.

Examining the earthworks on Hampstead Hill, Cochrane felt more encouraged. The defense line swarmed with people and ran right to the water's edge, but it didn't seem to extend very far back into the country. "I think it may be completely turned without the necessity of taking it in front," he wrote that afternoon in a letter addressed to General Ross. He also took the opportunity to outline his own plans: "At daylight

we shall place the Bombs and barges to bombard the fort.
You will find them over upon the eastern shore, as the enemy
have forts upon the western side which it is not necessary to
encounter."

At 7:30 P.M. the letter was returned unopened with the
shattering news that Ross was dead.

Cochrane immediately forwarded it to Colonel Brooke,
adding some observations that he thought might be useful to
the army's new leader. His main concern was that Brooke
might be too easy on Baltimore. Ross had been so soft at
Washington—all that nonsense about respecting private
property—this new man must be set straight right away:

> It is proper for me to mention to you that a system of retal-
> iation was to be proceeded upon in consequence of the bar-
> barities committed in Canada—and if General Ross had
> seen the second letter from Sir George Prevost he would
> have destroyed Washington and Georgetown. Their nature
> are perfectly known to Rear Admiral Cockburn and I be-
> lieve Mr. Evans. In them a kind of latitude is given for rais-
> ing contributions instead of destruction, but in this, public
> property cannot be compromised.

So there would be no leniency this time. "I do not like to
contemplate scenes of blood and destruction," the normally
placid Admiral Codrington wrote his wife that evening, "but
my heart is deeply interested in the coercion of these Baltimore heroes, who are perhaps the most inveterate against us
of all the Yankees, and I hope they will be chastized even
until they excite my pity, by which time they will be suffi-
ciently humbled."

Baltimore sensed its crisis was at hand. The day began in
ominous silence—"As yet all is hush; we have no clue to

the enemy's plans of operation," General Forman confessed in a quick note to his wife. But around 10:00 news spread of the British landings . . . by 1:30 P.M. the guns could be heard on North Point . . . and by 2:00 the British squadron could be seen crawling up the Patapsco toward Fort McHenry.

Commander George de la Roche, skipper of the *Erie*, was amazed. It never occurred to him that loaded frigates could get up the river, but he had discounted British seamanship. Now his own *Erie* was dangerously exposed, lying among the gun barges blocking the Northwest Branch. Her thin skin could never stand up against the broadsides of a frigate like the *Surprize*. On orders from Commodore Rodgers he hastily moved his ship to a safer berth close to the city.

Then he joined the men sinking the block ships that Rodgers hoped would tighten the barrier across the Northwest Branch. Until now the merchants of Baltimore had not taken kindly to this idea—they couldn't see the logic of sinking their fortunes to save them—but today, with the British on the doorstep, the mood was different. Down went John Donnell's handsome ship *Chesapeake* . . . John Craig's brig *Father and Son* . . . Elie Claggett's schooner *Scudder* . . . 24 vessels altogether. Ultimately the barrier was extended across the Ferry Branch too, although there was no time for that just now. As always, Sam Smith looked to the east; the west could take care of itself.

General Winder knew it all too well. For a whole week he had seen his western command neglected or nibbled away. Now a new order came from Smith to send his cavalry to Colonel Nicholas Ruxton Moore, operating east of the town. Winder of course complied, but sent at the same time a last, despairing note to headquarters: "This has finally robbed my command of its only means of availing itself of favorable opportunities of annoying the enemy. . . . In fine, I am now fairly destitute of every means by which I can render my command honorable to them or myself as essentially useful to the country, unless by mere accident."

As usual, Sam Smith was too busy to answer, nor did anyone else have time to worry about the ruffled feelings of a forgotten general this hectic afternoon. Around 4:00 P.M. word spread that Stricker was beaten—was falling back —and the whole city plunged into a frantic, last-second rush of preparation. Commodore Rodgers pulled Commander de la Roche off the block ships, hurried him to Hampstead Hill, where his skills in naval gunnery could be better used. The Committee of Vigilance and Safety ordered all lights out tonight—no point in giving the British gunners a mark to shoot at. Nervous citizens reread the morning *Telegraph*'s instructions on handling incendiaries. "Should Congreve rockets be thrown into the city," the paper advised its apparently well-heeled readers, "we should recommend to every housekeeper to have a servant ready with buckets filled with water to extinguish the flames."

The gunfire to the east drew closer; the number of British ships hovering off Fort McHenry grew to 16, plus numerous gigs, cutters and barges. Convinced that the final assault was about to begin, General Forman ordered the great ropewalk of Messrs. Calief and Shinnick set afire to keep it from falling into enemy hands. Shortly after 4:00 flames and smoke rolled skyward, consuming the hemp and cordage for the new frigate *Java* and throwing the city into even greater consternation.

At Fort McHenry, Major Armistead studied the ominous line of British ships lying just out of range. The gun ports were open; small craft were clustered along the sides. "From the number of barges and the known situation of the enemy," he wrote Sam Smith at 4:30, "I have not a doubt but that an assault will be made this night upon the Fort."

At the Lazaretto across the channel, Lieutenant Rutter

worried about British trickery. To guard against a surprise blow, he and Armistead quickly worked out a set of challenges for the night. The password would be "William," the answer "Eutaw."

Such precautions were wise and necessary, but at a time like this a man could also use a little inspiration. The defenders of Fort McHenry got theirs from a huge American flag that flew from a pole just inside the parade ground. Measuring 30′ x 42′, it seemed to dominate not only the fort but the outlying strong points and even the defenses on Hampstead Hill. Needless to say, it could also be seen by the newly arrived visitors from Britain.

That was just the way Major Armistead wanted it. During the invasion scare in the summer of 1813 he had written Sam Smith:

> We, Sir, are ready at Fort McHenry to defend Baltimore against invading by the enemy. That is to say, we are ready except that we have no suitable ensign to display over the Star Fort, and it is my desire to have a flag so large that the British will have no difficulty in seeing it from a distance.

He soon got his wish. Some time that summer a committee of three high-ranking officers—General Stricker, Commodore Barney and Colonel William McDonald of the Maryland 6th Regiment—called on Mary Young Pickersgill, a widow who normally specialized in making house flags for Baltimore's far-flung merchant ships. They explained their needs, and Mrs. Pickersgill accepted the order.

Recruiting her 13-year-old daughter Caroline to help, she spent the next several weeks cutting and measuring her bolts of cloth—15 white stars, each two feet from point to point . . . 8 red stripes and 7 white, each two feet across. Altogether she used some 400 yards of bunting.

Then came the job of piecing it together. Even the big upstairs bedroom in the Pickersgill house wasn't large enough,
so on an inspiration she borrowed the use of the malthouse in
Brown's brewery. Here she and Caroline continued working—often by candlelight—sewing and basting the colors
together.

That August the flag was delivered at a cost—meticulously calculated by Mrs. Pickersgill—of exactly $405.90.
For a year it wasn't needed, but this hot, dangerous evening
it blazed in the sunset—not an icon of might and power,
but rather an expression of earnest purpose . . . a mark of
defiance flown by a small, young and not always wise
country about to take its stand against the strongest nation
in the world.

CHAPTER ELEVEN

Fort McHenry

Major Armistead's big flag snapped in a damp, easterly breeze as the British bomb vessel *Volcano* weighed anchor at 5:00 A.M., September 13, and began edging toward Fort McHenry. Close behind came another "bomb," the *Meteor*, and the rocket ship *Erebus*. Also tagging along was the *Cockchafer*, a pugnacious little schooner that always seemed in the middle of things. Later they were joined by three more bombs—the *Terror*, *Devastation* and *Aetna*—while the frigates and sloops moved up to lend support.

At 6:30 the *Volcano* came to, and Captain David Price fired a couple of shots to check the range. Not close enough. The bombs and rocket ship crept on—now less than two miles away—but even before they were in position to fire, the perky *Cockchafer* let loose a broadside at the star-shaped ramparts.

At 7:00 the *Meteor* opened up. Then one by one the other

277

bombs and the *Erebus* joined in, while the *Cockchafer* continued banging away. The guns of the fort roared back, firing erratically but still within range. "The enemy shot falling short and over us," coolly noted the keeper of the *Meteor*'s log.

At 8:40 a cannon ball ripped through the mainsail of the *Cockchafer*, and Admiral Cochrane decided to play it a little safer. Shortly after 9:00 he pulled the squadron back to a point slightly over two miles from the fort. This meant sacrificing the firepower of the frigates and the *Erebus*, but that's why he brought the bombs along.

Compared to the stately frigates and ships of the line, these ungainly vessels weren't much to look at—the *Aetna*, for instance, was a stubby 102 feet long. Nor was service in them fashionable. They fired shells that burst—a bit unsporting, that—and their operation was left largely to the Royal Marine Artillery, who didn't seem to mind. Nevertheless, they were useful and in many ways remarkable ships. Armed principally with two guns—a 10- and a 13-inch mortar—they fired huge bombshells that weighed over 200 pounds and carried up to 4,200 yards.

It took enormous force to do that, and this in turn put enormous strain on the ships every time the mortars were fired. A complicated system of beams and springs tried to cushion the blow, but even so, the jar was terrific. It rattled the crew's teeth, shook loose anything not made fast, and sent the whole ship bucking and plunging like a frightened horse.

When the mortar was fired, that also lit a fuse in the bombshell itself. With luck, it exploded about the time it landed, scattering fragments far and wide. But not often. While every effort was made to cut the fuse to fit the distance, the shells were wildly erratic and quite likely to burst in mid-air.

At Baltimore, however, arithmetic was on Admiral Cochrane's side. A well-handled bomb vessel could hurl 45 to 50 shells an hour, and he had five of them. With all that firepower—and safe from the annoyance of any return fire—the fall of Fort McHenry seemed only a matter of time.

Major George Armistead tried to coax just a little more range out of his guns. He had already increased the elevation as much as he could, but that wasn't enough. Now he loaded them with extra charges of powder—a dangerous experiment, since the barrels could only stand so much. Happily they didn't burst, but three of the guns gave a mighty kick that threw them off their carriages. That could be fixed; the big problem remained. Armistead had tried everything, and the guns of Fort McHenry still couldn't reach the British fleet.

The best the fort could do was 1,800 yards with the 24-pounders and 2,800 yards with the big French 36-pounders. But since the British ships were over two miles out, he was just wasting his shots. At 10:00 A.M. Armistead grimly ordered his guns to cease fire, and the garrison settled down to a long, hard wait.

The gunners crouched by their parapets; the infantry huddled in a dry moat that ran around part of the fort. Trying to make himself small, Judge Nicholson felt that he and his Artillery Fencibles were all "like pigeons tied by the legs to be shot at."

By 9:30 A.M. Admiral Cochrane was feeling discouraged too. He was meant to be helping the army, yet this flashy bombardment had been going on for over two hours, and nothing had been accomplished. The firing was too slow; the shells were too erratic; and above all, the fort was too strong. He now dashed off a pessimistic note to Admiral Cockburn, presumably attacking by land with the troops:

> My Dear Admiral—It is impossible for the ships to render you any assistance—the town is so far retired within the forts. It is for Colonel Brooke to consider under such circumstances whether he has force sufficient to defeat so large a number as it is said the enemy has collected, say 20,000 strong, or even a less number and to take the town. Without this can be done, it will be only throwing the men's lives away and prevent us from going upon other services. At any rate a very considerable loss must ensue and as the enemy is daily gaining strength, his loss let it be ever so great cannot be equally felt. . . .

Thus by midmorning caution was again creeping over Admiral Cochrane. He had given up all idea of supporting Colonel Brooke. He wasn't even sure the army should go through with its attack. But assuming the troops did take the city, the navy must continue battering at the fort, hoping ultimately to open a passage through which he could join Brooke, share the glory, and remove the riches of Baltimore. The five bombs pounded on—11:00 . . . noon . . . 1:00 P.M. . . .

It was just about 2:00 P.M. when a British shell landed squarely on the southwest bastion of Fort McHenry, and exploded with a blinding flash. For a brief second everything was lost in a ball of fire and smoke; then it cleared away, revealing a 24-pounder dismounted and its crew sprawled at odd angles in the dirt.

Several members of Judge Nicholson's Fencibles rushed over—it was one of their guns—but they were too late to help Lieutenant Levi Claggett or Sergeant John Clemm, two of Baltimore's prominent merchants who served in the company. As the dead and wounded were carried off, Private Philip Cohen must have felt lucky indeed. He had been standing right next to Claggett when the shell landed, yet escaped without a scratch.

So many of the garrison seemed to live charmed lives. Captain Henry Thompson dashed through a hail of shrapnel carrying messages to and from Hampstead Hill. Master's Mate Robert Stockton constantly exposed himself as Commodore Rodgers's courier. And every man in the garrison had a horseshoe in his pocket that terrifying moment when a shell finally did crash through the roof of the magazine. It didn't go off . . . just lay there sputtering as some quick-witted hero doused the fuse in time.

This was too close a call for Major Armistead. He ordered the powder barrels cleared out and scattered under the rear walls of the fort. Better risk one or two than see the whole place go up. Private Mendes Cohen of the Fencibles joined the crew rolling out the kegs. It was dangerous work with the shells flying about, and he finally took a moment to rest —by sitting on the end of a full powder barrel.

Actually, there was nothing else to do but trust in luck, and perhaps that was why the men took it as such a good omen when a rooster appeared from nowhere, mounted a parapet, and began to crow. The exhausted troops laughed and cheered, and one man called out that if he lived to see Baltimore again, he'd treat that bird to a poundcake.

Toward 3:00 P.M. Major Armistead suddenly noticed that three of the British bomb vessels had weighed anchor and, together with the rocket ship, were moving toward the fort again. Apparently Admiral Cochrane felt he had softened it up enough—that it could no longer hurt his ships even if they came within range. Now they were closing in for the kill.

That was all right with Armistead. For six hours he had sat taking his punishment, firing only occasionally to reassure Baltimore he was still holding out. But most of his guns were sound and his gunners thirsting for a chance to work off their frustrations. Now they stood at the embrasures aching to go. At the Lazaretto across the Northwest Branch, Lieutenant Rutter stood ready too, as did Lieutenant Solomon Frazier's flotillamen on the gunboats in the channel. The British ships glided closer—two miles . . . a mile and a half. Then with a roar that shook the whole harbor, Armistead let go with everything he had.

The *Devastation* shuddered as a cannon ball plowed into her port bow, springing timbers and starting a leak. Another ripped through her main topsail. The *Volcano* took five straight hits—miraculously, none serious. A gunboat, observing fire 300 yards ahead, caught a freak shot that cut a Royal Colonial Marine in half.

Admiral Cochrane quickly reversed himself. The fort wasn't finished after all. In fact, despite all those bombshells it seemed barely damaged. Signal flags fluttered from the *Surprize*, ordering the squadron to disengage and pull back again out of range.

Farthest in, the rocket ship *Erebus* was slow to respond. Or maybe Captain David Ewen Bartholomew, like Nelson at Copenhagen, just didn't want to see the signal. He was that Royal Navy rarity, an officer up from the ranks—he had even been impressed—and was known to have a stubborn streak. Taking no chances, Cochrane sent a division of small boats with emphatic orders to tow out the *Erebus*.

By now the Admiral felt more frustrated than ever. This long-range shelling was getting him nowhere, but what else was there to do? His frigate captains had an answer to that:

they wanted to run the *Hebrus*, *Severn* and *Havannah* right alongside the fort and blow the place out of the water. No, said Cochrane, that might cost too many men.

He was, in truth, the prisoner of his own policies. There was little point in taking Baltimore unless he could lay his hands on the immense wealth of the city . . . yet there was no way to do that without taking Fort McHenry . . . and no way to do that without risking high losses—the sort that might ruin his plans for the south and the even greater wealth of New Orleans.

He felt the same about Colonel Brooke's attack. Even if the army succeeded in breaking into Baltimore, what good would it do unless the navy also took Fort McHenry and opened a passage for the ships? If Brooke's losses were low, there was much to be said for just burning the city, but if his losses were high, a mere bonfire wouldn't be worth the price.

And right now, it looked as if Brooke were already having problems. A long-delayed letter had arrived from him around 3:30 P.M. Written the previous midnight, it was full of optimism: he planned to advance in the morning, hoped to be in Baltimore "about twelve or one." But it was late afternoon now, and still no sound of his guns, no sign of commotion among the Americans on Hampstead Hill. Something must be holding him up.

Indeed it was, although Colonel Brooke's day had begun on a high note. After a wet night, his troops fell in at dawn in exceptionally good spirits—there was much joking about the military posture of the seamen's brigade—and all looked forward to the plunder of Baltimore. Tramping west, they were for the first time bothered by trees cut down to slow their progress, but the biggest problem was the rain. It was coming down hard now, and the men held their muskets close to their sides, using their elbows to cover the firelocks and keep them dry.

Reaching the Philadelphia Road about 10:00 A.M., they swung left and were now heading straight for Baltimore less than four miles away. Another three-quarters of a mile, and they found themselves on the crest of a hill that looked out toward the city. Their view, however, was blocked by an even higher rise about two miles away. This was, of course, Hampstead Hill, and along its crest they could see thousands of American troops waiting to receive them.

From the second-floor windows of Judge Thomas Kell's house just off the road, Colonel Brooke and Admiral Cockburn studied the American line. There were not only intricate earthworks, but ditches, palisades, and in front of the whole position every tree and house had been removed to provide a perfect field of fire. Brooke estimated there were 15,000 men altogether, and some staff officer counted 120 guns.

Could the position be turned? Cochrane's letter last night suggested the American left was weak, and now Brooke decided to explore this possibility. Toward noon he led the army on a reconnaissance, working his way north and west beyond the end of the earthworks.

To his dismay Brooke discovered the Americans had enough troops not only to man their line but to protect their flank as well. A large enemy force moved into position just where he hoped to go. The Colonel didn't know it, but these were Stricker's troops—the force he had beaten yesterday —ready to take him on again. And along with them, at last released from his western "exile," was General Winder with Douglass's Virginia brigade.

By 1:00 P.M. Brooke was back by the Philadelphia Road. The left end of the enemy line was indeed weak, but he had nowhere near the strength to assault those troops that shadowed him so effectively. Instead, he and Cockburn decided to wait for night. Then the Americans would lose the advantage of their artillery, and the panic-prone militia would be at their worst. At 2:00 A.M. all four brigades would hurl themselves at Hampstead Hill, and British bayonets would do the rest.

But in pulling it off, Brooke wanted the navy's help. If Admiral Cochrane could stage a diversionary attack on the Ferry Branch of the Patapsco—on the other side of Baltimore—it should confuse the Americans and draw off some of their troops. George Cockburn was of course all for it, and Lieutenant Scott was rushed to the fleet with a message outlining the plan and asking Cochrane for the diversion.

Sir Alexander was anything but pleased. At this point he had pretty well written off the whole Baltimore episode, and wanted only to get everybody back on the ships and start planning for New Orleans. Yet the Admiral felt he couldn't flatly order Brooke not to carry out his project. Lord Bathurst's instructions were very clear that the army commander should have the final say once the troops were ashore. Of course no one contemplated that a mere colonel would be in charge, but London was always strict about keeping the lines straight between the two services. The most Cochrane felt he could do was to throw all the weight of his position and rank against this harebrained scheme.

Addressing his answer to Cockburn (which seemed to be the way Sir Alexander preferred to deal with Brooke), he reiterated that the navy could lend no direct support: the block ships kept the fleet out of the harbor, and the town lay too far behind the fort to be bombarded directly. All things considered, he urged Brooke to return to the ships. If he went ahead anyhow and suffered high casualties, he would be responsible for any adverse effect on "ulterior operations."

By 8:00 P.M. Scott was back with the army and the message was in Cockburn's hands. The Admiral had been through all this before. It was the same as Washington, when

Cochrane had tried to stop that too. But with a little prodding Ross had gone ahead anyhow and won a glorious victory. Now he urged Brooke to do the same.

He was dealing with a different man. Brooke had just fallen into this job, and he wasn't going to ignore the Commander-in-Chief's advice. He told Cockburn he saw no alternative but to retire. When the Admiral again protested, he decided to assemble his staff and hold a council of war. He "invited" Cockburn to attend, but the Admiral wasn't used to invitations from colonels and coldly declined.

The staff wrangled till midnight, when a forlorn Colonel Brooke reported the outcome in a new note to Cochrane:

> From your letter to Admiral Cockburn this evening, I called a Council of War. Though I had made all my arrangements for attacking the enemy at three in the morning, the result was that from the situation I was placed in, they advised I should retire. I have therefore ordered the retreat to take place tomorrow morning and hope to be at my destination the day after tomorrow—that is, the place we disembarked from.

On the *Surprize* Admiral Cochrane had no idea whether the expedition commanders would take his advice or not. He only knew the last time he tried to stop an operation—the march on Washington—the army had gone ahead anyhow. Moreover, communications were so poor there was no chance of getting an answer before the time set for the attack. To be on the safe side he must stage the diversion as requested.

For leader he picked Captain Charles Napier, the colorful skipper of the frigate *Euryalus* and second-in-command on the recent expedition to Alexandria. The *Euryalus* herself wasn't here just now. Coming back down the Potomac, she ran aground so hard her guns had to be removed to get her off. But that didn't faze her dashing captain. He loaded the ship's cutter and two barges with marines and chased after the fleet to Baltimore. He clearly thrived on challenges.

Now he had a new one. Around midnight Napier was to take a picked force of seamen and marines in small boats, lead them quietly—with muffled oars—into the Ferry Branch, west of Fort McHenry. Continuing a mile or a mile and a half, they were then to anchor and wait. At 1:00 A.M. the bombs would open up again on Fort McHenry, and when signaled by skyrockets, Napier was to start firing too. To make as much uproar as possible, he would use guns, rockets, and mix in blank cartridges. It was all-important to put on a good show: "An attack is to be made upon their lines directly at two o'clock."

At 9:00 P.M. the fire of the bomb vessels slackened, then ceased altogether. Hopefully the Americans would take this as the end of the day's work. At 10:00 the small boats of the squadron, loaded with men, came alongside the *Surprize* for final instructions. Morale was sky-high, but to add that extra ounce of fortitude, a half-ration of rum was passed out to the men.

Midnight, and they were on their way—20 boats altogether, carrying perhaps 300 men. It was raining hard now —a pitch-black night—and with the guns of the fort and the fleet both silent, there was absolutely nothing to guide them. The last 11 boats lost the others in the darkness . . . missed the turn west into the Ferry Branch . . . and continued rowing straight for Baltimore Harbor. A less weary set of defenders might have seen them and caught them squarely between the guns of Fort McHenry and the Lazaretto. As it was, the lost boats managed to turn around and splash back to safety. Leaderless and confused, they returned to the *Surprize*.

Reduced to 9 boats and 128 men, Captain Napier led the remainder of his flotilla into the Ferry Branch, unaware of the fiasco behind him. Sticking close to the far shore—oars muffled as directed—he slipped safely by Fort McHenry. Now he was passing Fort Babcock and soon would be opposite Fort Covington—about where he should drop his hook and wait.

At Fort Babcock, Sailing Master John A. Webster cocked a shrewd ear to the roar of the British bomb vessels as they opened up at 1:00 A.M. It struck him that they were firing harder than ever . . . and that this just might mean trouble for him. He changed the charges in all six of his guns, this time double-shotting them with 18-pound balls and grapeshot. Finally satisfied, he wrapped himself in a blanket and, despite the rain, lay down on the breastwork for a nap.

He was dreaming of his home, Mount Adams, when he suddenly jerked awake. He could hear the unmistakable sound of oars and sweeps. Ordering the men to their posts, Webster peered into the night, noticed an occasional dim light moving up the Ferry Branch about 200 yards offshore. He quickly checked the priming and personally trained each of the guns, then gave the signal to open fire by shooting his pistol in the air. Just before 2:00 A.M. the battery thundered into action.

Five hundred yards upstream at Fort Covington, Lieutenant H. L. Newcomb also saw the lights and opened fire . . . some claimed even sooner than Webster. Then Captain Napier—realizing there was no longer any point in hiding—opened up too. Fort McHenry joined in, and the British ships fired their hardest yet. The fuses of their great 200-pound bombshells traced fiery arcs across the sky, while flights of Congreve and signal rockets gave a weirdly festive look to this deadly serious night.

At Fort Babcock Sailing Master Webster hammered away

at the silhouettes of the British boats and felt sure he was getting some hits. But it was hard work manhandling those big
18-pounders, and he dislocated his shoulder in the process.
Needing more hands, he sent a young midshipman named
Andrews to get back 30 men he had previously lent Lieutenant George Budd, a half-mile to the rear.

Budd refused to release them. He needed every man, he explained, to cover Webster's retreat when the British drove
him from the shore. This gloomy appraisal was too much for
young Andrews. Instead of reporting back to Webster, he
galloped off to Baltimore, spreading the news that Fort Babcock was lost.

Baltimore was almost ready to believe him. Every building
in town shook from the explosions. The rain-swept sky flickered and flared with the flash of bursting bombshells. To the
spectators who crowded the city's rooftops, it was hard to see
how anyone could get through this "most awful spectacle."
And it might be only the start. For there was also the British
Army to consider . . . lurking there in the silent blackness
beyond Hampstead Hill.

It was shortly after 3:00 A.M. in the British camp when the
orders went out to get everyone up. Lieutenant George
Laval Chesterton, Royal Artillery, tried to uncurl from his
square foot of floor in a crowded barn. His friend Captain
Mitchell of the marines had an easier time—he was quar-
tered all alone in a pigsty.

Several hundred yards to the north, three other officers
were called in from the best billet of all—Surrey, the fine
country place of Colonel Joseph Sterett, currently with his
regiment on Hampstead Hill. As they left, one of them
paused long enough to leave a waggish thank-you note on the
dining room sideboard:

Captains Brown, Wilcox and McNamara of the 53rd Regiment, Royal Marines, have received everything they could desire at this house, notwithstanding it was received at the hands of the butler, and in the absence of the colonel.

Spirits were high as the men fell in. Off toward the harbor they could hear the guns of the naval bombardment; they could see the flashes and trails of fire. The fleet was doing its part; soon it would be their turn. They were greatly outnumbered—one look at the American campfires on Hampstead Hill told them that—but they had handled militia before; they would do it again tonight.

Shortly after 3:00 the columns began moving—but not toward Hampstead Hill. To the general (but perhaps not universal) dismay of the troops, they were heading the opposite direction. Away from the hill . . . away from Baltimore . . . away from the sound of the fight. As decided at the midnight council of war, Colonel Brooke was returning to North Point and the ships.

How humiliating. The men ranted at Brooke . . . at cautious staff officers . . . at planners in general. Of course they could have taken the hill. Maybe they would have suffered a few casualties, but anything was better than this business of retreating, as one officer put it, "before a parcel of fellows who had scarcely even seen a gun fired in their lives . . . a parcel of tailors and shoemakers."

In the Ferry Branch Captain Napier was beginning to wonder. Admiral Cochrane's orders said to keep firing until he saw the army was "seriously engaged," then return to the *Surprize*. But it was now after 3:00 A.M., and still no gun flashes—no rumble of cannon—from the hills to the east. Something must have gone wrong. In any case, he had done his part: surely by now he had diverted all the Americans who could be diverted. So far he had miraculously escaped getting hit, but to stay any longer was courting disaster for no conceivable purpose. Signal lights flickered; Napier's boats swung around and began the long row home.

Passing Fort McHenry, they again hugged the far shore and almost slipped by unnoticed. But one of the officers chose this moment to fire a signal rocket to let the fleet know they were returning. The fort instantly responded with a hail of balls and grapeshot. Later, the British claimed only one boat was "slightly struck" and one man mortally wounded; the Americans, however, found the remains of at least two boats and the bodies of three seamen.

At 4:00 A.M. the boats were again alongside the *Surprize*, and the bombardment came to an end. Two or three of the vessels continued to take an occasional shot, but to all intents the fireworks were over, and the whole blazing, tumultuous night gave way to a black, predawn quiet.

Francis Scott Key wondered what to make of this strange new quiet, as he stood with John S. Skinner and Dr. Beanes on the deck of their flag-of-truce sloop. They were anchored with the transports at Old Roads Bay, some eight miles down the Patapsco—well out of the fight, yet near enough to follow most of the action. All day they had watched Fort McHenry's flag with a glass and knew it was still holding out. During the night the bombs and rockets were proof in themselves that Armistead had not surrendered. But this eerie silence, broken only by an occasional distant gun, gave no hint to the fate of the fort—or of the city itself.

Key found himself torn with anxiety. It was the climax of the whole, soul-searing experience he had been going through these past days. He loathed "this abominable war," yet here he was in the middle of it. He saw himself as a gentleman who would be quite at ease with the polished English officers, but he found them to be, with few exceptions, "illiberal, ignorant and vulgar . . . filled with a spirit of malignity against everything American." He detested the saber-rattling rowdiness of Baltimore—sometimes felt the place deserved any punishment it got—but now it was fighting for its life, and he knew where his heart really lay. He was first and last an American, and in these hours of suspense he fervently—desperately—prayed that the flag was still there.

The rest of the night the three Americans paced the deck, scarcely daring to think what daylight might bring. Again and again they pulled out their watches, trying to gauge when the dawn would come. Five o'clock, and the first light of day at last tinged the sky. Out came the spyglass, but it was still too dark to make anything out. At 5:50 it was officially sunrise, but there was no sun today. The rain clouds hung low, and patches of mist swirled across the water, still keeping the night's secret intact.

But it was growing brighter all the time, and soon an easterly breeze sprang up, flecking the Patapsco and clearing the air. Once again Key raised his glass—and this time he saw it. Standing out against the dull gray of the clouds and hills was Major Armistead's American flag.*

Capping the joy of the three Americans, at 7:00 the *Surprize* signaled the bombarding squadron to retire down the

---

* Skeptics have wondered how much Key could really see from his position eight miles down the Patapsco. From comments in the logs of nearby British ships, it seems clear that with the help of a spyglass he could easily watch the fort under fire. A recently uncovered account, however, raises a new riddle. Was it actually Major Armistead's big flag that Key saw, or a somewhat smaller "storm flag" (measuring 17 by 25 feet) supplied by Mary Pickersgill at the same time she turned out the larger one? For more detailed discussion, see Chapter Notes.

river . . . at 8:oo the *Erebus* and the five bombs were under way . . . and at 9:oo the supporting frigates followed. The attack on Fort McHenry was over.

Meanwhile other signs appeared, indicating to Key and his companions that the land attack too had failed. A steady procession of boats streamed out of Bear Creek, carrying scores of wounded to the various transports. To Key it was clear that the army had been "roughly handled."

He looked at the flag on the fort again, and it was about now that the turbulent, fervent thoughts racing through his mind began to take poetic shape. Using the back of a letter that happened to be in his pocket, Francis Scott Key began to jot down lines and phrases and likely couplets. . . .

"The enemy has been severely drubbed—as well his Army as his Navy—and is retiring down the river after expending many tons of shot, from 1800–2000 shells, and at least 700–800 rockets," Commodore Rodgers excitedly wrote Secretary of the Navy Jones on the 14th, while the British were falling back to North Point.

Others weren't that sure. "The enemy has retired, not departed—this retiring may be a stratagem to throw us off our guard," warned Sam Smith in a general order issued during the day. British deserters seemed to confirm the theory. Several said Brooke was pulling back only to pick up reinforcements.

Even on the 15th, when the enemy army was clearly re-embarking, Smith felt it might be just to hit Baltimore from another angle. That evening General Douglass's brigade prepared to thwart an assault on the south side of the city, and Sam Smith warned Fort McHenry that he believed "an attack would be made in the course of the night on this post and on the city by way of the Ferry Branch."

It was a bad moment for Fort McHenry to face such a prospect. Exhausted by five days of superhuman effort, Major Armistead was delirious with fever, and his subordinates were fighting over seniority. A new British attack would catch the place torn with dissension. Sam Smith hurriedly put Commodore Rodgers in charge. A little unorthodox, perhaps, to have a naval officer run an army fort, but as with most of Sam Smith's solutions, it worked.

September 16, Cochrane's ships still hovered off North Point, but they were now anchored out in the Bay. Slowly, imperceptibly, it finally dawned on Baltimore's defenders that they had actually accomplished what they scarcely dared hope—they had turned back the British. At Fort McHenry, the men found it hard to believe that only three days ago they were crouching behind the ramparts, praying for their lives, and relying on such a dubious talisman as a rooster crowing on the rampart. But one man remembered—and bought the rooster the poundcake he had promised.

On Hampstead Hill the troops were released from the earthworks and marched back to their regular quarters. Free from tension at last, the men exploded with a ribald joy that appalled Private John A. Dagg, the sometime clergyman from Virginia: "During the last few days every one had spoken softly and seriously, and no oaths had been heard, but this night our barracks were in an uproar with noise and profanity, giving painful proof of human depravity."

The noise and foolishness soon gave way to a deeper, quieter gratitude. For Baltimore it had been a very near thing, and everyone sensed it. Gifts poured in for the comfort of the wounded—not just money and medical supplies, but small things too from people who had little else to give except their thanks: two large pots of preserves from Mrs. Samuel Harris . . . one jar of crab apples from Mrs. William Lorman.

For the heroes there were dress swords and testimonial dinners; and for a convalescent Major Armistead, a fine silver punch bowl of the exact dimensions of a 13-inch British bombshell. But he won far more than that. His wife Louisa presented him with a baby girl that made him forget the son he had wanted. Professionally, Madison sent him a spot promotion, and even better, he had that dream of every soldier —a little military fame. "So you see, my dear wife," he wrote Mrs. Armistead, "all is well, at least your husband has got a name and standing that nothing but divine providence could have given him, and I pray to my Heavenly Father that we may long live to enjoy."

Baltimore was already celebrating when a small sloop arrived on the evening of September 16, inched past the block ships, and docked at Hughes' Wharf between eight and nine o'clock. Released at last by Admiral Cochrane, the flag-of-truce packet was back with John S. Skinner, Francis Scott Key, and their elderly charge, Dr. Beanes.

Bystanders eagerly pumped them for news. What would the British do next? Well, said Key, the officers spoke of going to Poplar Island for repairs, then Halifax. Was Ross really killed? Yes, said John Skinner, no doubt about it. But the main focus of attention was Skinner's list of 91 prisoners held in the British fleet. All Baltimore was desperate for news of missing friends and relatives; now a great surge of relief swept the city.

Breaking away, the three new arrivals retired to the Indian Queen Hotel—but there would be no sleep yet for Francis Scott Key. Vivid thoughts of the scenes he had witnessed raced through his poetic mind. He had tried to express his feelings—the thrill of seeing the flag at dawn—in a few random lines scribbled down right after the attack. Later he added more during the long wait and sail back to Baltimore.

Now these lines had jelled into a song, and he simply had to get it down on paper.

From the start, he almost certainly thought of it as being sung to the tune of "To Anacreon in Heaven," a familiar drinking song of the period. The same melody had already been borrowed in 1798 by Robert Treat Paine for a patriotic air called "Adams and Liberty," and Key himself had used it for an amateurish effort he composed in 1805, honoring the heroes of Tripoli.

Now it would do again, and he even relied, perhaps unconsciously, on some of the rhymes and images he had used nine years before. Taking a sheet of paper, he wrote it all out from beginning to end. Oddly enough, he gave it no title.

Next morning he showed it to John S. Skinner and also to his wife's brother-in-law, Judge Nicholson, free at last from the ordeal of Fort McHenry. One of them sent or took it to the offices of the Baltimore *American and Commercial Daily Advertiser* to be struck off as a handbill. Probably set by Samuel Sands, a 14-year-old printer's "devil," copies were soon circulating throughout the city. A brief introduction explained how it came to be written, and a guide line gave the tune as "Anacreon in Heaven." But it mentioned no author and carried no title except the modest heading, "Defence of Fort M'Henry." Weeks would pass before it became known as "The Star-Spangled Banner."

But the song caught Baltimore's fancy right away. Key's words somehow conveyed perfectly the strange combination of fear, defiance, suspense, relief and sheer ecstasy that went into that desperate night. The Fort McHenry garrison adopted it—every man received a copy—and the tavern crowds took it up. Resuming publication after a ten-day lapse, the Baltimore *Patriot and Evening Advertiser* ran it in full on September 20, proclaiming that it was "destined long to outlast the occasion, and outlive the impulse, which produced it."

It quickly spread to other cities too, as the whole nation rejoiced in the news from Baltimore. Within a month papers in towns as far away as Savannah and Concord, New Hampshire, were running Key's stirring lyrics. Everywhere they struck the right chord—the rare sense of exultation people felt about this totally unexpected victory.

For unexpected it was. As late as 7:15 A.M. on September 14 (15 minutes after Cochrane began his retirement), the vedettes at Elkton, Maryland, were warning the cities to the north that "the general opinion here is that Baltimore must fall." In Philadelphia crowds filled the streets all day, despite the rain, waiting for news that never came. Communications were out; the stage not running; the outlook bleak. Coming so soon after Washington, the situation had all the familiar earmarks of another disaster.

And now the impossible had happened. Joy and relief swept the country. At Norfolk the *Constellation* fired rousing salutes; at Salem, Massachusetts, the town cannon boomed in celebration. "Never have we witnessed greater elevation of public spirits," exclaimed the Salem *Register*. The triumph at Baltimore had erased all past impressions of the enemy's irresistible strength. "Ten thousand victories cannot give them their former hopes, and the spell is lost forever."

And almost at the same time word spread of an equally glorious victory on the Canadian front. On September 11 a large British invasion force under Sir George Prevost was thrown back at Plattsburg, New York. The naval arm of this expedition was annihilated on Lake Champlain by the brilliant tactics of Captain Thomas Macdonough, commanding a hastily assembled U.S. squadron; while Prevost's army of 11,000 Peninsular veterans retired in confusion before the far smaller numbers of Brigadier General Alexander Macomb.

It was another miracle, and the defenders of Baltimore responded appropriately. Promptly at noon on September 18, the guns of Fort McHenry sounded loud and long. But this time it was not in angry defiance—it was a "federal salute" in honor of the new, splendid victory on Lake Champlain.

It was just as well Admiral Cochrane knew nothing about the fiasco at Plattsburg; the retirement from Baltimore was discouraging enough. This time there were no huzzahs as the ships' boats collected the troops from the bluff at North Point on September 15. There was only silence, broken occasionally by the groans of the wounded. On the deck of the *Seahorse* alone 25 shattered forms lay on the main topgallant sail awaiting the surgeon's knife. Drenched with blood, the sail was finally thrown overboard. In a barrel on the *Royal Oak* the remains of General Ross were carefully preserved in 129 gallons of good Jamaica rum.

That evening Admiral Cochrane transferred back to the *Tonnant* with what must have been mixed feelings. He clearly liked being on the *Surprize* with his son Sir Thomas; on the other hand, the evidence suggests that the boy left much to be desired as a frigate captain. The log was a mess, and mishaps seemed to plague the ship: an upset gig, a drowned sailor, desertions, groundings, no one knew what next. This very afternoon two of her signal flags blew away.

All the 16th the fleet lay at anchor, taking stock. Carpenters went over the damage to the *Devastation* and *Volcano*; the wounded were transferred to the *Diomede*, which was refitted as a hospital ship; and the troops were generally sorted out. In the process it became painfully clear that desertions were again a problem: altogether some 237 men were listed as prisoners or missing. Something had to be done "to encourage the rest," and before the week was out two recaptured deserters were hung from the yardarm of the *Weser*. Boats from every ship in the fleet were ordered to be present, so the men could absorb the lesson.

Through it all Admiral Cochrane did his best to put on a confident front. On the 16th he issued a ringing proclamation to all hands, praising their exertions in the "demonstration and reconnaissance which it was deemed advisable to make upon the city of Baltimore." On the 17th he sent off by the *Rover* his official dispatch to the Admiralty. Again he vaguely described the attack as a "demonstration," and Brooke's modest success came off as a "decisive victory" . . . "a brilliant affair." The final withdrawal was easily explained: "The primary object of our movement had already been fully accomplished."

That was for the public. The same day he privately wrote Lord Melville that the entire project was "contrary to my opinion, but extremely urged by the General, to which I reluctantly consented but to preserve unanimity between the two services." Cochrane added that he now "extremely regretted" the whole operation. Even the tactics were bad: the army should have landed on the other side of Baltimore and attacked from the west.

But Sir Alexander was too lively a schemer to mope for long. "The ball is at our feet," he reassured Melville, "and give me but 6,000 men including a rifle and cavalry regiment, and I will engage to master every town south of Philadelphia and keep the whole coast in such a state of alarm as soon to bring the most obstinate upon their marrow bones."

That very afternoon the frigate *Vesta* arrived with a dispatch from London that gave Cochrane everything he wanted except the cavalry regiment. The government was sending out Lord Hill with 7,000 men. They would rendezvous with the fleet at Jamaica on November 20, and the united force would then proceed to the Gulf Coast. All this was entirely apart from Sir Alexander's own proposals for this area—his scheme had not yet reached Downing Street —but the development was no less pleasing.

Brimming with enthusiasm, Cochrane quickly dashed off a new letter to Lord Melville promising to be in New Orleans in December. But even as he wrote, forces far beyond his control were at work in London which would not only affect his plans for Louisiana but alter the whole course of the war.

CHAPTER TWELVE

Britain Struggles with Herself

Gazing at the clutter of perfumes, snuffboxes and wigs, Captain Harry Smith could hardly believe the truth. Here he was—an unknown junior officer—sitting in the Prince Regent's own dressing room, describing to His Royal Highness the capture of Washington.

After a remarkably fast passage from the Chesapeake, Smith had reached London with General Ross's dispatches early on the morning of September 27. He immediately reported to Lord Bathurst, who lost no time whisking him to Carlton House for a royal interview. Things were moving fast, even for a man of Smith's jaunty self-confidence. How should he act? he asked Bathurst. "Oh," said the Earl lightly, "just behave as you would to any gentleman."

The formula worked. The Prince Regent couldn't have been more gracious. He asked all the right questions as Smith unrolled a large plan of Washington with the burnt buildings neatly marked in red ink. Outside, the Park and Tower guns began thundering a mighty victory salute.

"War America would have, and war she has got. . . . Washington is no more," proclaimed the *Courier* that afternoon. "The reign of Madison, like that of Bonaparte, may be considered as at an end," declared the *Evening Star*. A few days later the *National Register* reported that in the hour of disaster the President had shot himself.

It was chastisement at last, and London especially savored every detail of the humiliating rout at Bladensburg. "History presents many examples of patriotic heroism in which, if success was not always attained, honor was never lost," pontificated the *Morning Post* on the 28th. "It remained for the Americans to display an example of pusillanimity hitherto unknown in the long course of ages."

In contrast: English valor. All in all, it was almost a morality play and, as the *Sun* observed, "a lesson for the past and an example for the future of how dangerous and fatal it is to rouse the sleeping Lion of the British Isles."

The victory capped a summer of almost continuous joy. Napoleon had been gone for six months now, but the celebration rolled on—the balloon ascension in front of Buckingham House . . . the great festival in Hyde Park, where "the consumption of bottled ale and porter exceeded almost the power of calculation" . . . the sham naval battle on the Serpentine that saw miniature British "frigates" crush their American counterparts. At the time a few spoilsports observed that it didn't always happen that way on the ocean, but the doubters were no longer in evidence.

Washington was an indisputable, glorious reality, and it silenced the war's critics—a small but persistent minority who pointed to the casualties, the drain on the economy, the strategic difficulties, the marginal gains to be won. The peace-minded *Spectator* had been among the most vocal, but now it swallowed its pride. Calling Ross's feat a "brilliant dash," the editors lamely added that they would reserve any questions about advisability for another time.

The government too changed its tune. As Prime Minister, Lord Liverpool was quite aware of the costs of the war. Only four days earlier he had written his Foreign Secretary, Lord Castlereagh, in Vienna, "I confess on many counts I wish we were well out of it. . . ." Liverpool was hoping the Peninsular regiments he had sent across the Atlantic would make this possible. Their victories should give him the leverage he needed to deal with both a bellicose public at home and the hardheaded American peace negotiators who were meeting the British representatives at Ghent in Belgium.

Now Liverpool had his leverage, yet his first thoughts were not of peace but of more victories. He and Lord Bathurst immediately decided to add two more regiments to Admiral Cochrane's force. This was quite a turnabout, for on sober second thought the government had previously cut back the big army promised Cochrane. New Orleans, it was felt, could be taken without Lord Hill and with far fewer troops. Now most of the cut (but not Hill himself) was restored. Together with reinforcements already on the way, Cochrane's force would be "upwards of 10,000 men."

This should be enough to accomplish all objectives, Bathurst wrote General Ross, who as far as London knew was still in good health. Moreover, Bathurst added, Ross and Cochrane had the government's approval to go wherever they liked—Rhode Island, the Delaware, the Chesapeake, the Carolinas, New Orleans, any or all these places. Again unaware of events, Bathurst added that if they went to Baltimore, he hoped they would "make its inhabitants *feel* a little more the effects of your visit than what has been experienced at Washington."

More men . . . a free hand . . . a hard line—all these a

grateful government rushed to bestow on the conquerors of Washington. Whitehall bustled with activity as Colonel Henry Torrens, the hard-working military secretary, set about assembling troops, supplies and transports. Even the Duke of York, nominally the Commander-in-Chief, snapped to life. Only yesterday Torrens had privately described him as "never more drowsy"; today His Royal Highness shuffled papers with the best of them.

The fall of Washington also had its effect at Ghent, where the British and American negotiators continued their fencing. "I hope you'll be able to put on a face of compress'd joy at least, in communicating the news to the American ministers," Bathurst wrote Henry Goulburn, the second-ranking member of the British delegation on September 27.

Goulburn was delighted to oblige. Although Admiral Lord Gambier supplied the gold braid and Dr. William Adams the technical expertise, it was Goulburn who provided the real muscle for "His Majesties True, Certain, and Undoubted Commissioners, Procurators, and Plenipotentiaries." He did most of the talking and continually pressed for harsh peace terms—often at cross-purposes with his more relaxed superiors in London.

Now at last he had a real go-ahead from Bathurst, and he took special pleasure in forwarding the latest London newspapers to the Hotel Lovendeghem, where the five-man American delegation lived in the disarray of unaccustomed bachelorhood. At the moment Henry Clay was off on a little junket to Brussels, and Goulburn's covering note dryly suggested that the papers might relieve his boredom in that uninteresting city.

Beyond such taunts the British tone became distinctly tougher, and any inclination to compromise seemed to vanish. Lord Liverpool and Bathurst, who called the shots from London, felt they had already compromised enough. When the negotiations began in August, they had presented a "shopping list" that included such stern demands as an Indian buffer state in the Northwest Territory and exclusive British control of the Great Lakes. The American negotiators flatly rejected all this, and by now London was willing to settle for considerably less: the prewar Indian boundaries; inclusion of the tribes as parties to the peace treaty; a chunk of Maine big enough for a short cut between Halifax and Quebec; British possession of both sides of the St. Lawrence, as well as certain key posts on the Great Lakes.

For John Quincy Adams and his colleagues this was still too much, and on September 26 they replied to that effect. Their note reached London just after the news of Ross's triumph, and Liverpool cheerfully wrote Bathurst there was no need to hurry a reply. "Let them feast in the meantime upon Washington."

Yet the Prime Minister didn't use the victory to increase his demands. Rising military expenditures, signs of a tax revolt, and the uncertain European political picture all suggested caution. He would like to end the war, he wrote the Duke of Wellington, "if it can be done consistently with our honor and upon such terms as we are fairly entitled to expect."

To get these, Liverpool was willing to be patient. Jonathan might be stubborn at the moment, but he should feel differently after Wellington's veterans had won a few resounding victories. Washington was a good start. . . .

The American commissioners were willing to wait too. They were in the happy position of wanting nothing but the status quo. Their only important demand—an end to impressment—had been quietly withdrawn as the storm clouds gathered over Washington during the summer. Now their main job was simply to stand up to the British, and they were more than equipped to do this.

Adams, the chairman, was clearheaded and implacable; Albert Gallatin, a man of unruffled poise; Henry Clay, the shrewdest of gamblers behind that lazy façade. The other two Americans were less striking figures, but James Bayard was tenacious and Jonathan Russell had a slavish devotion to Clay that made him utterly reliable in a crisis. As a group they towered intellectually over the three British commissioners and enjoyed a psychological edge as well. It was all too clear that London regarded its representatives as little more than messenger boys.

Nevertheless, the capture of Washington was darkly discouraging, and the effects were deeply felt on October 8 when a new British note arrived full of bombast, threats and an "ultimatum" that the Indians be restored to their prewar boundaries. Still depressed by the news from home, the Americans accepted the demand, consoling themselves that London no longer insisted that the Indians be a party to the peace treaty.

But the chief consolation for the Americans during these gloomy days was an abundance of evidence that European sympathy had swung to their side. The French press lashed at Ross's and Cockburn's free use of the torch in Washington. The *Journal des Débats* compared the invaders to pirates; the *Journal de Paris* likened the destruction to burning the Pantheon or St. Peter's at Rome. "How could a nation eminently civilized, conduct itself at Washington with as much barbarity as the old banditti of Attila and Genseric? Is not this act of atrocious vengeance a crime against all humanity?"

And the deed lost nothing in the telling. According to the French journalists, Washington was "annihilated" . . . "swept from the face of the earth." It had been "one of the finest capitals in the world" . . . "a city whose riches and beauty formed one of the most valuable monuments of the progress of the arts and of human industry"—descriptions which would have startled even the most chauvinistic of the capital's inhabitants.

In London the cry was still for chastisement, and what could be a more legitimate target than the public buildings of an enemy capital? "Such are the fruits which America has derived from this unnatural war," declared the *Courier*, adding, "But the vial of our wrath is not yet exhausted; a few days, perhaps hours, will bring us intelligence of further successes." The *Public Ledger* was more specific; the editors said they wouldn't be surprised to see Boston, Philadelphia, New York and Baltimore all turned into "heaps of smoldering rubbish" by the end of the year.

In fact, rumors swept London in the first week of October that Baltimore had already fallen. The details were convincingly specific: 100 sail taken . . . a prodigious amount of flour, "ready packed in barrels." Assuring its readers that this was no mere gossip, the *Morning Post* explained that the story came straight from the Cork *Reporter*, which got it from Admiral Sawyer at Cove, who got it from the brig *Charybdis*, which got it from a Spanish ship off the banks of Newfoundland. The *Morning Chronicle* provided no such authentication, but its version was even more exciting: Baltimore had not only fallen, but under the protection of the British forces it had "seceded from the Union and proclaimed itself neutral."

The government of course knew better, but optimism was sky-high by the middle of the month. Facing a pleasant interlude with no particular problems, on the 16th Colonel Torrens sent a note to his friend Major General Taylor, suggesting they go for a day's shooting during the coming week. He assured Taylor they had the chief's blessing: "HRH gave us *carte blanche* to destroy all the pheasants we can."

No pheasants fell to these particular guns, for the following morning the roof fell in. Captain Duncan MacDougall arrived with the latest dispatches from the Chesapeake: Ross was dead . . . the army and navy repulsed at Baltimore.

As soon as possible Lord Liverpool and Bathurst hurried to the Horse Guards, where they huddled with Colonel Torrens over the selection of a new general. Colonel Brooke was clearly too junior; so was Major General John Keane, now on his way out with the first of Cochrane's reinforcements. Sir Thomas Picton had the seniority but seemed a little too rough. In the end they picked Major General Sir Edward Pakenham—Wellington's brother-in-law and one of his most trusted staff officers.

While all this was being settled behind closed doors at Whitehall, the press struggled bravely with the disastrous news. "Another brilliant victory," proclaimed the *Morning Post*. If the results didn't seem too decisive, the paper continued, it was only because the cowardly militia refused to stand up to British bayonets. "All the victories of Alexander, Caesar, Scipio, and Hannibal are dimmed by the resplendent glories of the heroes of our isle. It is hard, then, it is indeed distressing that their immediate duty requires them to contend with a set of creatures who take the field only to disgrace the musket."

As for the death of Ross, that could be explained by another cowardly American trick: "the assassin-like manoeuver of *marking their man*, under the security of their impenetrable forests."

Nobody was really fooled. It was all too clear that the army had failed to reach its objective and had lost its leader in the process. Worse, the affair probably gave the Americans new spirit, canceling out whatever benefits might have come from Washington. "Victories which have effects like these," remarked the *Statesman* on sober reflection, "we think Britain had better be without."

Then, on top of Baltimore came the disaster of Lake

Champlain and Plattsburg, and now even the pretense of victory was ludicrous. "So *lamentable* an instance of weakness and imbecility has not been recorded in our military annals!" Colonel Torrens wrote the Marquis of Tweeddale in a letter that reflected the government's shock and anguish. "Good God! Is it to be borne that an officer in command of 9,000 British troops shall retreat before a handful of Banditti because he forsooth thinks that the object to be gained by an attack after the loss of the fleet would not justify the loss—as if there were no such thing as national honor and professional credit to fight for!"

On October 18, as the bad news came pouring in, Lord Bathurst dashed off new instructions to his peace commissioners at Ghent. Gone was the policy of calculated delay—the strategy of marking time until a few military victories gave Britain a solid bargaining position. Clearly there would be no more victories until the reinforcements reached America, and now the choice was to escalate the war or ask for less.

London asked for less. Out went the long list of territorial demands cooked up in August. Instead, Britain would settle for the doctrine of *uti possidetis*—each side to keep what it held. To Bathurst this meant Britain would get the northern half of Maine, Michilimackinac and Fort Niagara on the Great Lakes—the last a little anticipatory since it was still held by the Americans.

At Ghent, Henry Goulburn submitted the new British terms on October 21—just as the first details of Baltimore and Plattsburg arrived. It was a bad day to be asking Americans for anything. "The news is very far from satisfactory," Goulburn wrote Bathurst that night. "We owed the acceptance of our article respecting the Indians to the capture of Washington; and if we had either burnt Baltimore or held Plattsburg, I believe we should have had peace on the terms which you have sent us in a month at least. As things appear to be going on in America, the result of our negotiation may be very different."

As Goulburn feared, on October 24 the American commissioners flatly rejected the British demands. They wanted no part of *uti possidetis*. Instead, each side should keep what it had at the start of hostilities.

The continued stubbornness of the Americans caused new exasperation at Downing Street, for the disastrous military news had touched off a growing protest against the war. For some it was a matter of priorities. The Congress of Vienna was off to a rocky start . . . the Russians were taking over Poland . . . Prussia and Austria were eying Saxony . . . France seemed on the verge of another revolution—all with nearly half the British Army 3,000 miles away. This protracted conflict with America was tying down troops badly needed to strengthen England's hand on the all-important Continent of Europe.

There was also a growing clamor against military expenditures. As long as Napoleon was a threat, the British were willing to put up with back-breaking taxes—not only for their own forces, but their allies too. They had bankrolled the struggle for almost 20 years; now Bonaparte was gone and they wanted relief.

The American war was no way to get it. It cost a thousand guineas to ship a single cannon from Portsmouth to Lake Ontario. The Americans, on the other hand, were right on the spot. Even in their precarious financial condition they could wage war at minimum cost. Their tax bill came to about one-twentieth the horrendous amount paid by long-suffering Britons.

Worse, the cost of the war was rising. As always, the military had underestimated its needs and expenditures. "The continuance of the American war will entail upon us a prodigious expense, much more than we had any idea of," Lord

Liverpool wrote to Castlereagh, who was having his own troubles at Vienna.

Not only was the tax bill staggering, but business was surprisingly poor—and getting worse every day the war dragged on. The end of Bonaparte had not spelled prosperity. On the other hand, Cochrane's blockade and the American privateers were costing the country dearly. Some 1,400 vessels had been lost to privateers . . . insurance rates were higher than before Napoleon fell . . . 20,000 cases of goods lay on the docks at Liverpool, waiting for peace and shipment to America.

Even so, most Britons would be willing to make a great sacrifice if the purpose of the war were worth it. But it was one thing to defend a free hand for the Royal Navy—including the right of impressment—and quite a different matter to be demanding American territory. Even those not privy to the negotiations at Ghent could read the proclamation issued at Halifax claiming the west side of the Penobscot River. The *Morning Chronicle* considered this a dangerous escalation of the war that would only draw the Americans closer together.

Above and beyond these practical complaints, a moral revulsion crept over the public. When the Continental papers denounced the destruction at Washington, they pricked perhaps the most vulnerable point of Britain's anatomy—her national conscience. In ever-increasing numbers English critics too spoke of the "unmanly vengeance" exhibited in burning, say, the Library of Congress. "We are persuaded," the *Times* raged back, "that a single shelf in the Spencerian library would purchase all the scarce books that ever found their way across the Atlantic since the United States have had to boast an existence; and sure we are that if there were any scarce books at Washington, the readers that could read them were that much scarcer."

Such ranting accomplished nothing. Criticism continued to mount, and on November 1 the government quietly capitulated. Lord Bathurst ordered Cochrane to end his policy of retaliation.

But the larger question of the conduct of the war remained. It seemed to be leading nowhere, with nothing to look forward to but an open-ended commitment of more men, more money, more effort. "Think of the *expense* of such a war!" exploded William Cobbett even before the news of Baltimore arrived. "We *conquer* nothing, we *capture* nothing, and almost every action is followed by a *retreat*."

Indeed, it was the sheer endlessness of it all that discouraged people the most. Only a few weeks ago the *Naval Chronicle* was speculating on the dissolution of the Union; now the press wondered whether Canada could be saved. Early in October the guessing game was whether New York, Philadelphia or Baltimore would be taken next. A month later the Mayor of Liverpool was warning Lord Sidmouth of the city's "insufficient means of repelling attack in the event of such being made by the American government."

Criticism continued to mount, until finally on November 4 the government did what it always did in times of trouble —it turned to the Duke of Wellington. After a full cabinet discussion, Lord Liverpool wrote the Duke in Paris, where as British Ambassador he was trying to breathe life into the newly restored Bourbon monarchy. The French capital seethed with rancor, and stressing Wellington's personal danger, Liverpool said the cabinet was resolved to get him out. As a pretext, he could either go to Vienna and consult with Castlereagh or take command in America.

It was a curiously oblique way of approaching the matter, but there was no doubt how much importance Liverpool attached to the American assignment:

You should go out with full powers to make peace, or to continue the war, if peace should be found to be impracticable, with renewed vigour. . . .

The more we contemplate the character of the American war, the more satisfied we are of the many inconveniences which may grow out of the continuance of it. We desire to bring it to an honourable conclusion; and this object would, in our judgment, be more likely to be attained by vesting you with double powers than by any other arrangement which could be suggested.

Among other advantages, Liverpool wrote Castlereagh the same day, Wellington had the prestige to make unappetizing peace terms palatable to the British public.

The Duke was initially inclined to go, but the more he thought about the scheme, the less he liked it. Writing Liverpool on the 9th, he saw little chance of success: "That which appears to me to be wanting in America is not a General, or General officers and troops, but a naval superiority on the Lakes." Without this, no one—Prevost or anybody else —could accomplish very much . . . "and I shall go there only to prove the truth of Prevost's defense, and to sign a peace which might as well be signed now."

As to peace terms, Wellington went on to offer some unsolicited advice:

I confess that I think you have no right from the state of the war to demand any concession of territory from America. . . . You have not been able to carry it into the enemy's territory, notwithstanding your military success, and now undoubted military superiority, and have not even cleared your own territory of the enemy on the point of attack.

Then if this reasoning is true, why stipulate for the *uti*

possidetis? You can get no territory; indeed the state of your military operations, however creditable, does not entitle you to demand any. . . .

There could not have been a bigger jolt to the government's hopes and plans. Wellington was not only England's greatest general; he was the country's most respected, most revered public figure. All Britain deferred to his judgment, and it was almost unthinkable to go against his considered wishes. While he was too good a soldier to say so, he clearly didn't want this American assignment, and it was just as clear that he regarded the government's whole approach to peace as unrealistic.

It was a shaken group of ministers that faced the opposition in Parliament, which was now in session again. In the House of Lords, Lord Grenville deplored the destruction at Washington; in the House of Commons, George Tierney denounced the ever-growing deficit. When the Chancellor of the Exchequer Nicholas Vansittart presented a new list of mountainous military expenditures, the Whig benches exploded with indignation. Parliament was committed to tax relief—not more taxes—and the promise to end the detested property tax was "as strong a pledge as Parliament could give."

Far from ending the property tax, Vansittart conceded on November 17, the government planned to ask for an extension. Once more the Whigs erupted in anger, and Samuel Whitbread warned that the American war would prove a bigger drain than the struggle against Napoleon.

The government's spokesmen fought back, stressing the perils of a quick, easy peace . . . calling for patience . . . arguing that the war was fast approaching a turning point. All that was needed, the *Times* declared, was "a small degree of additional perseverance." Then Admiral Cochrane would win great new victories in the south, and the American economy would collapse.

Above all, it was argued, a little patience and the Union itself might dissolve. There were several hopeful signs: Nantucket had declared its "neutrality" . . . the people east of the Penobscot were swearing allegiance to the Crown . . . several of the New England states planned a convention at Hartford, Connecticut, that might lead to secession.

But the mail from America soon dashed these high hopes. The Foreign Office had good sources in Boston, and one of these contacts ("very respectable") sent in a report clearly showing that Cochrane's operations along the Atlantic seaboard had boomeranged. Whatever the Federalist old guard might say, New England as a whole was rallying to the colors. In the space of four weeks thousands of new men had joined the militia, and the coastal towns were all astir.

This was, of course, confidential information, but there was nothing confidential about the American newspapers that reached London on November 18, offering fresh proof that all sections of the country were closing ranks. Madison, it seemed, had released to the press those harsh British peace terms presented in August, and the nation exploded in anger. Even the President's old foe, Alexander Hanson of the Georgetown *Federal Republican*, stood by his side.

In vain Lord Liverpool cried "foul," complaining that it was an inexcusable breach of etiquette to release a confidential diplomatic exchange. The damage was done, and the British public knew all too well that the government had once again misassessed the situation. Its tactics had strengthened rather than weakened American unity, and the thrashing of Jonathan lay further off than ever.

Parliament went into a new uproar. In the House of Lords, the Marquis of Lansdowne declared that it was one thing to fight for a great principle like Britain's maritime rights, but a totally different matter to conquer territory, impose bound-aries, and generally hem in America. He didn't want any part of that. In the House of Commons, Alexander Baring de-clared that the whole business was like asking England to sur-render Cornwall.

Emotions ran high, but actually the government had already decided to give up its territorial demands. As early as November 13 Lord Liverpool privately wrote Wellington, reassuring him on the matter. On the 15th Bathurst warned Goulburn at Ghent to be prepared for this new retreat.

By now Goulburn was used to London's erratic ways. Still, he couldn't help expressing his personal disappointment. "You know," he wrote Bathurst, "that I was never inclined to give way to the Americans." As a loyal servant of the Crown, however, he promised that the British commissioners would do their best "to bring the negotiations to a speedy issue."

So a new note went off to the Americans on November 26. It abandoned the principle of *uti possidetis*, and from then on the two sides made steady progress. There was, in fact, little left to settle. The United States had given way on "free trade and sailors' rights"; Britain had dropped a strong stand on the Indians and any thought of territory. About all that remained were the questions of whether Massachusetts fishermen could dry and cure their catch on the shores of Newfoundland, and whether English vessels had freedom of navigation on the Mississippi. These issues were met by the simple expedient of silence: they were left out of the treaty altogether.

December 23, both parties agreed on a final draft. There was only one last-minute hitch: the British refused to return several small islands seized in Passamaquoddy Bay. They claimed these had always belonged to the Crown and would be held until future negotiations determined their title. This was nothing to fight a war about—the Americans acquiesced.

At 4:00 P.M., December 24, the five U.S. commissioners left the Hotel Lovendeghem, entered their carriages, and drove to the Chartreuse, a former monastery where the British had their quarters. For the next two hours all the diplomats sat together, going over the six copies of the treaty page by page. Then, at 6:00 P.M.—as the bells of St. Bovan began ringing in Christmas Eve—they carefully signed and sealed a "Treaty of Peace and Amity between His Britannic Majesty and the United States of America."

For five months' work it was an amazingly simple document. Mainly, it ended the war; returned all territory seized by either side (except the islands in the Passamaquoddy Bay); restored the Indians to their prewar status; and set up four commissions to deal with specific questions involving the Canadian boundary.

There was, however, one unusual provision. Normally treaties took effect when signed—but not this one. It would become operative only when unconditionally ratified by both parties, with the ratifications to be exchanged in Washington. "Even if peace is signed," Lord Liverpool explained in a letter to Castlereagh, "I shall not be surprised if Madison endeavours to play us some trick in the ratification of it."

To the end, the British wrote off the President as a sly, malevolent gnome—quite likely to reject the treaty altogether in some dark political maneuver . . . or equally likely to change a line here and there to snatch an undeserved advantage. So the war would go on—His Majesty's forces would press as hard as ever—until the treaty was actually ratified and this slippery man was nailed down to its terms.

These dark suspicions were carefully hidden on the 24th at

Ghent. All was perfect courtesy as the delegates sat at the long table in the Chartreuse, busy with their quills and ribbon and sealing wax. Speaking for the British, Lord Gambier said he hoped that peace would be permanent, and John Quincy Adams expressed the same wish. During the evening all joined together at the Cathedral for an impressively solemn service.

Christmas was appropriately merry. At noon John Payne Todd, Madison's wastrel stepson on hand as a minor secretary, gave a party that introduced eggnog to Ghent. The innovation was greeted with acclaim. At the Chartreuse the British sat down to roast beef and plum pudding, brought direct from England.

Across the Channel, London too was enjoying Christmas. The *Morning Chronicle* dotingly reported that the Viscountess Cremorne "exercised her usual benevolence" at her house on Great Stanhope Street, showering beef, bread and coals on thirty fortunate Irishmen. ("They were afterwards admitted to the servants' hall, wherein a liberal distribution of whiskey and ale took place.") At Highgate a Miss Mellon—otherwise unidentified—also made the poor happy: beef and bread to the elderly men; "and to every distressed aged female that applied, a chemise, a cloak, a blanket and wine; and to the children of poverty, one shilling each."

The damp air glowed with good fellowship this first Christmas since Napoleon, and now there were rumors of an early peace with America too. The *Times*—committed as always to total victory—scoffed at the notion as "madness." Yet the financial circles in the City had a way of knowing such things, and during most of the 24th the so-called "peace policies" showed unusual strength. At Amsterdam, where the shrewd Dutch bankers also had their sources, the American loan rose from 73 to 88—a high that hadn't been matched since the war began.

Around 2:00 P.M. on the 26th, Anthony St. John Baker, secretary to the British peace commission, arrived from Ghent with three copies of the treaty. He said nothing, but was immediately closeted with Bathurst at the Foreign Office. Soon afterward Lord Liverpool was observed hurrying to Carlton House to see the Prince Regent.

While most of London buzzed with curiosity, the City already knew—or at least that part of the City which enjoyed good Continental connections. Enterprising stock jobbers had raced ahead of Baker and beaten him to town. By 1:00 P.M. the "peace shares" were bounding upward, and knowledgeable gentlemen at Lloyds were giving 50 guineas to get 100, if a peace treaty were signed by midnight—a gamble that could only be described as a sure thing. "None were in on the secret for some time but those connected with the American junta," complained the *Evening Star*, which had none of these valuable contacts.

But by 4 o'clock the news was general . . . with reactions as divided as the country. When announcements were made that evening at the Covent Garden and Drury Lane theaters, there were cheers—but groans and hisses too. Next morning the *Times* thundered against "this deadly instrument," while the *Chronicle* congratulated the nation on a "desirable act." The *Public Ledger* was "mortified"; the *Morning Post* "astounded"; but significantly, the prowar *Courier* came around and accepted the treaty "with great satisfaction." Perhaps the *Sun* expressed the mood of war-weary London the best: the paper approved "with feelings which would prevent us, however, from blazing our windows with illuminations in honor of the event."

There were no such mixed emotions in the new, politically powerful manufacturing centers mushrooming through the Midlands. At Birmingham an immense crowd watched for the mail coach bearing the official announcement, then took the horses out of the traces, and with much shouting and cheering pulled the coach themselves to the Post Office. There was general rejoicing at Manchester, and at Britain's hard-hit ports as well. At Yarmouth the bells were rung for two days, and flags appeared everywhere.

At Downing Street, Lord Liverpool was more relieved than exultant. "You know how anxious I was that we should get out of this war as soon as we could do so with honor," he wrote George Canning, currently serving in Lisbon. This he felt had been done, and it was best to make peace "before the impatience of the country on the subject had been manifested at public meetings or by motions in Parliament."

Now Liverpool's main concern was to make the treaty stick. On December 27 he had it ratified by the Prince Regent, and that same day Anthony Baker was ordered to carry it to Washington for similar action there.

Along with the treaty went a batch of orders for Cochrane, Pakenham and His Majesty's other commanders in North America. If Washington unconditionally ratified, Baker was to inform them at once, sending along sets of orders that suspended hostilities. Cochrane was then to "return immediately to England" with all his ships, except a handful left for routine assignments. "My Lords further direct you to afford every facility and means of transport in your power for the conveyance back to England of the army under Sir Edward Pakenham with all its baggage and stores."

Besides coming home, Pakenham had a little tidying to do: "You will assure the friendly Indian Nations that Great Britain would not have consented to make peace with the United States of America, unless those Nations and Tribes who had taken part with us had been included in the Pacification." And if this sounded a little glib, the next passage was almost ominous: the General should do his utmost to persuade the Indians to accept the peace, "as we would not be justified in affording them further assistance if they should persist in hostilities."

All this, of course, assumed the Americans would ratify. But Downing Street remained fearful that Madison would do nothing of the kind. Even now it seemed likely that this tireless schemer would reject the treaty and continue the war as his one hope of staying in power. Or perhaps he would tinker with some phrase and change the whole meaning. "It must not be disguised," warned the *Evening Star*, "that every evil is to be apprehended from the delays that may be interposed by the quirking, quibbling chicanery of Madisonian pettifogging diplomacy." Or as Henry Goulburn put it more succinctly: "The Americans always cheat us."

In that event, Baker was to alert the various commanders that ratification had failed, and they already had their plans and orders. On the Atlantic coast a mighty hammer blow should be poised and waiting. Sir Edward Pakenham—with New Orleans safely under his belt—was slated to be in the Delaware or Chesapeake by the end of February or early March, and from here his 10,000 veterans could strike at any of the big eastern cities.

Meanwhile there would be no easing of pressure. The convoy system would be maintained. The troop reinforcements going out in January would leave on schedule. If Pakenham needed the men, this would save two months in getting them to him; if peace came, they could always be sent home—Anthony Baker had the orders in his pocket.

On January 2, 1815, Baker sailed from Plymouth on the sloop of war *Favourite* along with Henry Carroll, Clay's secretary at Ghent, who was bringing one of the three American copies of the treaty. Flying a flag of truce, the little vessel slipped out of the harbor, turned west, and clawed her way into the wintry Atlantic.

CHAPTER THIRTEEN

"The Dawn's Early Light"

Meanwhile the war went on.

All fall, while the diplomats played their game of thrust and parry, the fighting men dueled with real guns. In the Chesapeake, Admiral Malcolm resumed raiding the local creeks and inlets. Along the Maine coast, British frigates dipped in and out of the steeply wooded bays, cowing the inhabitants into submission. At Halifax, and later Jamaica, Admiral Cochrane planned his next expedition for the richest prize of all—New Orleans. From the Chesapeake, Malcolm sailed to join him with Ross's old force; three batches of reinforcements went out from England; Sir Edward Pakenham sailed to take over the military command.

Nothing went quite right. As originally planned, the expedition was to rendezvous at Jamaica by November 20; then sail to the Louisiana coast, where light-draft boats would ferry the troops through the lakes and bayoux to some landing spot near New Orleans. But the reinforcements left Britain in such piecemeal style that only the first group reached Jamaica by the rendezvous date. The rest—including Sir Edward Pakenham—would have to catch up later.

Worse, there were far too few flatboats. When Admiral Cochrane reached Jamaica, he found only a handful collected. Others had been promised from England, but London let him down too.

Even more serious, security collapsed completely. As early as August, Albert Gallatin warned from Ghent that a big expedition was fitting out, Louisiana the objective. In September James Monroe sent a separate warning to the district military commander, Major General Andrew Jackson. That same month Jean Laffite, leader of the freebooters operating out of Barataria Bay, reported a visit from a Royal Navy captain seeking his cooperation. And if Laffite was a bit of a chameleon, there was the proclamation issued by Major Edward Nicolls, the battle-scarred Royal Marine officer in charge of recruiting Indians, blacks and other dissidents. It appealed to the people of Louisiana for help in "liberating" their soil during the coming campaign.

Admiral Cochrane was blissfully unaware of all this, but he couldn't escape the situation in Jamaica. Captain William Fathergill, responsible for collecting the flatboats, had said they were for an attack on New Orleans. Word quickly spread all over the island, and at least one trading schooner slipped off, carrying the news to the Gulf Coast.

Undaunted, the expedition left Jamaica pretty much as scheduled on November 26 and 27. Packed aboard the transports were the four regiments from the Chesapeake plus the new arrivals from England—mainly the 93rd Foot, sporting tartan trews, and the 95th Foot, in their distinctive green rifleman's jackets. A day or so out more ships joined up, bringing the 5th West India, perhaps the best of the black colonial regiments. Altogether the army now totaled 5,700 men under Major General John Keane. He was young and untried but all they had, until someone more senior arrived. Meanwhile Admiral Cochrane would be pleased to give him guidance.

December 2, the leading ships were off the Apalachicola River, where Cochrane hoped to make contact with the thousands of Creek warriors promised by Major Nicolls. Only a handful appeared, dressed in red Guardsmen's jackets, huge cocked hats and no trousers at all.

The Admiral had just as bad luck with Negro recruits. Despite the poor turnout in the Chesapeake—and despite misgivings in London—all fall he had banked on winning thousands of slaves to his colors. But once again the blacks wanted no part of either side. Few enlisted.

And so the disappointments piled up. By December 12, when Cochrane's whole fleet had anchored off Lake Borgne, an admiral more respectful of his enemy—and less dazzled by the prize—might well have wondered whether he had any chance whatsoever.

At that, Sir Alexander almost pulled it off. For one thing, Andrew Jackson's stubbornness largely made up for the failure in British security. The tough, shrewd defender of New Orleans just couldn't believe that a "real military man" would attack through Lake Borgne, which meant a row of over 60 miles to some landing point near the city. As a result, he left the lake guarded by only a small flotilla of gunboats, which Cochrane quickly captured on December 14. This not only deprived Jackson of his "eyes," but added five desperately needed shallow-draft vessels to the Admiral's meager collection.

Even with these, Cochrane had enough boats to carry only 2,200 men at one time. But that was a start, and on December

16 he began the back-breaking job of ferrying the army from the ships to an advanced base established on Pea Island, roughly halfway across the lake.

Then came the luckiest break of all. Searching for a place to land, Cochrane's scouts ran across a village of Spanish fishermen, who turned out to be most cooperative. For $100, plus $2 a day as "head pilot," their leader Gabriel Farerr showed the English visitors the Bayou Bienvenu—the only waterway leading toward New Orleans that hadn't been blocked by Andrew Jackson. Disguised as fishermen, the scouts tried it out. Through a lacework of connecting branches and canals, they ultimately found themselves on the left bank of the Mississippi, less than eight miles below the city.

Actually, Andrew Jackson knew all about the Bayou Bienvenu and had specifically ordered it blocked. But Major Gabriel Villeré, to whom the job was entrusted, apparently felt there was little chance of the British coming this way. His family owned one of the plantations lying between the bayou and the river, and rather than obstruct such a useful means of communication, he decided a picket guard would be enough.

On the morning of December 23, a British advance force of 1,600 men under Colonel William Thornton of the 85th quietly entered the bayou . . . snapped up the pickets . . . and seized the Villeré plantation. The Major was enjoying a cigar on the gallery when he too was scooped into the net. Thus by a single stroke, all Admiral Cochrane's porous plans had been redeemed. His Majesty's troops were at the Mississippi, astride a good hard road, and just two hours' march from a totally unsuspecting New Orleans.

Colonel Thornton wanted to push on. That was the way they did it at Bladensburg. But General Keane said no. The men were tired; they were only 1,600 strong; they had but two small cannon; one of the captured pickets said Jackson

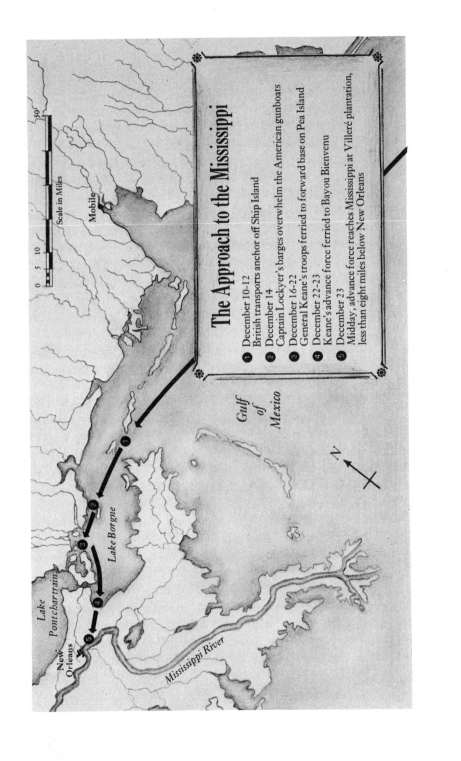

The Approach to the Mississippi

1. **December 10–12**
   British transports anchor off Ship Island

2. **December 14**
   Captain Lockyer's barges overwhelm the American gunboats

3. **December 16–22**
   General Keane's troops ferried to forward base on Pea Island

4. **December 22–23**
   Keane's advance force ferried to Bayou Bienvenu

5. **December 23**
   Midday, advance force reaches Mississippi at Villeré plantation, less than eight miles below New Orleans

Mobile

Scale in Miles

0   5   10   50

Gulf
of
Mexico

N

Lake Borgne

Lake
Pontchartrain

New
Orleans

Mississippi River

had 15,000 men armed to the teeth. It was better to rest until more troops, guns and ammunition could be landed. So the campfires were lit, and the men relaxed on the firm ground beside the levee. There was only one serious interruption— a volley of musketry when Major Villeré suddenly bolted from his captors, leaped through a window, and vanished into the woods behind his house.

"By the Eternal, they shall not sleep on our soil!" stormed Andrew Jackson when he heard the news. Gabriel Villeré had made good his escape, borrowed a horse, and raced to town, bursting in on the General about 12:30 P.M. Other riders were coming in too, setting the stage for later arguments over who really reached Jackson first. At the moment nobody cared. Far more important was the overwhelming fact that the enemy was almost within sight of the city, and not a gun had been fired.

"Gentlemen," Jackson told his staff, "the British are below. We must fight them tonight." At 1:55 P.M. the alarm gun sounded, and by 5:00 the available troops were marching— Colonel Thomas Hinds's Mississippi dragoons . . . the regulars in their tight blue jackets . . . the city battalion with their peacock finery . . . Brigadier General John Coffee's hard, lean Tennessee volunteers . . . 200 free men of color . . . a handful of painted Choctaws . . . some 2,100 men altogether.

At the same time the schooner *Carolina* slipped her moorings and floated downstream. Her crew were idle sailors drafted from the waterfront; her gunners were Baratarian freebooters happy to be in any sort of action. The plan was simple: when the *Carolina* opened fire on the British left, the troops would attack the enemy right.

It began at 7:30 P.M. with a withering broadside on Keane's unsuspecting men, gathered by their campfires eating supper. As planned, Coffee's troops then charged the British right, and a wild melee developed, which lasted till nearly midnight. Recovering from their surprise, Keane's regulars fought hard and well, finally forcing a standoff. But their own momentum was gone. The spearhead had been blunted.

The morning of the 24th found the British Army still at the Villeré plantation, occupying a strip of firm ground that lay between the Mississippi on the left and the maze of swamps and bayoux on the right. This narrow plain ran all the way to New Orleans, but two miles ahead the American Army was waiting. Pulling back after the battle, Jackson was now digging in behind the Rodriguez Canal, where the plain was less than 900 yards wide. Keane was in no hurry to find him. Thoroughly jolted, he decided to wait for the rest of the troops before resuming his advance.

Christmas, and Sir Edward Pakenham at last arrived . . . catching up with his army after an eight-week voyage and a final 19½-hour row. As he appeared at the Villeré plantation, the British gunners fired such a vigorous salute the Americans thought a major attack was coming.

Not yet. But Pakenham injected new life in the force, bringing up men, guns and ammunition as fast as possible. December 27, his gunners tested their skills, blowing up the *Carolina*, which had been a thorn in the British flank ever since the first night. This seemed a good omen, and that night Admiral Malcolm, up with the troops, hastened to write Admiral Cochrane, who was back with the boats: "The General proposes to move tomorrow at daylight. . . . I think he will be in possession of New Orleans tomorrow night—he appears determined on a bold push."

But the "bold push" did not work. As the army advanced in the early light of December 28, the American line erupted in gunfire. Then from the river the armed ship *Louisiana*— her guns also served by Baratarian volunteers—began raking the British left. The men wavered and stopped; and seeing the left in trouble, the right halted too. With his troops hopelessly pinned down, Pakenham finally called off the attack.

To the General, it was now clear he would never break the American line without some heavy guns of his own. So the next three days were spent bringing up ten 18-pounders and four 24-pound carronades, all courtesy of the Royal Navy. The seamen performed miracles, floating the guns in on canoes, then dragging them through the swamp to hard ground. Once again spirits soared, and on the night of the 29th Admiral Cochrane wrote his son Tom, "I hope to be in New Orleans in about eight days."

New Year's Day, 1815, Pakenham was ready to try again. During the previous night, under cover of darkness, his men had scooped out four batteries only 800 yards from Jackson's line. With too little time to do the work properly, sugar casks were used to build up the parapets. By dawn the guns were planted, and the army waited only for an early morning fog to burn off.

Across the Rodriguez Canal, the unsuspecting Americans were preparing for a New Year's Day review. Then at 9:00 the fog suddenly lifted, and the British guns crashed into action. Jackson's men scattered wildly to their positions, and the General rushed from his headquarters at the McCarty plantation house. By the time he reached his embankment, flights of Congreve rockets added to the din. "Don't mind those rockets," he reassured the troops, "they are mere toys to amuse children."

It was ten minutes before the American guns returned fire, but when they did, the effect was devastating. Sugar and splinters flew in all directions as Jackson's big 24- and 32-pounders pulverized the British batteries. In contrast, Pakenham's gunners did little damage. They were short on ammunition, their aim was bad, and most of their good shots

plowed harmlessly into the American earthwork. By 3:00
P.M. the guns were silent; Jackson's bands were playing
"Yankee Doodle"; and for the second time Pakenham con-
ceded failure.

Sir Edward now decided to wait for more men before
trying again. The 7th and 43rd Foot—two of Wellington's
best—should come any day and give him the extra strength
he needed to try new tactics. Next time would not be just
another frontal assault. He would also send a force across the
river to attack some American batteries on the other side.
This would remove an annoyance, create a diversion, and
outflank Jackson's line.

But boats would be needed, and they would have to come
from Cochrane's collection. For the next five days the men
shoveled away, deepening the bayou, extending the canal,
and cutting a breach in the levee. January 6, the work was
done, and the reinforcements arrived under Major General
John Lambert. To ease the shortage of ammunition, each man
carried a cannon ball in his haversack, and Sergeant Jack
Cooper of the 7th had only one complaint: he really needed
two for balance.

Behind the Rodriguez Canal Andrew Jackson was getting
ready too. He built up his embankment. He started two more
defense lines nearer New Orleans. He transferred guns from
the *Louisiana* to a new position he was digging across the
river. He strengthened his front by shifting men from other
points that no longer seemed threatened. On January 3 he got
some welcome reinforcements when the long-awaited Kentucky Militia arrived. But there was a hitch, someone reported: few of the newcomers had guns. "I don't believe it,"
snorted Old Hickory. "I have never seen a Kentuckian without a gun and a pack of cards and a bottle of whiskey in my
life."

As his preparations went on, from time to time Jackson

studied the British camp with his telescope. He noticed the enemy working on the canal, and rightly guessed they were planning an attack across the river. He also noticed them making scaling ladders, and decided the main blow would fall on his own position. And on January 7, when he saw them start cutting the levee and repairing the batteries in front of his line, he felt sure the attack would be coming tomorrow.

He was right. During the afternoon of the 7th Pakenham called his commanders together and announced they would strike at dawn. As a preliminary, Colonel Thornton would cross the river during the night with 1,400 men, capture the American guns on the other side, and turn them on Jackson's line. These would open fire when the general attack began, to be signaled by a rocket.

The assaulting force would advance in two columns, with the main blow delivered by the column on the right under Major General Samuel Gibbs, who had come out with Pakenham as his second-in-command. The other column, under General Keane, would advance in two parts. On the far left a picked force under Lieutenant Colonel Robert Rennie would assault a redoubt that anchored the right end of the American line. The rest of the column would stick more to the center, ready to support either Rennie or Gibbs, depending on how things went. Waiting in reserve would be General Lambert and his two fresh regiments.

In advance of them all would go Lieutenant Colonel Thomas Mullins's 44th Regiment, which had the job of picking up 16 ladders and 300 fascines needed to scale the American parapet. "The 44th will have the forlorn hope tomorrow," Mullins grumbled to his officers. "I think they will catch it."

Pakenham's plan went badly from the start. It proved incredibly difficult getting the boats from the canal into the Mississippi. The levee wasn't cut deep enough. . . . There

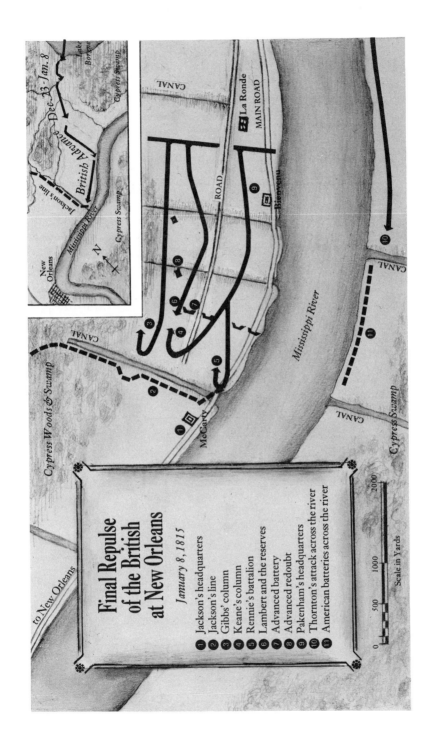

Final Repulse of the British at New Orleans

January 8, 1815

1. Jackson's headquarters
2. Jackson's line
3. Gibbs' column
4. Keane's column
5. Rennie's battalion
6. Lambert and the reserves
7. Advanced battery
8. Advanced redoubt
9. Pakenham's headquarters
10. Thornton's attack across the river
11. American batteries across the river

Scale in Yards

0   500   1000   2000

to New Orleans

Cypress Woods & Swamp

CANAL

McCarty

Mississippi River

CANAL

ROAD

La Ronde

MAIN ROAD

Bienvenu

CANAL

Cypress Swamp

Dec. 23–Jan. 8

British

Advance

Jackson's line

Lake
Borgne

Cypress Swamp

New
Orleans

Mississippi River

Cypress Swamp

N

was too little water in the canal. . . . The boats had to be dragged for 250 yards through mud and slime. Instead of getting off early in the evening, it was after 1:00 A.M. on the 8th before the first barge was finally afloat in the river.

Just about this time at the McCarty house, Andrew Jackson was awakened by a messenger from Commander Daniel Patterson across the river. Patterson reported "a very uncommon stir" in the British camp and asked for reinforcements. The main attack, Jackson answered, would be on his own side of the river and he had no men to spare. Then, turning to his aides: "Gentlemen, we have slept enough. . . ."

At 3:30 A.M. the first British troops began moving to the front. Colonel Mullins led his 44th Regiment forward to pick up the scaling equipment, but misunderstood his instructions. He went to the "advanced battery"—about 500 yards beyond the "advanced redoubt," where everything was actually stored. When he finally realized his mistake, he sent 300 men back on the double, but by now it was almost dawn—time for the attack to begin.

Both Gibbs and Pakenham learned of the fiasco, fumed a bit about blundering lieutenant colonels, but were reassured by staff officers that the 44th could get the equipment and be back in position in time. Pakenham was more worried about the failure of his scheme for a night attack across the river. It was now after 5:00, and Thornton hadn't started yet. At last it was decided to send the boats that were ready with as many men as they could hold. The Colonel finally shoved off toward 5:30 with only a third of his force.

"Thornton's people will be of no use whatever to the general attack," Pakenham fretted to his aide Captain Harry Smith. There was still time before daylight to call off the assault, Smith gently suggested. "This may be," Sir Edward replied, "but I have twice deferred the attack." As they talked, streaks of daylight began to appear, and the Captain urged more strongly that the advance be postponed. Pakenham could not be moved: "Smith, order the rocket to be fired. . . ."

Up, up the rocket went, signaling the start of the attack. Beneath the flicker of its falling stars Thornton's troops finally began to land across the river . . . Mullins's men struggled to bring up the ladders and fascines . . . and the rest of the army started for the American wall of earth. Behind the embankment crouched Jackson's men. They too had seen the rocket and knew what it meant.

At 500 yards a long brass 12-pounder near the left end of Jackson's line cracked into action. It was commanded by Garriques Flaugeac, a Napoleonic veteran who had witnessed scenes like this in Italy and Egypt. Then the rest of Jackson's artillery exploded with a roar. At 200 yards General Billy Carroll's Tennessee riflemen opened up, and the whole line soon blazed with fire. "Give it to them, boys," Jackson shouted. "Let's finish the business today!"

The British troops wavered on the right. The men of the 44th, returning with the ladders and fascines, failed to get back in time. Now they floundered about the rear of the column, confusing the other companies and feeling very jittery themselves. They began dropping their ladders and firing blindly at the American line. The leading troops—fired at from behind as well as in front—panicked and broke ranks.

General Gibbs rushed up shouting encouragement, but it was too late. The men streamed toward the rear, and Gibbs himself was cut down, four bullets in his body. Now Pakenham rushed over, waving his hat and shouting, "For shame! Remember you are British soldiers! This is the road you ought to take!" A volley of gunfire shattered his knee and brought down his horse. Borrowing Duncan MacDougall's mount, he was just back in the saddle when another volley tore into his groin and spine. Collapsing into MacDougall's arms, he mumbled, "Tell General . . . ," but he couldn't finish and died a few minutes later.

"Bayonet the rascals!" cried General Keane as the fleeing troops cut across his column to the left. Then he went down too, hit in the body and the thigh.

Leaderless, the remaining troops struggled on to the slaughter. Blinded by grape, Lieutenant Duncan Campbell of the 43rd was carried dying from the field, still clutching the hilt of his shattered sword. Colonel Rennie, a few others, reached the American lines before falling. Captain Thomas Wilkinson of Gibbs's staff died at the foot of the parapet, gasping, "Now why don't the troops come on? The day is our own!"

Back with the reserves General Lambert learned that he had inherited the command. Clearly there was only one thing to do. Around 8:00 he canceled the assault and pulled back what was left of Pakenham's army. Ironically, Thornton's attack across the river was a big success. But the day was lost by then, and Lambert decided to pull him back too. Admiral Codrington protested—they had to keep on or the army would starve. "Kill plenty more, Admiral," said Harry Smith bitterly. "Fewer rations will be required."

Candles gleamed from nearly every window along Pennsylvania Avenue in the early evening of February 4. Washington had just learned of Andrew Jackson's triumph, and a grand illumination seemed a fitting way to celebrate. As the word traveled northward to Baltimore, the guns of Fort McHenry—silent since the turbulent days of autumn—boomed out a national salute.

There was even more thrilling news in store. On the evening of the 11th the British sloop of war *Favourite*, still flying her flag of truce, slipped into New York Harbor bringing

Anthony St. John Baker and Henry Carroll with their copies of the peace treaty. Baker was held up by passport formalities, but at 8:00 P.M. Carroll landed at the Battery. He made no effort to hide his news, and within 20 minutes lamps blazed along lower Broadway, and cheering men were parading through the streets with candles.

The crowds ignored the fact that the treaty hadn't been ratified. A war-weary public assumed this would be automatic, and the celebration rolled on. By 9:00 P.M. the *Commercial Advertiser* had a special broadside on the streets. Bells were ringing, guns going off, and commercial messengers galloping in every direction to alert the country's network of enterprising speculators. Sunday was a holiday, but on Monday morning government 6% bonds shot up from 76 to 88, while the price of imports like tea and tin plummeted more than 50%.

By that time Carroll was well on his way to Washington, leaving Baker still tied up in red tape. As his post chaise lumbered south, the news continued to spread, further jarring prices and the nerves of the speculators.

At 4:00 P.M., February 14, Carroll's coach finally reached Washington . . . swung past the burnt shell of the Capitol . . . and rolled up Pennsylvania Avenue to James Monroe's residence at I Street. Carroll dashed inside as an excited crowd swarmed around the coach and its four steaming horses. A few moments later both Carroll and Monroe emerged and hurried down 18th Street to the President's temporary home at Octagon House. Here they joined Madison and retired upstairs to the circular room above the front hall. Other cabinet members soon joined them, and the little group huddled together, quietly dissecting the treaty paragraph by paragraph.

Downstairs all was excitement. Congressmen, officials, good friends streamed through the front door and milled around the drawing room embracing each other. For once party differences were forgotten, feuds buried, stilettos sheathed. Here again, nobody had seen the treaty but everyone was sure it would be all right—none more so than Dolley Madison, as she stood in the center of the room happily receiving congratulations. "No one could doubt," a guest recalled, "who beheld the radiance of joy that lighted up her countenance and diffused its beams all around, that all uncertainty was at an end. . . ."

And so it proved. Shortly after 8:oo the President appeared, pronouncing the terms as satisfactory. "Peace!" Mrs. Madison cried, and others took it up. "Peace! Peace!" the First Lady's cousin Sally Coles called from the top of the servants' stairs. Then the Madisons' butler John Freeman began pouring wine, while the pantry boy Paul Jennings got his fiddle and scraped away at the "President's March."

On the 17th the Senate unanimously ratified the treaty— just in time to have it ready for Anthony Baker, who arrived rather casually during the evening. At Monroe's suggestion the ratifications were exchanged at 11:oo P.M. that very night, and on the following morning the President formally promulgated peace.

Once again church bells rang and cannon boomed throughout the land. In Washington skyrockets were fired, and only three visitors from Massachusetts stood apart from the general rejoicing. In town to present the threatening demands of the recent Hartford Convention, Harrison Gray Otis and his colleagues knew that dissidence was finished.

The celebrations rolled on. At Schenectady James Freeman stood directly in front of a saluting cannon and paid for his carelessness with his life. At New York the citizens vied with each other in producing complicated illuminations. Most agreed that a Dr. MacNoon took the honors with an "elegant transparency" depicting a Tennessee rifleman shooting two redcoats labeled respectively "Booty" and "Beauty"—reputed to have been Admiral Cochrane's watchwords at New Orleans.

Off the New England coast the British sailors—weary of long months of blockade duty—staged their own celebrations. Rear Admiral Sir Henry Hotham gave his squadron double rations of rum, and the sailors of the *Superb* threw their caps into the sea.

It was different with the high command. Admiral Cockburn was operating off Georgia when the news reached him, and writing his friend Captain Palmer of the *Hebrus*, he couldn't conceal his disappointment: "That Jonathan should have been so easily let out of the cloven stick in which I thought we so securely had him, I sincerely lament."

Admiral Cochrane was deeply depressed. He had withdrawn his shattered force from Louisiana, seized Fort Bowyer at Mobile as a sort of consolation, and was just getting ready for new adventures in the Chesapeake—then suddenly, this peace. To Admiral Codrington, he seemed "most amazingly cast down," and Codrington decided it must be at the thought of missing so much prize money. It was perhaps a harsh judgment, for the two admirals—so congenial in the days of victory—were now barely on speaking terms.

Curiously enough, Cochrane's son Sir Thomas had a very different reaction to peace. Despite all his father's protection —all that parental pampering—the young man had a set of values that were quite his own. He would take his prize money with the rest of them, but the wanton destruction of farms and villages appalled him. He confided his thoughts to a private journal, and now, as word of the treaty arrived, he again picked up his pen:

I confess this intelligence gives me the most immense joy both on my own, and my country's account, and I de-

voutly hope the President will not hesitate as to whether he
will approve the treaty.

Already the war between Great Britain and some power
or other has lasted longer than I can recollect. . . . Our
country groans under the weight of its expense—and the
dreadful annual expense necessary to maintain the war
scarcely leaves wherewithal to support life to the middling
class of society. Relatives are torn asunder to supply men
for our Army and Navy, and there's scarcely a family in
England that does not mourn the loss of a father, husband
or brother.

Concern over the economic waste of war . . . "the middling class of society" . . . high casualties—it was the voice
of a new century speaking. And it was the voice of a new
and different England too, where manufacturers, shippers and
shopkeepers were beginning to push aside the fixed, closed
world of the eighteenth-century admirals and generals and
landed gentlemen.

Britain already reflected this new mood (it was what eased
Lord Liverpool's path in the face of demands for "chastisement"), but at the moment there was no time to ponder such
matters. On March 10—three days before the American
ratification reached London—devastating news arrived
from the Continent: Napoleon was loose again. Escaping
from Elba, he had landed on the southern coast of France and
headed north. The nation swarmed to his standards as the
whole rickety structure of Bourbon restoration collapsed. By
March 20 he was back in Paris, and Wellington was rushing
to reassemble his army.

A hundred days, and it was all over at Waterloo. Britain
once again relaxed in peace, but after the traumatic experience of the Emperor's return, the American war seemed an-
cient history and now lay quite forgotten.

Only a few unpleasant loose ends remained. There was, for

instance, the problem of jettisoning the Indians, wooed so ardently in the name of their "Great Father King George." Sailing away from the Gulf, Sir Alexander Cochrane entrusted this unpleasant task to Admiral Malcolm. He was instructed to urge the Creeks to accept the peace, to assure them that "they will grow rich, and being free from war, will be prosperous so as to be able to defend themselves from all future encroachments of the United States."

It turned out that wasn't enough. In August a Creek delegation appeared in London, shepherded by the indefatigable Major Nicolls, begging a "treaty of offensive and defensive alliance." For months they waited in vain for an audience with Lord Bathurst, while Nicolls was reduced to buying them socks and handkerchiefs out of his own pocket. Ultimately the government got rid of the visitors by a gift of 12 axes, 12 hammers and 24,520 nails.

Then there were the blacks who had heeded Admiral Cochrane's call to freedom. Here Sir Alexander's instructions to Malcolm were quite explicit: "You will endeavor to persuade them to go back to their former masters." Those who declined should be urged to join a West India regiment, and if they refused that too, they should be sent to Trinidad. Whatever fate awaited them there, they were probably better off than the blacks of the Chesapeake, who ended up shivering and destitute at Halifax.

And finally there was the prize money—none of the millions expected from New Orleans, but still a few thousand from here and there. Long after the Indians, the blacks and all the other issues were forgotten, the commanders continued their wrangling over the spoils of war. As late as 1817 Admiral Cochrane was still arguing that a minor raid in the Chesapeake was really a naval affair, thus cutting out any share for the army. It was April 1818 before the last of the claims, counterclaims and appeals were settled.

In America there were loose ends too. Washington had gone to war for free trade and sailors' rights, but London did not give an inch. Nor did land-hungry westerners have any better luck with their unannounced goal, the acquisition of Canada. The return of peace found Canada more firmly British than ever.

In the end, of course, these issues took care of themselves. Peace in Europe meant freedom to sail the seas, and the opening of the west gave expansionists all the land they could swallow. But these were fortuitous developments, not the achievements of warriors or diplomats. As far as war aims went, everything was left hanging.

Yet there were intangible results that went far beyond anything that could be written into a treaty. For one thing, America gained new respect abroad. For 20 years she had been regarded as a sort of semi-nation—almost a freak— by the great powers of Europe. Considered too weak to stand on her own, she had seen her rights ignored by both sides during the Napoleonic Wars.

Now all that was over. America had fought, and this fact alone gave her prestige. There had been some fiascoes, but there were skillful performances too, and these were occurring with ever-increasing frequency. "The war has raised our reputation in Europe," James Bayard wrote his son on Christmas Day, 1814, right after signing the treaty, "and it excites astonishment that we should have been able for one campaign to have fought Great Britain single handed. . . . I think it will be a long time before we are disturbed again by any of the powers of Europe."

Paralleling this new respect abroad went new confidence at home. Americans themselves had often wondered whether their flimsy federation could survive a real crisis. Many felt with Gouverneur Morris that "it was almost as vain to expect permanency from democracy as to construct a palace on the surface of the sea." Now they knew it could be done. True, there had been strains—economic chaos, poor military leadership, weak administration in Washington, dangerous dissension in New England—but this very catalogue of weaknesses made the ultimate survival all the more impressive.

And with this new self-confidence went a new freedom from dependence on Europe. Feeling they could now take care of themselves, Americans turned to developing their own vast resources. Soon, absorbed in internal development, they went to the opposite extreme and forgot about Europe completely. It was a state of mind that would last a hundred years.

But the most important result of all was a new feeling of national pride. "Who would not be an American?" rhapsodized *Niles' Register*, announcing the peace. "Long live the republic! All hail! Last asylum of oppressed humanity!" Such ecstasy would have seemed odd indeed in the years before the war, when Americans were united in their desire for independence but not much else. What was needed was a common experience, something to bring them together and drain the factions and dissensions that were tearing the country apart.

This the war had supplied, and none saw it more clearly than the French Minister Louis Serurier, who had witnessed so much from his perch in Washington. Drawing up for Talleyrand a sort of balance sheet on the results of the conflict, Serurier concluded: "Finally, the war has given the Americans what they so essentially lacked, a national character founded on a glory common to all."

This glory had many ingredients. There was Jackson's victory at New Orleans, so emphatic that it gave birth to a legend of American military invincibility that would live on and on. There were Perry's triumph on Lake Erie and Macdonough's on Lake Champlain—strategic turning points that were lasting tributes to courage and leadership. There were the single-ship engagements that offered the extra fillip of tweaking John Bull's nose. But of them all, nothing did as much to pull the country together as that searing experience of losing Washington—the people's own capital—followed by the thrill of national redemption when the same enemy force was repulsed at Baltimore.

In this swift turnabout new hopes were born, spirits raised, a nation uplifted. More than a banner of shining stars and stripes, a whole new sense of national identity shone forth in the smoky haze of what Francis Scott Key so lyrically called "the dawn's early light."

Acknowledgments

A shot rang out from the steeply wooded bank of the Patuxent and slashed the water not far astern of the ketch *Memory*. It was hunting season in Maryland, and some unknown marksman was trying his skill in the general direction of the river. Never dreaming that a large boat would be that far upstream, he added an uncomfortable touch of realism to an expedition that was retracing the British invasion route of 1814.

Such are the perils of research. And sharing them with the intrepid author was Charles C. Glover III, who generously lent both his boat and his navigational skills to the cause. Scores of others—though denied the opportunity to test their zeal under fire—also took endless time and trouble in helping me piece together this account.

Sometimes, as in the cruise up the Patuxent, the help was "on location." At Fort McHenry in Baltimore the enthusias-

345

tic staff of the National Park Service went all out—I'm especially grateful to Albert J. Benjamin, director, and Paul E. Plamann, the staff historian. They gave me the run of the place, opened up their splendid archives, and even contributed desk space in the old headquarters building. Working there late at night, it was easy to feel the ghosts of the past and picture the British squadron out in the dark, hurling its bombs and rockets at the sturdy ramparts.

For the Royal Navy's eye-view, the Maryland Port Administration generously made available its stylish tender *Nymph*. A fruitful morning was spent checking the various British positions and getting a reasonably clear picture of what Admiral Cochrane must have seen from the frigate *Surprize*. There was less success when it came to the question of what Francis Scott Key might have seen. The view of Fort McHenry from Old Roads Bay was lost in the smoky haze of a great industrial port, and it proved impossible to know whether "our flag was still there." Except for turning off the chimneys, Leonard Levering and Donald Klein of the Port Administration's dedicated staff performed miracles in providing a useful, productive day.

Some 120 miles south of Baltimore—and two centuries away in time—lies Tangier, the tiny Chesapeake island which the British developed as a base for their operations in the bay. With its old white houses, the clipped front yards, the narrow roadways so happily free of cars, Tangier seems part of an earlier time—a sort of American "Brigadoon"—which must have changed but little since Lieutenant Fenwick, Royal Engineers, laid out his neat rows of barracks and storehouses. They have been reclaimed by the bay now, but the memories and legends live on. Sydney Parks, Tangier's own historian, knows them all and has generously shared his knowledge.

Such visits to the scene are of course immensely helpful in

getting the feel of a subject. How else, in fact, to appreciate the tidal current of the Patuxent and what it meant to sail against it? But in the last analysis the full story of an event so long ago must depend on the holdings of libraries and archives. In this case some 28 different repositories contributed to the end result.

The patient staff at the National Archives in Washington pulled some 70 different reels of microfilm and innumerable dusty file boxes. Nothing was ever too much trouble for Mary Johnson, William Lind, Elmer O. Parker, or their cohorts. It was the same at the Library of Congress—whether at the Manuscript Division, the Map and Cartography Division, the Newspaper Division, or the Print and Photography Division, where Milton Kaplan performed miracles on short notice. At the library of the Office of Naval History Walter Bart Greenwood and Frederick Meigs were as helpful as always, and a special word of thanks goes to the National Park Service, which made available Dr. George J. Svejda's fine *History of the Star Spangled Banner from 1814 to the Present.*

No problem seemed too great or too small for the selfless librarians who took me under their wing. Sometimes the need was very specific: Charles Ball's account of Bladensburg at the Talbot County Free Library; or Sailing Master John Webster's interview at the Pratt Library in Baltimore; or copies of certain of Wellington's *Supplementary Despatches* at the Princeton University Library. Other times there seemed no limit to my needs: books, periodicals, newspapers, everything at the New York Public Library and the New York Society Library.

The historical societies deserve a paragraph of their own. Both history and its chroniclers would be lost without these painstaking custodians of the past, who do so much with so little. I'm especially indebted to the Columbia Historical Society, the Historical Society of Pennsylvania, the Maryland

Historical Society, the New-York Historical Society, and the Prince Georges County Historical Society. Their halls were filled with heroes, but none greater than P. William Filby, director of the Maryland Historical Society, who took time out from his own research on "The Star-Spangled Banner" to help me with mine.

The War of 1812 has been called a tie, and certainly this is the case when it comes to comparing British and American contributions to my research. The work involved tapping some 15 different repositories in England and Scotland, and without exception they were responsive and helpful.

At the Public Record Office in London Kenneth Timings gently guided this neophyte through the intricacies of learning the system, and Norman Evans in the Rolls Room kept the records flowing. As a single example, his uncomplaining staff produced 46 different ship logs—some of them trundled halfway across London.

More often it was a matter of going to the materials, and London offered a good test of both stamina and shoe leather. Yet the rewards were always waiting: the fine collection of regimental histories at the Ministry of Defense Library; the Codrington and Malcolm Papers at the National Maritime Museum; the Napier Papers at the British Museum; the splendid files at the Museum's newspaper library at Colindale; the priceless collection of old military and naval journals at the Royal United Services Institute, where the capable librarian John Dineen practically took me in as a tenant.

But London is only part of the story. The British cherish old documents, and countless collections are tucked away in local record offices, family muniments, and regimental headquarters. The National Register of Archives was of invaluable assistance in locating these sources, and I'm deeply grateful to Hugh Murray-Bailie and his fine staff for many valuable leads.

The Bury St. Edmunds and West Suffolk County Record Office made available an interesting memorandum, attributed to Sir Charles Napier, on the British strength at Washington and Baltimore. The West Sussex County Record Office gave me access to the informative Badcock-Lovell family papers. Through the kind intervention of the Scottish Record Office I was able to see a most important letter in the Hope of Luffness muniments, throwing much light on prize money as a factor in the Chesapeake and New Orleans campaigns.

The older regiments are very conscious of the past too, as anyone will soon learn who enjoys a cup of tea with Lieutenant Colonel W. W. M. Chard, Royal Regiment of Fusiliers, at the Tower of London. Along with his hospitality Colonel Chard showed me a most interesting notebook kept by Corporal James Brierly of the 7th Foot during the New Orleans campaign. I'm also indebted to Colonel H. J. Darlington (Retd) OBE, DL, Regimental Secretary of the Kings Own Royal Highland Fusiliers, for biographical information on members of the 4th Foot; to Captain A. J. Wilson (Retd), curator of the Royal Highland Fusiliers Museum, for similar data on members of the 21st Foot; and to the National Army Museum for making available several contemporary scrapbooks that supplied incidental background and color.

Finally, there is the National Library of Scotland in Edinburgh, with its voluminous papers of the Cochrane family. Most have never been used before in connection with this subject, but they are so beautifully organized that they were easily examined in the ten days allotted. Nothing could exceed the friendly helpfulness of James Ritchie and the fine staff of the library's Manuscript Division.

Apart from the many libraries and archives, there were numerous individuals—on both sides of the Atlantic—who filled important gaps in my knowledge. Alexander C. Brown came up with the exact location on the Pleasure House near

Cape Henry . . . Anne S. K. Brown supplied information on militia uniforms from her justly celebrated military collection . . . Howard I. Chapelle briefed me on gunboats . . . Jonathan Farber provided some useful photographs of North Point . . . Peter Kemp knew the answers to anything that had to do with the Royal Navy . . . Paul Lanham pinned down the location of the Bowie house at Bladensburg . . . Christopher McKee gave leads on little-known material at the National Archives . . . Roger McNamee checked out an important point in the Albany press . . . Philip S. Snyder let me examine his unique map of Bladensburg . . . Oliver Reeder was a gold mine on Baltimore harbor . . . Mary-Paulding Martin, director of the Star-Spangled Banner Flag House in Baltimore, shared her time and knowledge on a very busy day.

Then there were those to whom I turned for advice on almost anything. Outrageously imposed upon, they were good sports to the end. This gallant band included Francis F. Beirne, C. Carroll Davis, Richard von Doenhoff, Richard Hough, Myrick E. Land, and Cecil Wooddham Smith. A special niche must be added for Beth Straus, who took a hard look at Francis Scott Key and suggested the appropriate title.

Finally there are those who worked, as it were, in the boiler room and kept the project moving. Mildred Wretts-Smith did invaluable research in London. Jonathan Hornblower did the same in New York . . . then outdid himself collecting pictures in Washington. Randy Beehler first concentrated on Baltimore, but ended up all over the map. Margaret Brooks contributed her skills at translating French. Evan Thomas was as patient and competent an editor as always. And Florence Gallagher completed her silver anniversary year—it must seem to her a lifetime—of typing my scribbled foolscap.

Chapter Notes

It was the end of a long day at the Public Record Office in London, and it seemed almost unfair to find two pages of an old Admiralty letterbook stuck together with wax. The last reader, perhaps 150 years earlier, had evidently been careless with his candle.

That was only one of the difficulties of digging into an event that happened so long ago. The handwriting alone could be murder. For every Joshua Barney, with his neat clarity, there were a dozen like that incorrigible scribbler William H. Winder.

Even where the written word was clear and explicit, there remained the question of how much to believe. Admiral Codrington's daughter carefully deleted all critical references to Admiral Cochrane in publishing her father's memoirs. Jacob Barker and Daniel Carroll were still arguing 36 years later over who saved George Washington's portrait.

But the biggest problem of all was the sheer volume of material—mountains of file boxes, letterbooks, ships' logs, official records, historical society publications, newspapers, periodicals, books. And still they flow: In 1971 alone three extremely pertinent biographies appeared: Ralph Ketcham, *James Madison;* Harry Ammon, *James Monroe;* Frank A. Cassell, *Merchant Congressman in the Young Republic: Samuel Smith of Maryland, 1752– 1839.* With such a torrent of prose, it's impossible to list everything, but here are the sources that seemed most useful. . . .

Foreword

General background: Henry Adams, *History of the United States during the Administrations of Thomas Jefferson and James Madison;* Francis F. Beirne, *The War of 1812;* Harry L. Coles, *The War of 1812;* Reginald Horsman, *The War of 1812;* Marshall Smelser, *The Democratic Republic 1801–1815;* Glenn Tucker, *Poltroons and Patriots;* Leonard D. White, *The Jeffersonians;* and Henry Steele Commager's article "Second War of American Independence," in the June 17, 1962, *New York Times Magazine,* which first brought home to me the aptness of the war's older name.

1. Sails on the Chesapeake

British fleet sighted: National Archives, M124, R65, Joseph Middleton to Charles Gordon, 8/16/14; M222, R14, Thomas Swann to John Armstrong, 8/17; Alexandria *Gazette,* 8/20; Norfolk *Herald,* 8/23; New York *Evening Post,* 8/22. (All dates here and elsewhere, unless otherwise noted, are 1814.)

Washington's complacency during the early summer: supporting letters accompanying the report of the Congressional Committee appointed to investigate the capture of Washington, *Annals of Congress,* 1814–1815, 13th Cong., 3rd Ses.—especially letters of Armstrong, William Jones, John P. Van Ness. Also see *National Intelligencer,* 5/14; *Niles' Weekly Register,* 6/11, 6/18. James Madison's own misgivings: letters to Committee from Richard Rush, George W. Campbell. Madison's defense plan: J. S. Williams, *History of the Invasion and Capture of Washington;* Irving Brant, *James Madison, Commander in Chief, 1812–1836,* the sixth volume of a truly monumental biography.

Cabinet meeting of July 1: letters to investigating Committee from Armstrong, Campbell, Jones, Monroe, Rush. Also see Armstrong, *Notices of the War of 1812,* Vol. 2. Failure to implement decisions taken: undated "Memorandum," designated D21a, included among Winder Papers, Library of Congress. (Except where otherwise noted, I've relied on the Winder Papers at the Library of Congress, which largely duplicate the less legible file at the Maryland Historical Society.) Also see National Archives, M221, R67, "General Winder's Report on the Defense of District 10," 9/1; his better-known "Narrative" of 9/26, addressed to the investigating committee; and his correspondence with Armstrong, *American State Papers, Military Affairs,* I. Also see E. D. Ingraham, *A Sketch of the Events Which Preceded the Capture of Washington by the British in 1814.*

Armstrong's complacency: S. M. Hamilton, ed., *Writings of James Monroe,* Monroe to Jefferson, 12/21; Van Ness to investigating Committee; Ingraham; Williams. Winder's gyrations can be traced from his correspondence with Armstrong.

Washington developments, August 18: *National Intelligencer,* 8/18, 8/19; National Archives, RV, Prisoners and Prisons, Misc., July 1814–February 1815, Box 3, #583; Record Book 217, Letterbook 4, Tobias Lear to William Pratt, 8/18; *Bulletin of the Historical Society of Pennsylvania,* Vol. 1 (1845–47), Allen McLane, "Col. McLane's Visit to Washington, 1814"; Winder Papers, various, 8/18; letters to investigating Committee from Tobias Stansbury and Walter Smith.

Uncertainty as to British intentions: Van Ness to Committee; Charles J. Ingersoll, *Historical Sketch of the Second War between the United States of America and Great Britain,* Vol. 2; Library of Congress, Sam Smith Papers, Box 6, Levin Winder to Smith, 8/18. Also, Brant; Williams.

Monroe's mission to reconnoiter the enemy: Hamilton, *Writings,* Monroe to Madison, 8/18; New York Public Library, Monroe to George Hay, 9/7; letters to investigating Committee from Monroe, Van Ness, Robert Young.

2. *"Chastise the Savages"*

British mood toward America, spring of 1814: London *Times; Military Register;* Major Barber Beaumont in Parliament, 5/21, quoted in *National Intelligencer,* 8/15; Public Record Office (P.R.O.), WO 3/607, Henry Torrens to H. Clinton, 4/14; National Library of Scotland, Cochrane Papers 2265, R. Dundas to Sir Thos. Cochrane, 7/1; Henry Adams, *Writings of Albert Gallatin,* Gallatin to Monroe, 6/13. Wellington's doubts: J. Gurwood, *Wellington's Despatches,* Wellington to Bathurst, 2/22.

Evolvement of British expedition: P.R.O., WO 1/658, Duke of York to Earl Bathurst, 4/13; WO 3/607, Torrens to Sir John Murray and to Sir Henry Clinton, 4/14, 5/18; ADM 1/4229, Bathurst to John Croker, 4/26, 5/18; Bathurst to Major General Barnes, 5/20; ADM 2/1380, Croker to Sir Henry Bunbury, 4/27; Croker to Sir Alexander Cochrane, 5/19; WO 1/853, George Harrison to Commissary in Chief, 5/6. Also, Arthur R. Wellesley, 2nd Duke of Wellington, ed., *Supplementary Despatches, Correspondence and Memoranda of Field Marshal Arthur Duke of Wellington,* Vol. 9, York to Wellington, 4/14; Bathurst to Wellington, 5/18. Reasons for cutting back force: Cochrane Papers 2574, Melville to Cochrane, 5/22, 8/10.

Cochrane's plans for Atlantic coast: P.R.O., ADM 1/505, Cochrane to Croker, 3/31; ADM 1/506, Cochrane to Croker, 6/20, 7/18, 7/23; WO 1/141, Cochrane to Bathurst, 7/14; Cochrane Papers 2345, Cochrane to Melville, various; 2346, Cochrane to George Cockburn, 5/27, 7/1; 2326, Sir George Prevost to Cochrane, 6/2; 2333, Cockburn to Cochrane, 7/17, 2574, Cockburn to Cochrane, 4/2, 5/10, 7/17. Also see Library of Congress, Cockburn Papers, Vol. 24, Cockburn to Cochrane, 7/17; Vol. 38, same, 4/8, 4/26, 5/26, 7/21; Vol. 45, same, 7/17.

Cochrane's early planning for New Orleans: P.R.O., ADM 1/506, Hugh Pigot to Cochrane, 6/8; Cochrane to Croker, 6/20, 7/23; WO 1/141, Cochrane to Bathurst, 7/14; Cochrane Papers 2345, Cochrane to Melville, 3/25.

The lure of prize money: Cochrane Papers 2574, Cockburn to Cochrane, 4/2; Booth Johnson to Cochrane, n.d.; Cochrane Papers 2265, Cochrane to Sir Thomas Cochrane, 11/21; Cockburn Papers, Vol. 12, Cockburn to G. P. Hurlburt, 6/25; to Captain Watts, 7/18, 7/22; Vol. 38, Nourse to Cockburn, 7/23; *Louisiana Historical Quarterly*, Vol. 9, Duke of Wellington to Lord Longford, 5/22/1815; Hope of Luffness MSS, Major G. Brown to Lieutenant General Sir A. Hope, 4/4/1815; *Niles' Register*, Vol. 8, letters intercepted by privateer *Chasseur*, dealing with prize money. For knowledgeable comment, see J. W. Fortescue, *History of the British Army*, Vol. 10, and Michael Lewis, *A Social History of the Navy, 1793–1815*.

First-hand accounts, France to the Chesapeake: letters and diaries quoted in C. R. B. Barrett, *The 85th King's Light Infantry;* David Brown, *Diary of a Soldier;* Frederick Chaumier, *The Life of a Sailor;* George Laval Chesterton, *Peace, War and Adventure,* Vol. 1; G. R. Gleig, *A Narrative of the Campaigns of the British Army at Washington and New Orleans,* and its companion volume, *A Subaltern in America;* Sir Charles Napier, *Life and Correspondence; United Service Journal,* 1840, articles signed "an Old Sub," entitled "Recollections of the Expedition to the Chesapeake and against New Orleans"; same, 1841, articles signed "R.J.B." (Robert J. Barrett), entitled "Naval Recollections of the Late War"; Sir James Scott, *Recollections of a Naval Life;* Sir Harry Smith, *Autobiography.* Special mention should go to the collection of intimate letters from Sir Edward Codrington to his wife, designated as COD 7/1 among the Codrington Papers at the National Maritime Museum.

For years bibliophiles have conducted a medievalists' debate whether G. R. Gleig really wrote both the *Narrative* and the *Subaltern* cited above. They are anonymous and differ on minor points. All doubt is removed by Gleig's Diary, as included in Barrett; it is obviously the source of both books.

3. *Face to Face*

Last-minute preparations in Washington: National Archives, M221, R67, Winder to Armstrong, 8/19; RG 45/1, Jones to John Rodgers and to David Porter, 8/19; RG 45/7, Jones to Barney, 8/19, 8/20; RG 80/1, Jones to Wharton, 8/20; Winder Papers, Armstrong to Winder, 8/19; Winder to Stricker, 8/19. Also, Winder's "Report," 9/1; Van Ness to investigating Committee; Armstrong, *Notices;* McLane; Williams.

Militia muster and departure: letters to investigating Committee from John Law, Walter Smith, Van Ness; *National Intelligencer*, 8/20; Baltimore *Patriot and Evening Advertiser*, 8/24; *Niles' Register*, 8/27; Winder Papers, D23, "Minutes of Gen'l Winder's Proceedings"; James Wilkinson, *Memoirs of My Own Times*, Vol. 1; McLane; Williams. For analysis of District of Columbia Militia, see *Records of the Columbia Historical Society*, Vol. 50, Frederick P. Todd, "The Militia and Volunteers of the District of Columbia."

Monroe's scouting: Monroe to Madison, 8/20, 8/21; Monroe to Winder, 8/21; Monroe to investigating Committee—all accompanying the Committee's report. Also, National Archives, M124, R65, Monroe to Jones, 8/21; Winder Papers, Monroe to Winder, 8/21; New York *Evening Post*, 8/26.

British advance, 8/20–8/22: Cockburn to Cochrane, 8/22, included in William James, *Naval Occurences of the Late War between Great Britain and the United States of America* (This and James's parallel *Military Occurences* are the sources for all British official letters and dispatches, unless otherwise noted.) Also, Barrett; David Brown; and other British accounts cited above. General Ross's doubts: Gleig; Ingersoll; Scott; Ross's dispatch of 8/30; Baltimore *Patriot*, 5/29/1849; John S. Skinner's account. Also see J. Ralphe, *The Naval Biography of Great Britain*, Vol. 3, with material probably provided by Cockburn himself.

Destruction of Barney's flotilla: Cockburn to Cochrane, 8/22; *Niles' Register*, 11/5; Baltimore *Patriot*, 8/24; William M. Marine, *The British Invasion of Maryland, 1812–1815*; Mary Barney, *Biographical Memoir of the Late Joshua Barney*; Hulbert Footner, *Sailor of Fortune*; William James, *Naval History of Great Britain*, Vol. 6. Also, Chesterton; Scott.

American movements, morning of 8/22: National Archives, M221, R67, "Statement by General Winder," 9/1; Winder Papers, "Minutes of General Winder's Proceedings"; Major George Peters to J. S. Williams, 5/24/1854, quoted in Williams; letters to investigating Committee from Winder, Benjamin Burch, Monroe, John Law, Hanson Catlett, Walter Smith; *National Intelligencer*, 8/23; McLane; Williams. For Monroe's warning to Madison, 8/22, 9:00 A.M., see data accompanying investigating Committee's report. Some confusion has arisen because this warning is misdated in Armstrong's letter of 10/17 to the Committee.

Panic in Washington: saving records and property: *American State Papers, Misc.*, Vol. 2; National Archives, RG 45/350, Mordecai Booth to Thomas Tingey, running account; RG 217, Fourth Aud. Accts., petition of Daniel Renner and Nathaniel Heath; Library of Congress, William Thornton Papers, Mme. Serurier to Mrs. Thornton, 8/20. Fear of spies: National Archives RG 217, Letterbook 70–71, John Mason to Washington Boyd; Baltimore *Patriot*, 8/23; Williams; Ingraham. Fear of black revolt: New

York *Evening Post*, 8/22, 8/24; Richmond *Enquirer*, 8/27. Fleeing from city: New York *Commercial Advertiser*, 8/26; Mrs. Richard Rush to Rush, 8/21, copy at Fort McHenry.

American camp at Long Old Fields, 8/22–8/23: Gaillard Hunt, ed., *Writings of James Madison*, Madison to Mrs. Madison, 8/23; letters to investigating Committee from Jones, Law, Monroe, Winder; T. L. McKenny, *Memoirs and Travels;* Armstrong's *Notices;* Barney; Brant; Ingersoll; McLane; Wilkinson; Williams.

Winder's "victory plan," skirmish of 8/23, and American retreat to Washington: National Archives, Winder's "Report," 9/1; Winder Papers, "Minutes of Gen's Winder's Proceedings"; Peter to J. S. Williams, 5/24/-1854; letters to investigating Committee from Burch, Laval, Law, Walter Smith, Stansbury, Winder; Barney's official report, 8/29, included in John Brannan, *Official Letters of the Military and Naval Officers of the United States during the War with Great Britain.* (Unless otherwise noted, Brannan is the source used for all American official reports of battles and engagements.) Also see Baltimore *Patriot*, 8/27; Armstrong, *Notices;* Ingersoll; McKinney; McLane; Williams.

Mission to Cochrane for authority to move on Washington: Scott.

4. *Sleepless Hours*

Colonel George Minor's search for arms: letters to investigating Committee from Minor, Henry Carberry; *Records of the Columbia Historical Society*, Vol. 4, account of James Ewell. Also, Ingersoll; Ingraham. Winder's movements: various Winder letters, statements, and reports cited above; Barney's official report, 8/29; Peter to J. S. Williams, 5/24/1854; letters to investigating Committee from Burch, Laval; Baltimore *Patriot*, 8/27; *National Intelligencer*, 9/10. Armstrong's attitude: Campbell to investigating Committee; Hamilton *Writings*, Monroe to Jefferson, 12/21; Jacob Barker, *Life of Jacob Barker.* Also, Brant; Williams.

Stansbury's camp at Bladensburg: letters to investigating Committee from Monroe; William Pinkney; Stansbury; Joseph Sterett. Also, H. T. Tuckerman, *The Life of John Pendleton Kennedy;* Baltimore *Patriot*, 8/27, 9/5, 9/6; Armstrong, *Notices;* Ingersoll; McLane; Wilkinson; Williams. British camp, Ross's doubts finally resolved: "Old Sub"; Ralfe; Scott; Sir Harry Smith.

5. *Time Runs Out*

Morning conference at Winder's headquarters: Hunt, *Writings*, Madison's "Memorandum—Aug. 24, 1814"; Historical Society of Pennsylvania, U. C. Smith Collection, Williams Jones Papers, "Memorandum of Occurences on the 24th August, 1814"; Rush to J. S. Williams, 7/10/1855, quoted in Williams; Barney's official report, 8/29; Booth's running account to Tingey; various Winder letters and statements cited above; letters to investigating Committee from Armstrong; William Beall; Campbell; Hanson Catlett; Jones; Monroe; Rush; William Simmons. Also Armstrong, *Notices;* Barker; Ingersoll; Wilkinson; Williams.

Madison's exchange with Armstrong en route to Bladensburg: Library of Congress, G. W. Campbell Papers, Rush to Campbell, 11/2; Madison to Campbell, 11/2; Campbell to Madison, 12/15; Madison's "Memorandum"; letters to investigating Committee from Armstrong, Campbell, Rush. Also, Barker; Ingersoll; Williams.

Monroe's redeployment of Stansbury's troops: letters to investigating Committee from Pinkney; Stansbury; Sterett. Monroe never publicly took responsibility, but privately conceded his role—see Monroe to George Hay, 9/7, cited above.

British march to Bladensburg: Cockburn's official letter to Cochrane. Also, Barrett; Gleig; "Old Sub"; Scott; Sir Harry Smith. Decision to attack immediately: Ingersoll; Sir Harry Smith.

6. *Bladensburg*

First-hand accounts, American side: Winder's official report, 8/27; various other Winder letters, statements and reports, cited above; Barney's official report, 8/29; Library of Congress, Jenifer Sprigg to J. Hughes, 8/25; Peter to J. S. Williams, 5/24/1854; Rush to J. S. Williams, 7/10/1855; Madison's "Memorandum"; letters to the investigating Committee from all participants previously cited; Maryland Historical Society, John Stricker Papers, reports from Henry Thompson and other scouts to Stricker, 8/24; Thornton Papers, statement by William Elliot, 3/11/1815.

Also, New York *Commercial Advertiser*, 8/27, 8/31; New York *Evening Post*, 9/2, 9/5; Philadelphia *General Advertiser*, 8/29, 8/31; Georgetown *Federal Republican*, 8/30; *National Intelligencer*, 9/9; Norfolk *Herald*, 8/30; *Niles' Register*, Vol. 7 Supplement, pp. 159-160, containing undated letter from Barney.

Later recollections in books: Tuckerman, J. P. Kennedy's account; Marine, Henry Fulford's and John Webster's accounts; Mary Barney, *Biographical Memoir*, Commodore Barney's account; Charles Ball, *Slavery in the United States: Narrative of the Life and Adventures of Charles Ball.* For the unseemly flight of Barney's aide George W. Wilson, see Footner; also Jones Papers, Barney to Jones, 9/7.

First-hand accounts, British side: Cochrane's dispatch, 9/2; Ross's dispatch, 8/30; Cockburn's official letter to Cochrane, 8/27. Also see David Brown; Gleig; "Old Sub"; Scott; Sir Harry Smith; Barrett, for letters of

R. Gubbins and J. J. Knox; Ingersoll, for recollections of Colonel William
Wood; *Magazine of American History*, Vol. 4, Horatio King, "The Battle
of Bladensburg," for later recollections by Gleig.

A minor riddle involves the strength of British artillery at Bladensburg.
The generally accepted figure is three guns, but strong evidence indicates no
more than one gun reached the field in time for the battle. See Chesterton;
Scott; Cockburn to Cochrane, 8/27.

General commentary: Benson J. Lossing, *Pictorial Field Book of the
War of 1812*; Charles G. Muller, *The Darkest Day: 1814*; Neil H. Swan-
son, *The Perilous Fight*; Andrew Tully, *When They Burned the White
House*. Also, Adams (especially for his devastating indictment of Winder);
Ammon; Brant; Coles; Fortescue; Ingersoll; Tucker; Wilkinson; Williams.

The Thomas Barclay affair: National Archives, RG 217, John Mason
Letterbook, running correspondence 9/8–10/11; P.R.O., ADM 1/3767,
Barclay to Commissioners for Transport Service, 12/3.

7. *Ordeal by Fire*

Fleeing the President's House: Dolley Madison to Lucy Todd, 8/23–8/24,
included in L. B. Cutts, *Memoirs and Letters of Dolly Madison*; Katharine
Anthony, *Dolly Madison, Her Life and Times*; A. C. Clark, *Life and
Letters of Dolly Madison*; Paul Jennings, *A Colored Man's Reminiscences
of James Madison*; Anne H. Wharton, *Social Life in the Early Republic*.
Also, Barker; Brant; Ingersoll; Lossing. Saving the portrait of George
Washington: Daniel J. Carroll, letter to the editor, New York *Herald*,
1/31/1848; Jacob Barker to Carroll, 2/8/1848; Dolley Madison to R. G. L.
de Peyster, 2/11/1848; and Barker to Carroll, 5/5/1848, all included in
Barker's *Life*.

Abandoning the city: Hamilton, *Writings*, "J. M. Notes Respecting the
Burning City in 1814," n.d.; Madison's "Memorandum"; Jones's "Memorandum"; Booth's running account to Tingey; various Winder letters and
statements; letters to the investigating Committee from Catlett, Jones, Laval,
Monroe, Simmons, Tingey.

Also see Tingey to Jones, 8/27, included in the Committee's supporting
data; New-York Historical Society, Mary Hunter to Susan Cuthbert, 8/30;
Library of Congress, Michael Shiner, "Journal"; Maryland Historical Soci-
ety, John Webster to Brantz Mayer, 7/22/1853; Anne H. Wharton, *Social
Life in the Early Republic*, "Miss Brown's" account; *Records of the
Columbia Historical Society*, Vol. 19, Mrs. William Thornton's Diary; same,
Vol. 24, John P. Van Ness's bill for whiskey given to exhausted soldiers.
Eyewitness newspaper accounts: Baltimore *Patriot*, 8/27; Richmond *En-
quirer*, 8/27; Georgetown *Federal Republican*, 8/30, 9/20; New York

Commercial Advertiser, 9/3. General comments: Armstrong, *Notices;* Ingersoll; Lossing; Williams.

British entering the city: Gleig; Scott; Cockburn to Cochrane, 8/27; Royal United Services Institute, *Military Extracts,* Vol. 2, account of Captain Bennett, 4th Foot; James, *Naval History;* Ingersoll; Ingraham. Watched by local citizens: Baltimore *Patriot,* 8/30, 8/31, 9/6; Georgetown *Federal Republican,* 8/30; Norfolk *Herald,* 8/30. Also see Booth; Ewell; Mrs. Hunter; Shiner.

Burning the Capitol: Saul K. Padover, *Jefferson and the National Capital,* Benjamin Latrobe to Jefferson, n.d.; Horatio King, "The Battle of Bladensburg"; *Records of the Columbia Historical Society,* Vol. 24, Hallie L. Wright, "Sketch of Elias Boudinot Caldwell"; *American State Papers,* Misc., Vol. 2, letters dealing with loss of House records and Library of Congress; London *Times,* 9/29. Also see Hunter; Ingersoll; Lossing; Scott; Williams. Moving up Pennsylvania Avenue: London *Times,* 9/29, Chester Bailey's account; Georgetown *Federal Republican,* 9/16, William P. Gardner's account; New-York Historical Society, John W. Taylor to Mrs. Jane Taylor, 10/8; Margaret Bayard Smith, *Forty Years of Washington Society;* James, *Naval History.*

Burning the President's House: *Archives des Affaires Étrangères, Correspondence Politique, États Unis,* Louis Serurier to Talleyrand, 8/27 (copy in Library of Congress); *United Service Journal,* Part I (1829), Ross to "Ned," 8/30 c.; letters of participants in London *Morning Post,* 10/2; *Courier,* 10/3; and R.U.S.I., *Military Extracts,* Vol. 5. Also see Barrett; Chesterton; Gleig; Ingersoll; Scott; Sir Harry Smith; Margaret Bayard Smith. Supper at Mrs. Suter's: Ingersoll; McLane; Scott. Visiting *National Intelligencer* offices: New York *Commercial Advertiser,* 8/29; London *Times,* 9/29; *Records of Columbia Historical Society,* Vol. 7, Maud Burr Morris, "Life of Pontius D. Stelle." Also see Ewell; Ingersoll; Margaret Bayard Smith; Taylor to Mrs. Taylor.

Events of 8/25. Death of John Lewis: Ingersoll. Saving the Patent Office: New York *Commercial Advertiser,* 9/10, William Thornton's account; Ingersoll. Potomac bridge burned: John Morton to investigating Committee; Codrington Papers, COD 7/1, Codrington to wife, 8/31; Ingersoll; Williams. Explosion at Greenleaf's Point: Baltimore *Patriot,* 8/31; New York *Evening Post,* 9/13; *Niles' Register,* Vol. 7 Supplement, pp. 149–150; P.R.O., WO 1/141, 9/2, casualty figures; Ingersoll; Scott. The great storm: *Records of the Columbia Historical Society,* Vol. 3, Mrs. V. C. Moore, "Reminiscences of Washington"; Vol. 12, A. C. Clark, "The Abraham Young Mansion." Also Ewell; Gleig; Ingersoll; Shiner; Wharton; Tingey to Jones, 8/27; Horatio King, "The Battle of Bladensburg." Loosely called a "hurricane" or a "tornado," the storm was clearly an exceptionally violent thunder squall—see logs of British ships in Potomac and Patuxent.

British withdrawal: Barrett; Chesterton; Ewell; Gleig; "Old Sub"; Scott; Sir Harry Smith; Ross's dispatch, 8/30; Catlett to investigating Committee; Philadelphia *General Advertiser*, 8/31, 9/20. British desertions: P.R.O., WO 1/141, 9/1, official returns. Seizure of Dr. Beanes: see Norfolk *Herald*, 9/6, for account attributed to "a gentleman just from Marlborough"; and Tucker for similar account taken from Baltimore *Federal Gazette*.

8. *Shock Waves*

American Army scattered: National Archives, M221, R64, McLane to Armstrong, 8/27; R67, Winder to Armstrong, 8/25; Sam Smith Papers, Box 6, Winder to Stricker, 8/25, 8/26; Thompson to Stricker, 8/25; Box 14, Daniel Parker to Sam Smith, 8/27; Winder Papers, Stansbury to Winder, 8/26 (*sic*); Monroe, "Notes Respecting the Burning City"; J. L. Daggs, "Autobiography," copy at Fort McHenry; letters to investigating Committee from Walter Smith; Sterett. Also see Barker; McKinney; Margaret Bayard Smith; Sprigg; Webster; and various statements and reports of General Winder.

The government in flight: The Madisons' movements are convincingly traced in Brant. Supporting correspondence: Booth's running account to Tingey; Ingraham, Madison to Monroe, 8/26; Hunt, *Writings*, Madison to Mrs. Madison, 8/27; Historical Society of Pennsylvania, Jones Papers, Madison to Jones, 8/27. Also see Georgetown *Federal Republican*, 8/30; New York *Commercial Advertiser*, 8/31; Monroe, "Notes"; and Margaret Bayard Smith.

Shambles in Washington: *National Intelligencer*, 8/31, 9/24; New York *Commercial Advertiser*, 8/31, 9/10; Tingey to investigating Committee; National Archives, M179, R30, James Blake to Madison, 8/27. Also see Ingersoll; Jennings; Shiner; Mrs. Thornton's Diary.

Alexandria captured: *American State Papers*, 16, Military Affairs, 1; John Hungerford to Monroe, 9/6; and to investigating Committee; Norfolk *Herald*, 9/2, 9/30; Richmond *Virginia Patriot*, 9/10; New York *Evening Post*, 9/5, 9/13; P.R.O., logs of *Aetna, Devastation, Erebus, Euryalus, Meteor, Seahorse;* ADM 1/507, 8/29, list of prizes taken at Alexandria; Gordon's official letter to Cochrane, 9/9; James, *Naval History;* Napier.

Washington recovers: Serurier to Talleyrand, 8/27; New York *Commercial Advertiser*, 9/10, Thornton to "the Public"; *National Intelligencer*, 9/10; Monroe to George Hay, 9/7; Monroe's "Notes"; Library of Congress, Joseph H. Nicholson Papers, Box 7, Monroe to Nicholson, 9/21. Armstrong forced out: Ingraham, Armstrong to editors of Baltimore *Patriot*, 9/3; Madison, "Memorandum," 8/29; New-York Historical Society, Nicholson to Mrs. Gallatin, 9/4; Library of Congress, Campbell Papers, Armstrong to Madison, 9/4. Also see Barker, Brant, Ingersoll, McKenney. Efforts to block

British squadron on Potomac: *Niles' Register*, 10/1, official reports of Perry, Porter, and Rodgers; logs of *Erebus, Euryalus, Seahorse;* Gordon to Cochrane, 9/9; Napier. Sir Peter Parker killed: Baltimore *Patriot* 9/5, 9/6; T. H. Palmer, *Historical Register*, Vol. 4, Philip Reed to Benjamin Chambers 9/3; Henry Crease's official letter to Cochrane, 9/1; Sir George Dallas, *Biographical Memoir of the Late Sir Peter Parker.*

The warning that might have saved Washington: Maryland Historical Society, Winder Papers, A69, "Friend" to Madison, 7/27/14.

America reacts: National Archives, M124, R65, Henry Fulton to Jones, 9/6; M179, R30, John Jacob Astor to Monroe, 8/27; M221, R60, J. A. Coles to James Monroe, 9/11; R65, Sam Ringgold to Armstrong, 8/27; R66, John Sterett to Armstrong, 8/30; M222, R13, Richland Citizens Committee to War Department, n.d.; Library of Congress, Rodgers-Macomb Papers, Minerva Rodgers to John Rodgers, 8/25; M. E. Bartgis, "Journal," copy at Fort McHenry; Pierre Irving, *Life and Letters of Washington Irving.* Newspapers: Boston *Daily Advertiser, Repertory;* New England *Palladium;* New York *Evening Post, Commercial Advertiser, Gazette and General Advertiser;* Norfolk *Herald;* Philadelphia *General Advertiser, United States Gazette;* Richmond *Enquirer.* See Lossing for the grog-spliced schedule of the Philadelphia volunteer diggers.

British decision to leave Chesapeake: P.R.O., WO 1/141, Cochrane to Bathurst, 8/28, 9/2; Cochrane Papers 2345, Cochrane to Melville, 9/3; 2450, Cochrane to Sir Thomas Hardy, 9/4; Cochrane to Cockburn, 9/5; Malcolm Papers, MAL/103, Cochrane to Malcolm, 9/4; Codrington Papers, COD 6/4, General Memorandum to entire force, 9/4. Also see Scott; Sir Harry Smith.

9. *Focus on Baltimore*

Initial panic: Nicholson Papers, Nicholson to Mrs. Gallatin, 9/4; Marine, Henry Fulford's account; Annie Leakin Sioussat, *Old Baltimore*, David Winchester to James Winchester, 8/25; Library of Congress, Rodgers Family Papers, Rodgers to Jones, 8/27; National Archives, RG 45/464, Porter to Jones, 8/27. Also, New York *Commercial Advertiser*, 8/27, 8/29; New York *Evening Post*, 8/27, 8/29.

Sam Smith takes over: Samuel Smith Papers, Resolution of Committee of Vigilance and Safety, 8/25; Levin Winder to Smith, 8/26; Smith to Armstrong, 8/27. Frank Cassell's biography gives Smith long-overdue recognition, but the General was not an easy man to live with: Library of Congress, Monroe Papers, Joseph Nicholson to Monroe, 9/1, and Paul Bentalou to Monroe, 9/24, copies of both at Fort McHenry; Winder Papers, Tilghman to Winder, n.d.; Singleton to Winder, 9/10; Smith Papers, T. M. Forman to Smith, 10/3; *Maryland Historical Magazine*, Vol. 40, R. H. Goldsborough to wife, 9/21.

Smith-Winder controversy: National Archives, M221, R67, correspondence of Smith, Winder, and Monroe, 8/26–9/11. This is generally, but not always, duplicated by letters in Smith and Winder Papers. Analyzed in *Maryland Historical Magazine*, Vol. 39, Ralph J. Robinson, "Controversy over the Command at Baltimore."

Baltimore mobilized: Sam Smith Papers, Boxes 5 and 6, various; National Archives, M221, R59–60 (help pouring in); M222, R12, Committee of Vigilance to War Department, 10/11 (money raised); Maryland Historical Society, the Reverend James Stevens to Mrs. Julian Pernell, 9/29; Forman to wife, various; Baltimore *Patriot*, August–September; New York *Evening Post*, 9/5. Also, *Maryland Historical Magazine*, Vol. 2, F. M. Colston, "Battle of North Point"; Vol. 39, W. D. Hoyt, Jr., "Civilian Defense in Baltimore," extracting the minutes of the Committee of Vigilance and Safety; Vol. 54, Franklin M. Mullaly, "The Battle of Baltimore"; S. Sydney Bradford, "Fort McHenry, 1814." Additional details: Cassell; Marine; Swanson.

Key-Skinner mission: National Archives, M625, R77, John Mason to John S. Skinner and Francis Scott Key, 9/2; Mason to Skinner, 9/2; Mason to Ross, 9/2; Skinner to Mason, 9/5; Ross to Mason, 9/7; M179, R30, Skinner to Monroe, 9/2; RG 217, Mason Letterbook 95, Mason to Colonel Thornton, 9/12 (*sic*). Also, Marine, Levin Winder to Ross, 8/31; Maryland Historical Society, Key to John Randolph, 10/5; Library of Congress, Key to "My Dear Mother," copy at Fort McHenry; Roger B. Taney Papers, Taney to Charles Howard, 3/17/1856; Baltimore *Sun*, Skinner to editor, 5/29/1849. Mission received by British fleet: P.R.O., logs of *Royal Oak*, 9/6; *Tonnant*, 9/7; *Surprize*, 9/8; *ADM* 50/87, Malcolm's Journal, 9/6; ADM 50/119, Codrington's Journal; Cochrane Papers 2336, Malcolm to Cochrane, 9/6; National Maritime Museum, MS 64/044, Malcolm to Barclay and to Mason, 9/6.

Name of Key's boat: extensive research by Ralph J. Robinson, *Baltimore* magazine, January 1955, suggests that the vessel was Ferguson's sloop *President*, and this is pretty much accepted by P. W. Filby and Edward G. Howard, *Star-Spangled Books*. But to one student of riddles, it's not that simple. For instance, Robinson made much of the fact that Skinner did use the *President* in December 1813, and his expense account submitted in 1817 lists $545 paid to B. Ferguson "for the use of his vessel"—in the singular. All very well, but Ferguson's receipt for the very same payment is "for the use of our packets"—in the plural.

British decision to attack Baltimore: Cochrane Papers 2329, Sir Peter Parker to Cochrane, 8/30; 2345, Cochrane to Melville, 9/17; Codrington Papers, COD 6/4, Letterbook, orders to *Asia*, 9/7; COD 7/1, Codrington to wife, 9/10, 9/13; also see Ralfe, Scott, Sir Harry Smith. Temporarily diverted to Potomac: logs of *Royal Oak*, *Surprize*, *Tonnant* and other ships of fleet, 9/7–9/9; COD 7/1, Codrington to wife, 9/10. Heading back up the bay: ships' logs; Gleig; COD 6/4, Letterbook.

Baltimore reacts: Maryland Historical Society, the Reverend James Stevens to Mrs. Julian Pernell, 9/29; Severn Teackle to Philip Wallis, 9/23; Mendes I. Cohen, recollections as told to B. I. Cohen; George Armistead to wife, 9/10. Also, Baltimore *Sun*, 9/13/1847, recollections of Thomas Beacham, copy at Fort McHenry; Rogers-Macomb Papers, Solomon Rutter to John Rodgers, 9/11; National Archives, RG45, Report of H. S. Newcomb, 9/18; log of U.S. sloop-of-war *Erie*; John Stricker's official report, 9/15; *National Intelligencer*, 9/13, 9/14; Philadelphia *General Advertiser*, 9/13; *National Advocate*, 9/14; *United States Gazette*, 9/16; New York *Evening Post*, 9/17; *Commercial Advertiser*, 9/19. Also, Lossing, Marine, Sioussat, Swanson.

10. *North Point*

First-hand accounts, American side: Stricker's report, 9/15; Smith's report, 9/19; Sam Smith Papers, various; Maryland Historical Society, L. Hollingsworth to Ann Hollingsworth, 9/13; Baltimore *Sun*, 10/31/1846, account by "one of the Forlorn Party"; 9/13/1847, account by the Reverend Thomas Beacham. Contemporary newspapers with first-hand accounts: *United States Gazette*, 9/16, 9/19; New York *Evening Post*, 9/17; *Commercial Advertiser*, 9/19; Georgetown *Federal Republican*, 10/7; *Niles' Register*, 9/24.

First-hand accounts, British: Cockburn's official letter to Cochrane, 9/15; Arthur Brooke's dispatch, 9/17; Cochrane's dispatch, 9/17; Cochrane Papers 2345, Cochrane to Melville, 9/17; *Niles' Register*, 10/27, account by unidentified British officer. Also see Barrett; Gleig; "Old Sub"; Scott.

Death of Ross: Ralfe's authorized biography of Cockburn is as close as we are likely to get to a first-hand account by the Admiral himself. Other details: P.R.O., WO 3/608, Torrens to Vansittart, 11/11; ADM 1/509, John Lambert to Cochrane, 2/18/1815; log of *Royal Oak*, 9/12; Cochrane Papers 2345, Cochrane to Melville, 9/17; William Stanhope Lovell (Badcock), *Personal Narrative of Events;* New York Public Library, Gordon Gallie MacDonald, MS account; London *Examiner*, 10/23. The question remains, who fired the fatal shots? Contemporary sources usually gave the credit to Daniel Wells and Harry McComas of Captain Aisquith's rifle company. Later authorities were skeptical, contending that Ross was killed not by rifle but by musket fire. Yet most British sources—including Cochrane's private letter of 9/17 to Melville—say that the General was indeed killed by a rifle.

General comment on the battle: Beirne; James, *Military Occurences;* Lossing; Marine; Muller; Ralfe; Sioussat; Swanson; Tucker.

Cochrane's advance up the Patapsco: logs of *Surprize* and other vessels involved; Codrington Papers, COD 6/1, Codrington to Joseph Nourse, 9/12; "R.J.B." (Robert J. Barrett) account; James, *Naval History*. Cochrane's communications with the army ashore, discovered among his papers in Edinburgh, throw fresh light on British plans and problems: Cochrane Papers 2329, Cochrane to Ross, 9/12; Cochrane to Brooke, 9/12; Brooke to Cochrane, 9/13, 12:30 A.M.

Last-minute preparations at Fort McHenry: The block ships were not mere hulks, but mostly sound vessels that meant a real sacrifice—see National Archives, Fiscal Division File No. 6; Report No. 70, accompanying HR 412, 20th Cong. 2nd Ses. Armistead's fears: Smith Papers, Armistead to Smith, n.d.; Winder Papers, Nicholson to Winder, 9/12. Passwords: Rogers-Macomb Papers, Rutter to Armistead, 9/12. The flag: Mary-Paulding Martin, *The Flag House Story;* Victor Weybright, *Spangled Banner*.

11. *Fort McHenry*

Bombardment during the day, British accounts: logs of 15 of the 16 ships that participated (none could be found for *Rover*); Cochrane's dispatch, 9/17; Codrington Papers, COD 6/3, Codrington to fleet carpenters, 9/13; "R.J.B." (Robert J. Barrett); "Old Sub"; E. Fraser and L. G. Carr-Laughton, *The Royal Marine Artillery*, Vol. 1; James, *Military Occurences;* James, *Naval History*. Cochrane's mounting frustration: Cochrane Papers 2329, Cochrane to Cockburn, 9/13. American accounts: Armistead's official report, 9/24; Nicholson to Monroe, 9/18, copy at Fort McHenry; and at Maryland Historical Society, see Teackle to Wallis, 9/23; James Piper to Mayer, 4/17/1854; M. I. Cohen account. Also see *Niles' Register*, 9/24; J. Thomas Scharf, *Chronicles of Baltimore;* Lossing; Marine; Sioussat.

British land operations. Plans and hopes: Cochrane Papers 2329, Brooke to Cochrane, 9/13. Advance to the American lines: Brooke's dispatch, 9/17; Cochrane's dispatch, 9/15; Barrett; Chesterton; Gleig; Ralfe; Scott. American countermeasures: Stricker's official report, 9/15; Sam Smith's official report, 9/19; Lossing; Sioussat; Swanson. Naval diversion requested: Gleig; Scott. Decision to withdraw: Cochrane Papers 2329, Brooke to Cochrane, 9/14; Cockburn's official letter to Cochrane, 9/15; Ralfe; Scott; Smith Papers, James McCulloh, Jr., to Smith, 9/14 (*sic*). Retirement: Chesterton; Gleig; "Narrative of North Point by a British Officer," copy at Fort McHenry.

Ferry Branch diversion: Cochrane Papers 2329, Cochrane to Captain Charles Napier, 9/13; Elers Napier, *Life and Correspondence of Admiral Sir Charles Napier;* James, *Military Occurences;* John S. Skinner, account in the Baltimore *Sun*, 5/29/1849. As seen from American side: Armistead's official report, 9/24; Rogers's official report, 9/23; Lieutenant H. S. Newcomb's report, 9/18; John A. Webster to Brantz Mayer, 7/22/1853; also

Webster's undated account at Pratt Library, Baltimore; Philadelphia *National Advocate*, 9/19.

Key's experiences: he was some eight miles down the river; the weather was stormy; and Armistead said the bombardment continued till 7:00 A.M., over an hour after sunrise. Under the circumstances, it has been asked whether Key really saw what he wrote. Subject to minor poetic license, the evidence suggests he did:

1. The logs of the British ships *Ramilles, Thames, and Trave*—all anchored near Key's boat—independently note watching the fort under bombardment.

2. The British ceased fire at 4:00 A.M., then resumed only occasional fire from several of their ships until 7:00 A.M., when they stopped altogether. See logs, *Aetna, Cockchafer, Devastation, Hebrus, Meteor, Terror.* The fort's return fire seems to have ceased by 4:00 A.M.

3. John S. Skinner's account, Baltimore *Sun*, May 29, 1849, corroborated Key and is remarkably accurate on other counts when checked against British sources.

Oddly enough, three years of research have unearthed only one first-hand account that refers to the flag without apparent knowledge of "The Star-Spangled Banner." It is the article by "R.J.B." (Midshipman Robert J. Barrett) of the *Hebrus*, appearing in the *United Service Journal*, April, 1841. Describing the squadron's withdrawal from Fort McHenry, Barrett recalled, "As the last vessel spread her canvas to the wind, the Americans hoisted a most superb and splendid ensign on their battery. . . ."

This raises an intriguing possibility. At the time Armistead bought the big flag from Mary Pickersgill, he also bought a smaller "storm flag" for $168.54. During the windy, rain-swept night of the bombardment, could he have substituted this storm flag; then in the early morning again hoisted his big flag in triumph as the British retired? Was it the storm flag—and not its famous counterpart—that Key actually saw?

Key's return and publication of "The Star-Spangled Banner": P. W. Filby and Edward G. Howard, *Star-Spangled Books*, which clearly supersedes earlier research in this area. For contemporary accounts of Key's return, see Severn Teackle to Philip Wallis, 9/23; New York *Evening Post*, 9/20; *Gazette and General Advertiser*, 9/20; Philadelphia *United States Gazette*, 9/21. The *Frederick-town Herald*, 9/24, seems to be the first paper that specifically attributes the song to Key. For additional background, see Skinner's account; Taney to Howard, 3/17/1856; Ralph J. Robinson, "The Birth of the National Anthem," *Baltimore* magazine, December 1953; O. G. T. Sonneck, *The Star-Spangled Banner;* George J. Svejda, *History of the Star Spangled Banner from 1814 to the Present.*

America reacts: New York *Commercial Advertiser*, 9/16; Norfolk *Herald*,

9/20; Salem *Register*, quoted in Baltimore *Patriot*, 9/27. British withdrawal: logs of ships mentioned; Cochrane's "victory message," Codrington Papers, COD 6/4, 9/16; Cochrane's dispatch, 9/17; Cochrane Papers 2345, Cochrane to Melville, 9/17.

12. *Britain Struggles with Herself*

British reaction to the capture of Washington: P.R.O., WO 3/608, Torrens correspondence in general, 9/27–10/1; Cochrane Papers 2574, various, 9/28–10/2; correspondence of Lord Liverpool and other leaders included in Wellington's *Supplementary Dispatches*, Vol. 9, especially Liverpool to Wellington, 9/27. Newspapers: *Courier, Evening Star, Examiner, Morning Chronicle, Morning Post, News, Public Ledger and Daily Advertiser, Sun, Times.* Periodicals: *Bell's Weekly Messenger, Cobbett's Weekly Register, Military Register, Naval Chronicle, Spectator, Statesman.* Decision to reinforce Cochrane: P.R.O., WO 6/2, Bathurst to Ross, 9/28, 9/29; WO 3/608, Torrens to Ross and to Cochrane, 9/30.

The impact at Ghent: For over-all analysis, both here and later, I've leaned heavily on two splendid books: George Dangerfield, *The Era of Good Feelings;* and Bradford Perkins, *Castlereagh and Adams.* For incidental detail, I've depended greatly on the correspondence of various American participants: Charles F. Adams, ed., *Memoirs of John Quincy Adams*, Vol. 3; Worthington C. Ford, ed., *The Writings of John Quincy Adams*, Vol. 5; James F. Hopkins, ed., *The Papers of Henry Clay*, Vol. 1; Henry Adams, ed., *Writings of Albert Gallatin*, Vol. 1; American Historical Association, *Annual Report*, 1913, Vol. 2, "Papers of James Bayard"; Count Gallatin, ed., *The Diary of James Gallatin.* Two useful magazine articles: *American Heritage*, December 1960, Fred L. Engelman, "The Peace of Christmas Eve," and *Maryland Historical Magazine*, Vol. 66, Chester G. Dunham, "Christopher Hughes, Jr., at Ghent, 1814."

British reaction to Baltimore and Lake Champlain: P.R.O., WO 3/608, Torrens correspondence, various, especially letter of 11/26 to Marquis of Tweedale; Wellington's *Supplementary Despatches*, Vol. 9, Liverpool, to Castlereagh, 10/21; Torrens to Wellington, 11/3; also newspapers and periodicals noted above.

Growing pressure for peace: debates in Parliament as reported regularly by the *Times;* files of *Morning Chronicle, Statesman, Cobbett's Weekly Register*, and other critics of the war; also Wellington's *Supplementary Despatches*, Vol. 9, Liverpool to Castlereagh, 10/28, 11/2, 11/18, 12/23. For the government's efforts to enlist Wellington's support, and the Duke's own influence for peace, see Francis Bickley, ed., *Report on the Manuscripts of Earl Bathurst*, Wellington to Bathurst, 11/4; Wellington's *Supplementary*

Despatches, Vol. 9, Liverpool's correspondence with Wellington and Castlereagh, 11/4, 11/7, 11/9, 11/13, 11/18.

The peace treaty signed: published writings of Adams, Bayard, Clay, Albert Gallatin, James Gallatin. Also see Dangerfield; Dunham; Perkins. Reaction in London: Wellington's *Supplementary Despatches*, Vol. 9, various, but especially Liverpool to Canning, 12/28; also newspapers and periodicals cited above. Treaty ratified, and sent to America: P.R.O. ADM 2/1381, Croker correspondence, 12/27–12/30; ADM 1/4360, Admiralty orders, 12/27; WO 6/2, Bathurst to Pakenham, 12/27; Cochrane Papers 2574, Melville to Cochrane, 12/27.

Through the years there has been speculation that Anthony Baker's instructions included a provision aborting the treaty if he received word of a British triumph at New Orleans. This is not so. Baker's orders clearly show his authority was limited to securing Washington's unconditional ratification: P.R.O., FO 115/23, Bathurst to Baker, 12/30; FO 5/105, Bathurst to Baker, 12/31. Nor could he have had special unwritten instructions on this point, for it made no difference who delivered the treaty. On the chance Baker might not reach America, a spare copy was sent to General Sherbrooke in Canada, to be forwarded to Washington by any messenger of his choice: ADM 1/4360, orders of 12/27.

13. *"The Dawn's Early Light"*

British planning for New Orleans: P.R.O., ADM 1/506, Cochrane to Croker, 6/20; ADM 1/4360, Croker to Cochrane, 8/10; Cochrane to Croker, 10/3; WO 6/2, Bathurst to Ross, 8/10; Cochrane Papers 2574, Melville to Cochrane, 7/29, 8/10. Failure on flatboats: ADM 1/508, Cochrane to Croker, 12/7; Cochrane Papers 2343, Middleton to Croker, 9/7; 2330, comments by Cochrane, pp. 28–36. Collapse of security: Adams, *Writings*, Gallatin to Monroe, 8/20; National Archives, M6, R7, Monroe to Jackson, 9/5; *Niles' Register*, 11/5; Edward Nicolls to Jean Laffite, 8/31; Proclamation, Nicolls to "Natives of Louisiana," 8/29; ADM 1/508, Cochrane to Croker, 12/7; Cochrane Papers 2326, Cochrane to Melville, 12/29/1815.

Jamaica to Gulf Coast: Wellington's *Supplementary Despatches*, Vol. 10, John Keane, "A Journal of the Operations against New Orleans"; Malcolm Papers, MAL/104, squadron list; Cochrane Papers 2348, Cochrane to Croker, 12/16. Also, Barrett; Chesterton; Codrington; Gleig.

Advance to the Mississippi: J. S. Bassett, ed., *Correspondence of Andrew Jackson*, Vol. 2, Jackson to Monroe, 12/10; *National Archives*, M222, R12, Jackson to Monroe, 12/13, 12/16; Marquis James, *Andrew Jackson, Border Captain*, quoting Jackson to Monroe, 2/18/1815; Thomas ap Catesby Jones, official letter, 3/12/1815; Nicholas Lockyer to Cochrane, 12/18; Cochrane's dispatch, 1/18/1815; Keane's "Journal"; Keane's official letter, 12/26; Cochrane Papers 2330, n.d., Captain Robert Spencer's memorandum on payments to guides. On American failure to block Bayou Bienvenu, see James; *Louisiana Historical Quarterly*, Vol. 44, Carson I. A. Ritchie, "The Louisiana Campaign."

Operations, 12/23–1/8/1815, American accounts: Jackson's official reports, 12/27, 12/29, 1/8/1815, 1/9/1815, 1/13/1815; Daniel T. Patterson's official reports, 12/28, 1/13/1815. Also see *Niles' Register*, 2/11/1815, 2/18/1815, and the Vol. 8 Supplement for letters from various American participants; *Louisiana Historical Quarterly*, Vol. 9, "A Contemporary Account of the Battle of New Orleans by a Soldier in the Ranks"; A. Lacarrière Latour, *Historical Memoir of the War in West Florida and Louisiana*.

British accounts: Keane's official letter, 12/26; Keane's "Journal"; Thornton's official letter, 1/8/1815; John Lambert's dispatch, 1/10/1815: Cochrane's dispatch 1/18/1815; Cochrane Papers 2336, Maclolm to Cochrane, 12/27; 2330, Pakenham to Cochrane, 12/28; 2265, Cochrane to Sir T. Cochrane, 12/29; Hope of Luffness MSS, G. Brown to Sir A. Hope, 4/4/1815; Royal Fusiliers Museum, Corporal James Brierly, MS, "Observations, Notes etc. Whilst on Service"; *Niles' Register*, 5/20/1815, extracts from letters in British press; *Blackwood's Magazine*, September 1828, Captain R. Simpson, "Battle of New Orleans"; *Louisiana Historical Quarterly*, Vol. 9, "General Court-Martial for Trial of Lt. Col. Thomas Mullins" (transcript); *Military Register*, 9/20/1815, findings of Mullins court-martial; *Louisiana Historical Quarterly*, Vol. 44, account by Alexander Dickson edited by Carson I. A. Ritchie; Hugh F. Rankin, *The Battle of New Orleans, a British View*, account by Charles R. Forrest; *Naval Chronicle*, Vol. 33, account by unidentified officer with Thornton's force, 1/30/1815; J. H. Cooke, *Narrative of Events in the South of France and of the Attack on New Orleans;* J .S. Cooper, *Rough notes of Seven Campaigns;* W. Surtees, *Twenty-five Years in the Rifle Brigade;* G. Wrottesley, *Life and Correspondence of Sir John Burgoyne.* Also, Barrett; D. Brown; Chesterton; Codrington; Gleig; "Old Sub"; Harry Smith.

For general comment: Charles B. Brooks, *The Siege of New Orleans;* Samuel Carter III, *Blaze of Glory;* Jane L. de Grummond, *The Baratarians and the Battle of New Orleans.* Also, Coles; Fortescue; Horsman; Marquis James; William James, *Military Occurences;* Latour; Lossing; Tucker; and the fine analysis by Carson I. A. Ritchie in *Louisiana Historical Quarterly*, Vol. 44, cited above.

Peace treaty ratified in Washington: P.R.O., FO 115/24, Baker to Castlereagh, 2/19/1815; Georgetown *Federal Republican*, 2/14/1815, 2/16/1815; *National Intelligencer*, 2/16/1815; *Niles' Register*, 2/18/1815; Gaillard Hunt, *Life in America One Hundred Years Ago.* Also, Anthony; Brant;

Jennings; Ketcham; Lossing; Nicolay; Perkins; Tucker. Celebrations: *Niles'*
Register, Supplements to Vols. 7 and 8 contain many local accounts.

British reaction: Cockburn Papers 25, Cockburn to Edmund Palmer, 2/8/
1815; Codrington Papers, COD 7/1, Codrington to wife, 2/13/1815;
Cochrane Papers 2584, Sir Thomas Cochrane's "Journal," 2/8/1815. Abandoning the Indians and blacks: P.R.O., ADM 1/508, Cochrane to Malcolm
2/17/1815; WO 1/143–1/144, Nicolls correspondence, various dates. Wran-
gle over prize money: P.R.O., PC 1/4109, 5/29/1817, 4/3/1818; National
Maritime Museum, Robert Ramsay to William Ely Cook, 2/7/1817.

Meaning to America: James Bayard, quoted in American Historical Association, *Annual Report*, 1913, Vol. 2, Bayard to R. H. Bayard, 12/26;
Gouverneur Morris, quoted in *New York Times Magazine*, 6/17/1962,
H. S. Commager, "Second War of American Independence"; peace announcement, quoted from *Niles' Register*, 2/18/1815; Louis Serurier, quoted
in Brant. For over-all thoughts and conclusions, I've been especially impressed by Brant, Coles, Commager, Dangerfield, Horsman, Perkins, and
Smelser, all previously cited.

Index

Adams, John Quincy, 240, 305, 306, 318
Adams, Dr. William, 304
"Adams and Liberty," 296
Aetna, 199, 277, 278
Aisquith, Capt. Edward, 190, 260, 263–64
Albion, 50, 224, 225
Alcock, William H., 235
Alexander, Capt. Thomas, 208
Alexandria, 26, 78, 119, 182, 203; surrender of, 198–201, 202, 210; Monroe attempts to trap British at, 207
Alston, Joseph, 221
American and Commercial Daily Advertiser (Baltimore), 296
Anderson, John, 74
Andre, Lt. Gregorius, 264
Andrews (midshipman), 289
Andrews, T. P., 136

Annapolis, 24, 29–30, 48, 59, 60, 68, 82, 83, 87, 238, 247
Apalachicola River, 325
Argus, 162
Armistead, Maj. George, 229, 249, 254–55, 273, 274, 277–95 *passim*
Armistead, Louisa, 255, 295
Armstrong, John, 21, 22, 23, 28, 29, 30, 59, 61, 83, 216; background and personality of, 21; complacency of, 21, 22, 25, 30, 60, 73, 81, 92; opposes Winder's appointment, 23; relations with Winder, 24–25; at Long Old Fields with Madison, 81–82; reluctance to advise on military preparations, 94–95, 102, 103, 104, 105, 106; Bladensburg and, 105, 106–7, 116–17, 124–25, 130; during Washington's evac-

371

Armstrong, John (*continued*)
uation and capture, 145, 146,
149, 150, 154, 171–72, 191, 193;
return to Washington, his
resignation, 204–7; *see also*
Washington, D.C.
Asia, 245
Astor, John Jacob, 220, 221
Atlantic News, The, 41

Babcock, Capt. Sam, 238
Back River, 252, 253
Bacon, Captain, 154
Bailey, Chester, 170
Baker, Anthony St. John, 319, 320,
321, 337, 338
Ball, Charles, 131, 140, 180
Baltimore, 22, 29, 30, 48, 55, 60,
68, 96, 110, 111, 140, 148, 171,
191, 192, 193, 207, 239, 261, 292,
307, 308, 343, 344; British plans
for attacking, 222, 223–25, 244–
45, 246, 255–56, 280, 282–83;
fears being next British target,
227–29; defense preparations
under Smith, 229–38, 247–55;
attempt to assemble Maryland
Militia, 233; volunteers pour
into, 235–36; generals assembled
in, 237; British fleet approaches,
253–55, 271–73; attack on,
284–91; American reactions to
victory at, 294–98; British reactions to repulse at, 308–9; *see
also* Fort McHenry; North Point
Bank of Maryland, 147
Bank of Washington, 177
Barataria Bay, 324; freebooters
based at, 328, 329
Barclay, Thomas, 27–28, 142–43
Baring, Alexander, 316
Barker, Jacob, 95, 146, 147, 150,
151, 171, 191, 212
Barker, Major General, 221
Barlow, Mrs. Joel, 75

Barney, Com. Joshua, 60, 64, 69,
70, 74, 79, 83, 89, 94, 102, 103,
104, 154, 161, 177, 180, 255, 274;
in the Patuxent, 21, 26–27, 54,
59, 61, 66, 71–72; at the Wood
Yard, 72; at Long Old Fields,
78; Bladensburg and, 105, 107,
108, 117, 130–31, 132, 135, 136,
137–39, 142, 184
Barney, Maj. William, 221, 238;
reports on British fleet headed
for Baltimore, 247, 251
Barrett, Midshipman Robert J., 270
Bartholomew, Capt. David Ewen,
282
Barton, George, 143, 211
Bathurst, Earl, 36, 38, 39, 47, 69,
223, 225, 285, 301, 303, 304–5,
308, 309, 312, 316, 319, 341
Bathurst, Lady, 47
Bayard, James, 22, 306, 342
Bayou Bienvenu, 326
Beall, Col. William D., 69, 83–84,
87, 112, 115, 131, 132, 136, 137,
190
Beanes, Dr. William, 79, 186, 256,
291, 295; negotiations for release
of, 239–44
Beaumont, Maj. Barber, 34–35
Bell, Maj. John, 154
Benedict, Md., 59, 63, 67, 81, 89;
inhabitants aid British, 27; Brit-
ish planning and, 48, 54; British
at, 56, 61, 63
Bentalou, Paul, 233, 236, 237
Bentley, Mrs. Caleb, 192
Bermuda, 37, 42, 239
Bigelow, Abijah, 194
Biscoe, Maj. George, 105–6
Blacks, attitudes of, 45, 76–77, 180,
325
Blackwell, Maj. Hiram, 20
Bladensburg, 24, 27–28, 29, 63, 78,
83, 84, 85, 86–87, 96, 97, 98, 102,
184, 191, 214, 228, 229, 232, 252,

253; preparations to defend, 68–69, 73, 97, 104–18; battle of, 118–21, 123–43, 203, 214, 302
Blake, Mayor James, 76, 110, 146, 195, 196, 202
Block Island, 225
Blodgett's Hotel, 175, 212
Bolin, Joe, 148
Bomb ships, 277, 278–80
Bonaparte, Napoleon, see Napoleon/Napoleonic Wars
Booth, Mordecai, 74, 156–58, 161, 171
Bouldin, John, 234
Bowie, Robert, 185–86
Boyd, Washington, 76
Bradley, Dr. Phineas T., 141
Bradley, William A., 101
Brengle, Capt. John, 218, 250
Brent, Col. William, 61
Brooke, Col. Arthur, 134, 271, 299, 308; takes over command, 262; Battle of North Point and, 266, 269; advance on Baltimore, 280, 283–86; retreat to Flect, 290
Brookeville, Md., 192, 193, 194
Brown (informant), 211
Brown, Miss, 155–56, 172
Brown, Maj. George, 119, 120, 133, 262
Brune, 246
Brush, Mrs., 70
Budd, Lt. George, 289
Bunbury, Major General, 39
Burch, Capt. Benjamin, 62, 87, 93, 94, 104, 105, 114, 128, 129
Burch, Samuel, 74–75
Burrall, Postmaster, 228, 254
Burrell, Lieutenant, 63
Byron, Lord, 210

Calder (informant), 79–80, 211
Caldwell, Capt. Elias, 177–78, 196
Calhoun, James, 236

Calief and Shinnick, ropewalk of Messrs., 273
Cameron, Governor, 47
Campbell, Lt. Duncan, 336
Campbell, George W., 94–95, 104, 106, 107, 151, 171–72, 191, 193, 204
Canada, 14–15, 20, 30, 35, 37, 46, 47, 49, 61–62, 118, 222, 255–56, 271, 297, 312, 317, 342
Canning, George, 320
Cape Henry, 19
Capitol, description, 149; burning of, 162–65
Carberry, Col. Henry, 25, 92, 108
Carmichael (dispatch rider), 20, 28
Carolina, 328
Carroll, Maj. Gen. William, 335
Carroll, Charles, 146, 147, 150, 151, 205
Carroll, Daniel, 212
Carroll, Henry, 321, 337
Castlereagh, Viscount, 303, 311, 312, 313
Catlett, Hanson, 103
Cedar Point, 239
Chalmers, the Rev. John, 178
Chaptico, Md., 51, 52
Charlotte Hall, Md., 67
Chartreuse, the, 317–18
Chase, Jeremiah T., 247
Chase, Samuel, 235
Chaumier, Lt. Frederick, 34, 51
Chesapeake, 272
Chesapeake Bay, 15, 19–20, 49–50, 54, 56, 222, 224, 234, 238, 239, 242, 244, 323, 341
Chesterton, Lt. George, 289
Chittenden, Martin, 217–18
Choctaw Indians, 328
Claggett, Elie, 272
Claggett, Lt. Levi, 280
Clark, L. A., 211
Clay, Henry, 304, 306
Clemm, John, 280

Clinton, Lt. Gen. Sir Henry, 35
Cobbett, William, 39, 312
Cochrane, Vice Adm. Sir Alexander, 37, 38, 54, 56, 64, 76, 79, 80, 89, 97, 160, 177, 180, 221, 225, 239, 242, 243, 267, 303, 311, 312, 314–15, 320, 323, 339, 341; background, 42–43; plans for eastern seaboard, 43–46, 53; plans to take New Orleans, 46–47; attack on Washington and, 48–50, 53–54, 55; post-Washington plans, 222–25; decision to attack Baltimore, 244, 245, 246, 256; attack on Fort McHenry and, 269–71, 278–95 passim; land attack on Baltimore and, 285–87; withdrawal from Baltimore, 298–99; New Orleans expedition, 299–300, 323–26, 330, 331; reaction to peace, 339
Cochrane, Capt. Sir Thomas, 43, 246, 298, 339–40
Cockburn, Rear Adm. George, 27, 45, 50, 70, 71, 72, 79, 80, 104, 120, 186, 198, 210, 213, 225, 239, 240, 244, 246, 270, 271, 280, 306, 339; background and personality, 50–51; communications with Cochrane, 44; attack on Washington, D.C. and, 48, 53, 54–55, 59–60, 69, 80, 89–90, 97–98; raiding parties, 51–52, 53, 54; attitude toward Americans, 52–53; attitude toward Cochrane, 53–54; in the Patuxent, 64, 66, 67, 71, 72; at Bladensburg, 133–34, 138–39; in Washington, D.C., 160, 163, 165–68, 169–70, 172–73, 176–77, 179–80, 181; attack on Baltimore and, 223–24, 245, 246, 255, 257, 261–63, 266–67, 284–86

Cockchafer, 277, 278
Codd, Lieutenant, 63, 125, 133
Codrington, Capt. Edward, 46, 49, 50, 56, 57, 89, 222–23; as Rear Admiral, 243, 271, 339
Coffee, Brig. Gen. John, 328–29
Cohen, Mendes I., 252, 281
Cohen, Philip, 281
Colborne, Sir John, 120, 139
Coles, Col. J. A., 218
Coles, Sally, 338
Columbia, 162
Columbia, District of, see Washington, D.C.
Commercial Advertiser (N.Y.), 214, 227, 337
Congreve, Sir William, 126
Coombs, Griffith, 102
Cooper, Sgt. Jack, 331
Corn Laws, 39
Courier (London), 302, 307, 319
Cox, Walter, 158
Craig, John, 272
Crawford, William, 21
Creek Indians, 46–47, 325, 341
Creighton, Capt. John O., 107, 154, 158, 161, 200–1
Custis, George Washington, 136, 147
Cutts, Richard, 146, 148, 204, 212
Cutts, Mrs. Richard, 146, 148

Dagg, the Rev. John A., 189, 294
Daschkoff, Russian Minister, 153
Davidson, Capt. John, 62
de Peyster, Robert G. L., 147, 151, 152, 171, 191
Devastation, 208, 277, 282, 298
Diadem, 41, 42, 49
Diomede, 298
Dixon (barber), 161
Donaldson, Capt. Lowrie, 268
Donnell, John, 272

Doughty, Capt. John, 114
Douglass, General, 237, 284, 293
Dover, burning of, 46
Dover, Mary, 220
Doyhar, Mr., 27
Duffield, Capt. Thomas, 220
Duvall, Edward, 204
Dyson, Capt. Sam, 197, 205

Edmonston, William, 268
Elba, 340
England, see Great Britain
Enquirer (Richmond), 215
Erebus, 208, 270, 277, 278, 282, 293
Erie, 254, 272
Euryalus, 55, 196, 209, 286–87
Evans, Lt. George de Lacy, 63, 80, 98, 163, 224, 239, 244–45
Evening Star (London), 309, 319
Ewell, Dr. James, 91–92, 145, 155, 165–66, 177, 179, 180, 182, 183, 184, 195, 211
Ewell, Thomas, 150

Fairy, 256
Falls, Capt. Tom, 98, 119
Falls Church, 91
Farerr, Gabriel, 326
Father and Son, 272
Fathergill, Capt. William, 324
Favourite, 336
Fay, Lt. H. A., 247
Federal Gazette and Daily Advertiser (Baltimore), 214
Federalists, 14, 26, 205, 217
Federal Republican (Georgetown), 101, 205, 216, 217, 315
Fenwick, Father Edward Dominic, 142
Flaugeac, Garriques, 335
Florida, 34
Flotillamen, 153, 154, 161, 190, 249, 288–89; see also Barney, Com. Joshua

Forman, Gen. Thomas, 236, 237, 250, 272, 273
Forrest, Lieutenant, 104
Fort Babcock, 249, 288–89
Fort Bowyer, 339
Fort Covington, 249, 288
Fort Erie, British repulsed at, 61–62
Fort McHenry, 229, 233, 242, 254–55, 273, 336; defense preparations, 248–49, 273–74; flag flown at, 274–75, 292–93; attack on, 270–71, 277–95 passim
Fort Mifflin, 230
Fort Washington, 25, 68, 70, 72, 78, 81, 87, 196–97, 205
Foxhall's Foundry, 151
France, 25, 37, 40, 306, 312, 340; see also Napoleon/Napoleonic Wars
Fraser, Midshipman John West, 201
Frazier, Lt. Solomon, 282
Frederick, Md., 76, 107, 154, 172, 204, 218
Freeman, James, 338
Freeman, John, 148, 338
Fries family, 171
Frost, J. T., 74–75, 155, 164
Fulford, Henry, 129, 228
Fulton, Robert, 221
Furlong, Lieutenant, 118

Gales, Joseph, Jr., 170, 176, 194
Gallatin, Albert, 22, 35, 160, 230, 306, 324
Gallway, Captain, 128
Gambier, Lord, 304, 318
Gardner, William P., 167
Gathen, John, 219
Gazette (Winchester, Va.), 215
Gazette and General Advertiser (N.Y.), 213, 214–15

Gazette (London), 40
General Advertiser (Philadelphia), 140, 219
George III (of England), 40
Georgetown, D.C., 29, 74, 76, 102, 108, 148, 149, 150, 155–56, 171, 182–83, 203, 241
Ghent, peace negotiations at, 303, 304–6, 309–10, 316–18; *see also* Peace
Gibbs, Maj. Gen. Samuel, 332, 334, 335
Gibson, Mrs. Gerard, 172, 182
Gleig, Lt. George Robert, 41, 49, 63, 66, 89, 118, 119, 125, 133, 134–35, 141, 171, 181–82, 186, 187, 246, 255, 256, 262–63, 266
Glendy, the Rev. John, 253
Gohegan, Captain, 154
Golden Fleece, 49, 264
Gordon, Capt. James Alexander, 55, 182, 196; Alexandria surrenders to, 197–201; escapes from the Potomac, 207–9, 221, 239, 244, 245
Gorsuch, Robert, 254, 259, 262
Gossaway, Jonathan, 247
Goulburn, Henry, 304, 309–10, 316, 321
Graham, John, 192, 221
Great Britain, 340; peace negotiations and treaty, 22, 35, 309–10, 313–21; anti-American sentiments in, 33–35; expedition planned to attack east coast, 36–39; celebrates Napoleon's defeat, 39–40, 302; invasion force leaves, 40–41; reaction to capture of Washington, D.C., 301–4, 311; learns of defeats at Baltimore, Lake Champlain, and Plattsburg, 308–10; antiwar sentiments, 310–12, 314, 315–16; Wellington called on, suggests settlement, 312–14; reac-

tions to peace treaty, 319–20; effect of peace on, 340–41
Great Lakes, 35; *see also specific lakes*
Green, Maj. Josiah, 238
Greenleaf's Point, 102, 162; explosion at, 180, 183, 184
Grenville, Lord, 314
Grey, Capt. Charles, 66
Gruber, the Rev. John, 251

Halifax, 341
Hamilton, Captain, 133
Hampstead Hill, 235, 238, 254, 270, 273, 283, 284, 289, 290, 294
Hanchett, Captain, 41
Hanson, Alexander C., 216, 217, 315
Haradan, Lieutenant, 173
Hardy, Capt. Sir Thomas, 225, 239
Hare, John, 74
Harris, Mrs. Samuel, 294
Harrison, Captain, 80
Harrison, Maj. Gen. William Henry, 217
Hartford Convention, 315, 338
Havannah, 283
Hay, George, 203
Haymes, Lieutenant, 263
Hazlehurst, Andrew, 169
Heath, Nathaniel, 178
Heath, Maj. Richard, 260, 263, 264
Hebrus, 242, 283
Herald (Norfolk), 140
Hill, Lord Rowland, 40, 45, 47, 299, 303
Hines, Lt. Christian, 62
Homans, Benjamin, 155, 172, 212
Hood, Colonel, 236
Hood, Adm. Lord, 51
Hopewell, Mr., 53
Horseshoe Bend, 47
Hotham, Rear Adm. Sir Henry, 339

Howard, Capt. Benjamin, 260
Howard, John Eager, 228–29
Howard, John Eager, Jr., 137
Huffington, Jesse, 138
Hungerford, Brig. Gen. John P., 29, 198, 200
Hunter, the Rev. Andrew, 101–2
Hunter, Mary, 101–2, 162, 165, 177

Impressment, right of, 13, 305, 311, 316, 342
Indian Head, Md., 209
Indians, Adm. Cochrane's plans for using, 46–47, 325; British policy toward, 305, 306, 309, 316, 317, 320–21, 341
Ingle, Mary, 179
Iphigenia, 56, 225
Irving, Washington, 216
Izard, Gen. George, 221

Jackson, Maj. Gen. Andrew, 46–47, 324–36 *passim*, 343
Jamaica, 323, 324
Jane, 244
Java, 229, 273
Jefferson, Thomas, 22, 175, 212
Jennings, Paul, 146, 167, 338
Johnson, Mr. (stagecoach passenger), 150, 155
Jones, Eleanor, 88
Jones, Maj. Timothy, 174, 175, 176
Jones, William, 21, 27, 28, 59, 60–61, 74, 77, 83, 102, 107, 110, 155, 172, 174, 192, 193, 203–4, 221, 293; *see also* Washington, D.C.
Journal de Paris, 306
Journal des Débats, 306
Judah, Dr. (stagecoach passenger), 150, 155

Keane, Maj. Gen. John, 308, 325, 326, 328, 329, 332, 336
Kearney, John, 62

Kell, Judge Thomas, 284
Kelly, Edward, 185
Kennedy, John P., 97, 129
Kentucky, 331
Key, Francis Scott, 113, 114, 150, 156; mission on behalf of Dr. Beanes, 240–45, 256, 291–93, 295, 344; writes "Star-Spangled Banner," 293, 295–97
Key, Polly, 156
King, Rufus, 217
Kinsale, 53
Knox, Capt. John James, 133
Kramer, Lieutenant Colonel, 115, 131, 132

Labrobe, Benjamin, 163
Laffite, Jean, 324
Lake Borgne, 325
Lake Champlain, 35, 297–98, 308–9, 343
Lake Erie, 15, 343
Lambert, Maj. Gen. John, 331, 332, 336
Lansdowne, Marquis of, 315–16
Laval, Lt. Col. Jacint, 68, 70, 85, 105, 107, 115, 130, 153
Law, John, 87, 114
Law, Thomas, 212
Lawrence, Assistant Commissary General, 183
Lawrence, Lt. John, 125–26, 134
Lear, Tobias, 28
Lee, Richard H. (suspected spy), 211
Lee, Richard Henry, 228
L'Eole, 249
Levering, Capt. Aaron, 253, 260, 261, 263
Lewis, John, 174
Library of Congress, burning of, 164, 177, 212, 311
Liverpool, Earl, 40, 303, 304–5, 308, 310–11, 315, 316, 317, 319, 340

London, 39–40, 302, 318–19
Long Log Lane, 253
Long Old Fields, 77–79, 81, 84, 85, 86, 87, 92
Lorman, Mrs. William, 294
Louis XVIII (of France), 75
Louisiana, 329, 331
Louisiana, *see* New Orleans
Love, Mathilda Lee, 172
Lovendeghem, Hotel, 304, 317
Lowndes Hill, 120
Luffborough, Captain, 82, 83
Lynx, 173, 182

McComas, Pvt. Harry, 264–65
McCormack, the Rev. Alexander, 165, 194
McCormick, Thomas, 235
McCulloch, James, 129
McDaniel, Jeremiah, 126, 134
McDonald, Col. William, 274
Macdonough, Capt. Thomas, 297, 343
MacDougall, Capt. Duncan, 262, 263, 307–8, 335–36
McKean, Thomas, 217
McKenney, Thomas L., 27, 82, 85, 86, 206
Mackenzie, Alexander, 264
McKeowin's Hotel, 29, 92, 102, 150, 155
McKim, Alexander, 118
McLane, Col. Allen, 28, 62–63, 78–79, 189–90
McLeod, James, 179
McNamara, Michael, 185
MacNoon, Dr., 338–39
Macomb, Brig. Gen. Alexander, 298
Madison, Dolley, 15, 77, 83, 88; flight of, 146–48, 150, 151–52, 167, 168, 172, 191, 193; return of, 204; on news of peace, 338
Madison, James, 14, 27, 30, 61, 72,

88, 92, 95, 102, 136, 146, 148, 210, 230, 231, 240, 295, 302, 315, 317, 321; appearance and personality, 21–22; British opinion of, 34, 35, 317, 321; at Long Old Fields, 77, 78, 81, 82, 83; Bladensburg and, 106–7, 108, 116–17, 124–25, 130, 131; flight of, 150–53, 157, 167, 168, 170, 172, 179, 191–92; return, 193, 194, 195; Monroe put in charge of defense effort, 202–3; Armstrong removed, 206–7; seaman's letter warning of attack on Washington, 212–13; public opinion and, 216; ratifies peace treaty, 337–38; *see also* Washington, D.C.
Maffitt, the Rev. John, 152
Magraw, Tom, 147
Magruder, Col. George, 61, 115
Magruder, Patrick, 74
Maine, 323
Malcolm, Rear Adm. Poultney, 41, 42, 47, 49, 55, 225, 239–40, 242, 323, 341
Marie Antoinette, 72
Marines, U.S., 21, 61, 68, 105, 107, 108, 130–31, 132
Martin, Sailing Master, 137
Martin, Dr. Sam, 264
Maryland, 23, 24, 26–27, 51–52, 62, 68, 73, 76, 91, 93; *see also specific locations*
Mason, Gen. John, 142, 150, 192, 211, 240, 241–42, 244
Massachusetts, 316
Matthews, William, 171
Melville, Viscount, 43, 44, 46, 267, 299
Melwood, 85, 89, 90, 97, 119
Menelaus, 41, 55, 56, 209, 244
Merry, Anthony, 153
Meteor, 171, 277–78
Middleton, Joseph, 19
Militia, 22, 23–24, 26, 29, 83, 87–

88, 189–91, 328; District of Columbia, 29, 61–62, 68, 70, 93, 105, 107–8, 114–15, 136, 149–50; Maryland, 26, 29, 60, 68, 96–97, 108, 111–13, 118, 232–33, 247–48; Pennsylvania, 60, 233, 236; Virginia, 29, 91–92, 108, 148, 198, 200, 233, 249; *see also* battle sites; *officers commanding*
Miller, Capt. Samuel, 68, 105, 108, 131, 132, 137
Miller, Thomas, 157
Minor, Col. George, 91, 92, 108, 139, 148
Mississippi River, 316, 327–36
Mitchell, Captain, 289
Monroe, James, 21, 22, 23, 27, 59, 196, 218, 220–21, 237, 238, 240, 250, 324, 337, 338; background and personality of, 30; scouting activities, 30–31, 63, 67–68, 70, 72–73, 85, 96; Bladensburg and, 102–3, 110, 111, 112–13, 115, 117, 124, 127, 130, 203; during Washington's evacuation and capture, 149, 172, 192–93; in charge of defense effort, 202–3, 206; made acting Secretary of War, 207; attempt to trap British squadron at Alexandria, 207; *see also* Washington, D.C.
Monteath, Dr., 211
Montgomery, Capt. John, 253
Montgomery Court House, Md., 189, 190, 191, 192
Moore, John, 208
Moore, Col. Nicholas Ruxton, 272
Moorfields, British repulse at, 209–10
Morgan, Major, 141
Morning Chronicle (London), 307, 311, 318, 319
Morning Post (London), 302, 307, 308, 319

Morris, Gouverneur, 342
Muir, the Rev. James, 182
Mullins, Lt. Col. Thomas, 332, 334–335
Mullins, Mrs. Thomas, 42
Murray, Maj. Gen. Sir George, 36

Nantucket, 315
Napier, Capt. Charles, 196; Ferry Branch diversionary tactic, 286–89, 290–91
Napoleon/Napoleonic Wars, 13, 15, 22, 33, 34, 39, 43, 75, 302, 310, 311, 314, 340, 342
National Intelligencer (Washington), 53, 73, 101, 140–41, 210; wrecking the offices of, 170, 176
National Register (London), 34, 302
Naval Chronicle, 312
Navy Yard (Washington, D.C.), 21, 93–94, 102, 154, 156–57, 158, 195; burning of, 161–62, 165, 173–74
Nelson, Horatio, 51, 282
Neutral rights, American, 13, 14
Newcomb, Lt. H. L., 288
Newfoundland, 316
New Orleans, 34, 47, 222, 283, 285, 300, 321; British attack on, 323–36; action on December 23, 328–29; action on December 28, 329–30; action on January 1, 330–31; action on January 8, 335–36
New York, 14, 55, 60, 336–37, 338
Nicholson, Judge Joseph H., 238, 249, 251, 252, 279, 280, 296
Nicolls, Sergeant, 85
Nicolls, Maj. Edward, 47, 324, 325, 341
Niles' Weekly Register, 216–17, 343
Nomini, Va., 51
Non-Intercourse Act, 13

Norfolk, Va., 19
North Point, 234, 238, 248, 255, 272, 290, 293, 294; battle of, 252–54, 256–57, 259–69
Nottingham, Md., 64–66, 68, 69, 70, 72–73, 186
Nourse, Captain, 53, 56, 270

Octagon House, 75–76, 95, 153, 168, 212
Oden, Benjamin, 70, 72, 78
O'Neill, William, 74
Orders in Council, 13, 14
Orr, Mrs., 155, 165
Otis, Harrison Gray, 338

Pactolus, 42, 47
Paine, Robert Treat, 296
Pakenham, Maj. Gen. Sir Edward, 308, 320, 321, 323, 324, 329–36
Parish, Elijah, 14
Parker, Maj. Daniel, 191
Parker, Capt. Sir Peter, 55, 209–10, 244
Parker, Lt. Col. R. E., 199
Parrott, Richard, 204
Parsons, Barry, 127
Passamaquoddy Bay, 316, 317
Patapsco River, 224, 234, 244, 253, 254, 269–70, 292; Ferry Branch of, 237, 248, 249, 272, 285, 287–89, 290–91; Northwest Branch, 248, 251, 270, 272
Patent office, saving of, 175–76
Patriot and Evening Advertiser (Baltimore), 207, 233, 296–97
Patterson, Cdr. Daniel, 334
Patterson, Edgar, 73–74
Patuxent River, 20, 48, 53, 54, 55, 56–57, 63, 64, 67, 71, 89, 222, 239; *see also* Barney, Com. Joshua
Peace, negotiations for, 22, 35, 303, 304–6, 309–10, 316–17; treaty signed, 317–18; ratified by Britain, 320; ratified by

America, 338; celebrations, 338–39; reaction of British leaders to, 339–40; effect on Britain, 340–41; effect on America, 342–44; *see also* Ghent
Peake, Dr., 91
Peale, Rembrandt, 254
Pennsylvania, 24, 29, 60, 68
Penobscot River, 311, 315
Perry, Com. Oliver H., 15, 207, 209, 229, 343
Peter, Maj. George, 62, 70, 84–85, 94, 104, 105, 114–15, 131, 135, 193
Peter, John, 182–83
Philadelphia, 55, 60, 214, 219–20, 221
Pickersgill, Caroline, 274, 275
Pickersgill, Mary Young, 274–75, 292
Picton, Gen. Sir Thomas, 308
Pig Point, 71
Pilot Stage, 214
Pinkney, Maj. William, 111, 114, 117, 127, 129, 253
Piscataway, 29, 68
Plattsburg, 297–98, 309
Pleasanton, Stephen, 73–74
Point Lookout, 20
Point Patience, 56
Porter, Com. David, 60, 200, 207, 208, 209, 211, 232
Potomac River, 15, 20, 48, 51, 54, 178, 193, 233, 239; British squadron on, 55–56, 68, 81, 82, 83, 87, 196–201, 204, 207–9, 245, 246; bridge at Washington, burning of, 178–79
Pratt, Lt. George, 163, 164, 169
Pratt, Col. William, 28
President's House, description of, 23; burning of, 167–69
Prevost, Gov. Sir George, 37, 46, 255–56, 271, 297–98, 313
Price, Capt. David, 277

Prize money, British concern with, 46–47, 52, 225, 227–28, 270, 283, 323, 339, 341
Prosser, Uriah, 268
Public Ledger (London), 307, 319

Quantrill, Capt. Thomas, 253

Ragan, Col. John, 111, 127, 128, 129
Ramilles, 239
Ramsay, Peter, 211
Randall, Captain, 128
Regiments, British, 4th Foot, 41, 63; 7th Foot, 331; 21st Foot, 49, 63, 160; 43rd Foot, 331; 44th Foot, 41, 63, 332, 334–35; 85th Foot, 41, 63, 185, 327; 93rd Foot, 324; 95th Foot, 324; *see also battle sites; officers commanding*
Register (Albany), 217
Register (Salem), 297
Renner, Daniel, 74
Renner & Heath, 74, 178
Rennie, Lt. Col. Robert, 332, 336
Reporter (Cork), 307
Resolution, 80
Retaliation, British policy of, 46, 223, 255–56, 271, 311–12
Rhode Island, 54, 222, 239, 244
Richland District (South Carolina), 218–19
Ridgely, Lt. Charles, 254
Riggs & Badon, 74
Ringgold, Col. Sam, 218
Ringgold, Tench, 178
Robyns, Captain, 89, 90
Roche, Cdr. George de la, 272, 273
Rockets, 55, 120, 124, 125–26, 128, 161, 264, 270, 273, 277, 281
Rodgers, Com. John, 60, 110, 204, 207, 214, 215, 236, 293, 294; Baltimore's defense and, 232, 233, 250–51, 272, 273
Rodgers, Minerva, 214, 215

"Rodgers Bastion," 248, 253
Rodriguez Canal, 329, 330, 331–32
Rokeby, 172, 191
Ropewalks (Washington, D.C.), burning of, 178
Ross, Maj. Gen. Robert, 41, 47, 53, 71, 72, 78, 83, 89, 104, 136, 180, 198, 211, 227, 239, 242, 256, 264, 269, 270, 271, 286, 295, 298, 301, 303, 305, 306, 308; to command British troops, 37; instructions given to, 38–39; doubts about attacking Washington, 54, 69, 79–81, 97–98; march to Nottingham, 64–66; in Upper Marlboro, 79–81, 84–85; at Melwood, 97–98; Bladensburg and, 98–99, 119–21, 126, 132, 133–34, 138–39, 141; in Washington, 158, 160, 163, 165, 166, 167, 177, 178, 179, 181, 183–84; rejoins fleet, 184–85; imprisons Dr. Beanes, 186; decision to attack Baltimore and, 223–25, 245, 255, 257; negotiations for Dr. Beanes's release, 240, 241, 243–44; death of, 261–263
Rowley, Sir Joshua, 51
Royal Oak, 40, 41, 47, 55, 239, 242, 298
Rush, Richard, 77, 78, 103, 104, 107, 117, 118, 130, 150, 172, 192, 193, 196, 202
Rush, Mrs. Richard, 77
Russell, Jonathan, 306
Rutter, Lt. Solomon, 254, 273–74, 282

St. Marys River, 54
Salona, 152, 172, 191
Sands, Samuel, 296
Sawyer, Admiral, 307
Schutz, Col. Jonathan, 111, 128, 129
Scorpion, 71

Scott, Lt. James, 71–72, 80, 89, 90, 97, 98, 134, 158, 160–61, 163, 178, 268, 269, 285
Scott, Col. William, 105, 108, 115, 131, 135, 136
Scudder, 272
Seahorse, 55, 198, 199, 201, 207, 208, 209, 269, 298
Serurier, Louis, 75, 95, 110, 168–69, 201–2, 212, 343
Severn, 56, 270, 283
Sewall, Robert, 160, 162, 194
Shewning, Col. John, 20
Shiner, Michael, 161, 180
Shower, Captain, 128
Sidmouth, Lord, 312
Simmons, William, 116, 123, 152–53
Simms, Charles, 199, 200, 201
Sinclair, Robert, 195
Singleton, General, 237
Sioussa, Jean Pierre, 88, 147, 152, 153
Skinner, John S., 27, 240–45, 256, 291, 295, 296
Slaves, Adm. Cochrane's plans for using, 43–44, 45, 76, 180, 325, 341; British policy toward, 38–39, 44, 341; American fears of uprising of, 76, 180, 193; *see also* Blacks, attitudes of
Smith, Capt. Harry, 56, 120, 134, 139, 167, 168, 185, 224–25, 301–2, 334, 336
Smith, James, 53
Smith, Jim, 146
Smith, John, 253
Smith, Margaret Bayard, 201
Smith, Maj. Gen. Samuel, 26, 29, 60, 191, 274, 293; background and personality, 229–30; takes command at Baltimore, 229–32; preparing Baltimore's defenses, 233–38, 247–51, 252; *passim* 254, 260, 272–73, 294

Smith, Sam W., 235
Smith, Brig. Gen. Walter, 61, 85, 86, 107–8, 113, 115, 148, 149, 193, 205–6
Smith Point, 20, 245
Snell's Bridge, 192
Spectator (London), 302–3
Spence, Capt. Robert T., 229
Sprigg, Capt. Jenifer, 136–37, 141
Squires, Capt. Jacob, 236
Stansbury, Brig. Gen. Tobias, 60, 68, 83, 84, 86, 87, 103, 104, 148–49, 190, 228, 231, 233, 237, 263; Bladensburg and, 96–97, 108–18, 123–32 *passim*, 135, 140
"Star-Spangled Banner, The," 295–97
State, War, and Navy Dept. Building, burning of, 174
Statesman (London), 308
Stelle, Mrs. Pontius D., 170
Sterett, Lt. Col. Joseph, 68, 83, 87, 96, 111, 112, 123, 127, 128–29, 140, 228, 233, 289
Sterrett, Capt. John, 218
Stewart, James, 44
Stockton, Master's Mate Robert, 281
Stoddert's Bridge, 93
Stricker, Brig. Gen. John, 60, 189, 229, 237, 284; North Point and, 252–54, 259–69, 273, 284
Stull, Capt. John J., 61, 62, 84, 85, 105
Sukey (maid), 148
Sun (London), 302, 319
Surprize, 246, 256, 270, 272, 282, 287, 290, 291, 292
Suter, Mrs. Barbara, 167, 169
Swann, Thomas, 20
Swift, Jonathan, 198

Talleyrand, Charles M. de, 202, 343
Tangier Is., Va., 44, 242, 245

Tayloe, Col. John, 75, 153, 212
Telegraph (Baltimore), 273
Tenleytown, 171, 190
Terror, 277
Thompson, Capt. Henry, 190
Thompson, Robert, 218
Thornton, Captain, 30–31
Thornton, Col. William, 120, 126, 133, 210–11, 241; New Orleans expedition, 326–28, 332, 334, 335, 336
Thornton, Dr. William, 101, 146, 152, 211, 240; background and personality, 175; saves Patent Office, 175–76; helps restore order in Washington, 195–96; fears British return, urges surrender, 202–3
Thornton, Mrs. William, 75, 156, 202
Tierney, George, 314
Times (London), 33, 34, 35, 36, 311, 314, 318, 319
Tingey, Capt. Thomas, 94, 103, 104, 154–55, 156–57, 158, 173, 174, 182, 210; burns Navy Yard, 161–62
"To Anacreon in Heaven," 296
Todd, John Payne, 318
Todd, Lucy Washington, 147
Tonnant, 47, 49, 50, 55, 56, 224, 245, 298
Torpedoes, 270
Torrens, Col. Henry, 35, 36, 39, 304, 307, 308, 309
Treasury Building, burning of, 169
Trimble, Col. Henry, 236–37
Tripoli Monument, 173

United Service Journal, 34
United States Gazette (Philadelphia), 215
Upper Marlboro, Md., 70, 71, 72, 77, 79–81, 82–85, 89, 90, 110, 185
Urquhart, Lt. Beau Colclough, 168

Uti possidetis, doctrine of, 308–10, 313–14, 316

Van Ness, Maj. Gen. John P., 25, 29, 60, 61, 110, 150, 212
Vansittart, Nicholas, 314
Vienna, Congress of, 310
Villeré, Maj. Gabriel, 326, 328, 329
Virginia, 23, 24, 29, 51–52, 140, 172, 178, 191
Virginia Patriot (Richmond), 221–22
Volcano, 277, 282, 298

Wadsworth, Col. Decius, 73, 110, 111, 114, 125, 126
Wainwright, Captain, 50, 80, 138–39, 142, 173
Warner, Sailing Master, 137
Warren, Adm. John Borlase, 42, 222
Washington, D.C., 33, 34, 69, 70, 88, 141, 193, 194, 198, 224, 229, 233, 235, 286, 320, 342, 343, 344; officials' attitude toward safety of, 20–22, 29–30; Madison's defense plan, 22–23; 10th Military District set up, 23; Winder's problems, Armstrong's indifference, 23–26; no over-all defense plan, 26; reports from Barney, 26–27; British invasion fleet reported, 28–29; whether Washington target, 29–30; British plans for attack on, 48–49, 53, 54–55, 68–69, 79, 80; learns British in Patuxent, steps taken, 59–63; actual landings reported, 61; District Militia assembles and marches, 61–62; Ross reported heading for, 72–73; removal of records, 73, 74–75; Winder retreats to, 87, 88; British orders disapproving attack on, 89; defense and destruction of Eastern Branch bridges, 93–94, 96, 98, 104, 105,

Washington, D.C. (*continued*)
154; conflicting reports on British advance, 101–4; evacuated after Bladensburg, 145–60; capture and occupation of, 158–84, 301–4, 306–7, 309, 311; looting after British departure, 194–95; order restored, 195–96; fears British will return, 201–2; picking up the pieces, 210–11; hunt for spies and traitors, 211; British prisoners a problem, 211; resuming normal governmental functions, 211–12; public reaction to capture of, 213–19; flooded with offers and requests, 220–21; British reaction to capture of, 301–4; European reaction to capture of, 306; celebrates New Orleans victory, 336; peace treaty ratified, 337–38

Washington, George, 155, 164, 230; portrait of, 147, 152, 171, 212

Washington, Martha, 136

Washington Theater, 27

Waterloo, 340

Waters, Major, 176

Watts, Captain, 52

Weaver, Capt. Lewis, 267

Webster, Sailing Master John, 136, 153, 190, 249, 288–89

Weightman, Roger Chew, 27, 168

Wellington, Duke of, 36, 39, 40, 312–14, 340

Wells, Daniel, 264–65

Weser, 41, 42, 299

West, Richard, 240

Wharton, Lt. Col. Franklin, 61

Whetstone Point, 248–49

Whitbread, Samuel, 314

White House, *see* President's House

White House, Va., 208–9

Wilberforce, William, 38

Wilkinson, Brig. Gen. James, 104

Wilkinson, Capt. Thomas, 336

Williams, Maj. John, 206

Wilson, George W., 138

Wilson, William, 199, 211

Winchester, David, 228

Winder, Gov. Levin, 23, 26, 229, 231, 238, 240, 247

Winder, Brig. Gen. William Henry, 29–30, 59, 60, 61, 86, 96, 98, 106, 110, 111, 197, 202, 213, 214, 218, 229, 233, 251, 284; made commanding general of 10th Military District, 22–23; background and personality, 22–26; inadequately supported, 23–25, 26; ineffectual efforts of, 25–26; measures to counter British landings, 28–29, 60–61; advance to the Wood Yard, 62–63; at the Wood Yard, 67–69; orders Sterett and Stansbury to Bladensburg, 68–69; march on Nottingham, 70, 72–73; retreat from the Wood Yard, 72; at Long Old Fields, 77–79, 81–83, 86; plans to attack British at Upper Marlboro, 83–84, 86; retreats to Washington, 87–88, 92–95; Bladensburg and, 97, 102–6, 108, 113–14, 117, 118, 123, 124, 125, 128–29, 130, 135–36, 137; during Washington's evacuation and capture, 148–49, 153, 161, 171, 189–90, 191, 192, 193; conflict with Sam Smith over command at Baltimore, 231–32, 237–38, 249–50, 272–73, 284; *see also* Washington, D.C.

Wirt, William, 216

Wood, Lt. Col. William, 133

Wood Yard, Md., 28, 61, 62, 68, 70, 72, 77

York, Duke of, 40, 304

Young, Brig. Gen. Robert, 139, 193